BRAIN SCHOOL

HOWARD EATON, ED.M.

STORIES OF CHILDREN WITH LEARNING DISABILITIES AND ATTENTION DISORDERS WHO CHANGED THEIR LIVES BY IMPROVING THEIR COGNITIVE FUNCTIONING

GLIA PRESS
VANCOUVER, B.C.

Library and Archives Canada Cataloguing in Publication

Eaton, Howard

Brain school : stories of children with learning disabilities and attention disorders who changed their lives by improving their cognitive functioning / Howard Eaton.

Includes index.

ISBN 978-0-9867494-0-7

1. Learning disabled children—Education—British Columbia. 2. Attention-deficit-disordered children—Education—British Columbia. 3. Cognitive learning. 4. Social learning. 5. Remedial teaching. 6. Eaton Arrowsmith School. I. Title.

LC4706.C32B75 2010 371.909711 C2010-906473-9

Editing by Arlene Prunkl
Interior Book Design by Fiona Raven

First Printing 2011
Printed in the United States of America

www.HowardEaton.com

Glia Press Publishing
204 - 6190 Agronomy Road
Vancouver, BC Canada
V6T 1Z3

www.GliaPress.com

---

1. Arrowsmith Program® is a registered trademark of Barbara Arrowsmith Young.

To my wife, Karen Orth,
who is a remarkable mother to Chris, Sean, and Lin,
and who inspired me when we first met
to finish my university education.
I am so fortunate to share my life with you.

Instead, consider the possibility that any man could,
if he were so inclined,
be the *sculptor of his own brain*, and that even the least gifted may,
like the poorest land that has been well cultivated and fertilized,
produce an abundant harvest.

—SANTIAGO RAMÓN Y CAJAL (1852–1934), SPANISH NEUROSCIENTIST
AND WINNER OF THE NOBEL PRIZE IN PHYSIOLOGY OR MEDICINE, 1906

Contents

Acknowledgements

This book exists because of Barbara Arrowsmith Young. She has helped over three thousand children with learning disorders over the last thirty years. Over those years she developed nineteen cognitive functioning remediation exercises that have been studied, researched, refined, and implemented to improve the lives of these children. I have been fortunate to learn from her insights into neuroplasticity and learning disabilities. Arrowsmith Young has shed a new light on developmental possibilities for children with learning disorders. Her work is creating a dramatic paradigm shift in the field of learning disabilities and attention disorders. Following the lead of Arrowsmith School in Toronto, at Eaton Arrowsmith School we have begun to work with a few children with acquired brain injuries, and we are seeing promising cognitive functioning improvements in these children. Thus, Arrowsmith Young's work could one day transfer to other professions concerned with cognitive functioning remediation.

I will always be grateful to my parents for their determination in seeking out early intervention for my dyslexia. My mother and father steadfastly refused to listen to my elementary school teachers regarding my chances of finding academic success. As well, my mother's parents, Grandma and Grandpa Bissett, provided financial support for me to attend one of the best private schools for boys with dyslexia in Bucks County, Pennsylvania—the Kildonan School (now located in Amenia, New York). My parents also mortgaged their home to further cover the private school tuition and boarding fees. Most parents and grandparents will do anything to get their children the right kind of educational support, and mine were no different.

In addition, the tutors and teachers who gave me hope and a sense of possibilities are always on my mind. In particular, Sue Wyness and Jane Unger, Orton-Gillingham tutors, taught me how to read. Diana Hanbury King, the founder of the Kildonan School, provided an educational environment that allowed me to flourish and believe in myself as a student. I am so grateful that she had the passion and resilience to start one of the first schools for children with dyslexia in North America.

Over the past twenty years, my understanding of the field of learning disabilities, attention disorders, and neuroscience has also been developed by the following friends, colleagues, or experts in their respected fields of study: Dr. Loring Brinckerhoff, Dr. Robert Brooks, Dr. John Ratey, Dr. Jeffrey Schwartz, Sharon Begley, David Shenk, Dr. Edward Hallowell, Richard Lavoie, Stanislas Dehaene, Dr. Mel Levine, Dr. Max Cynader, Dr. Adele Diamond, Dr. Don Maiette, Dr. Donna Lehr, Dr. Norman Doidge, Dr. William Lancee, Dr. Carl Kline, Leslie Coull, Dr. Michael Merzenich, Dr. Gabor Mate, Desiree Wilson, Daphne Beams, Dr. Jane Garland, Helen MacDonald, Rick Stuible, Sarah Howard, June Green, Marilyn Wardrop, Ken Langford, Sandra Heusel, Ron Pearson, and so many others. My apologies to those I inadvertently did not name.

In order to start Eaton Arrowsmith School I also needed the support of parents. One of the most passionate and dedicated parents was Michele Thom. I am very thankful for your encouragement during the first four years of the school.

My administrative and teaching staff at Eaton Arrowsmith School/Vancouver, Eaton Arrowsmith School/Victoria, Eaton Brain Improvement Centre, and Magnussen School provided me with a large amount of time to write this book. They all have such talent that I had full confidence in the children's progress and well-being. These intelligent and dedicated individuals include Mark Watson, Sarah Cohen, Jason Cruickshank, Alexandra Dunnison, Mark Bleasdale, Sandra Heusel, Rose Atkins, Karen Ho, Naoko Yamaguchi, Peter Heusel, Louise Richardson, Katherine Quitzon, Erin Kim, Carrie Boutilier, Luciana Johnson, Simon Hayes, Natalie Poirier, Leah Meinhardt, Jean Coyle-Roach, Jenna Garrat, Sarah McArthur, Kelsey Hanna, Jessica Panjer, Daniela Francis, Paul Williamson, Celina Johnson, Adrianne Poulos, Amy Wong, Meagan Trayers, Danielle Unger, Roger Brunson, Kristin Harbut, Judy O'Donnell, Eric O'Donnell,

Melanie Sidney, Camelia Kasirer, Leanne McNivin, Angie Ho, Swiya Nath, Victoria Tool, Fiji McAlpine, Alvin Bonifacio, Amy Spralja, Jyoti Pawar, Pinder Dhesi, Erin Poettcker, Jennifer Poole, Shannon Mitchell, and Miriam Leo Gindin.

I am not one to have time for many friends. Working with families in need of support and guidance can take large amounts of time, and I want to devote the time remaining in a day to my own family. I would, however, like to express my deep gratitude to my good friend Alan for being such a great supporter of my family and work. As well, Henriette Orth, my mother-in-law, has been a constant source of inspiration for me. Her inquisitive mind and generous spirit have helped me to believe in myself during my struggles to complete post-secondary education. She has been a role model for me ever since I met my wife over twenty-six years ago. To the rest of my family—Renee, Daphne and Tony, Peter and Sarah, Jenny and Rob, and all their children—thanks for being there.

I am grateful for the guidance and editing of Annette Goodman, chief education officer of the Arrowsmith Program. Annette's keen knowledge and insight into the Arrowsmith Program helped shape the chapters. I have never been overly concerned with grammar, syntax, or style in matters of the written word—something many people with dyslexia contend with. Thus, without the additional editorial assistance of Louise Richardson, Rose Atkins, Alexandra Dunnison, Sandra Heusel, Karen Ho, Luciana Johnson, and interview transcriber Karmen Ho, this book would never have reached publication. They have all spent many hours reviewing my writing and making the necessary edits to improve the readability of this book. Additional gratitude goes to Arlene Prunkl, the professional editor who further honed the manuscript and gave it its final structure and polish, and to Fiona Raven, who contributed her superior artistry to the book's design.

My father, Howard Eaton, Sr., has been a great inspiration in getting this book completed. It began as an idea two years ago at a meeting in Santa Barbara, California, where my father lives. We met at the University of California Santa Barbara campus with Bob Nishi, a brilliant colleague and friend of my father's, and Bob's daughter Kira. Over several days, the brainstorming sessions produced the initial concepts behind the book, and the project was underway. Each subsequent month, my father would send me encouraging e-mails, and I am thankful for his persistence in supporting this book. In addition, he spent hours suggesting changes, additions, and formatting the manuscript. Thanks, Dad, for your constant encouragement!

I am also fortunate to have a wonderful wife who understands my determined focus on helping children with learning disabilities and attention disorders. Karen, thank you—I love you, always. To my children, Chris, Sean, and Lin—you mean more to me than anything in the world!

Finally, my gratitude goes to all the children and families whose stories fill this book. All names have been changed to protect their confidentiality, although many of the children wanted to use their real names; they were proud of what they had accomplished. The names of some schools and professionals involved in the children's education were changed to further protect their identities.

Introduction

The world is full of people who have never, since childhood, met an open doorway with an open mind.

—E.B. WHITE, AUTHOR, *CHARLOTTE'S WEB*

This book is about children who struggled in school and subsequently changed their cognitive[2] functioning and altered their lives. They struggled with learning disabilities and, in many cases, attention disorders as well. This book is about their resilience and determination to improve their lives. It is about their parents, who resisted accepting the common opinion that cognitive functioning is fixed, focusing instead on giving their children futures filled with possibilities. It is about a cognitive functioning remediation approach called the Arrowsmith Program. It tells the story of an exceptional woman, Barbara Arrowsmith Young, and how she is revolutionizing the field of learning disabilities and attention disorders. It is also about a group of talented teachers at Eaton Arrowsmith School (EAS) who worked with these children to sustain active engagement in challenging cognitive exercises. Each of these children's stories provides a fascinating look into the potential of the human brain to change itself and into the educational community that is needed to support this change.

Brain School is also about an educator, a specialist in learning disabilities and attention disorders. The educator has dyslexia. Despite this disability—and not knowing the brain is "plastic"—he completed graduate

2. Throughout this book, the adjectives *cognitive* and *neurological* are used interchangeably. For example, *cognitive remediation* and *neurological remediation* have the same meaning.

school and developed a business in testing children with learning disorders. He was intent on doing his job the same way every day until he retired. He believed that children who struggle in school must all have assessments and subsequently be labelled as having a *lifelong* disability. They could then receive educational support services in their schools. He believed this approach was the only way to provide the necessary scaffolding to get these children through school—support that included extra tutoring, special education classes, learning strategies, and "accommodations" (accommodating the student with, for example, extra time on tests, use of a reader or scribe, use of a computer for written exams). The person I am describing above, if you haven't guessed, is me. However, I changed.

Neuroplasticity, or brain plasticity, refers to the brain's amazing ability to reorganize itself. In other words, neuroplasticity is the alteration of neuronal structure and the reorganization of neural networks and their function through environmental stimuli. Research is showing that glial cells in the human brain play an important role in neuroplasticity.[3] For example, glial cells (also referred to as *astrocytes* or star-shaped glial cells) in the human brain and spinal cord increase in number when nerve cells grow through environmental stimulation. As well, they play a role in creating and sustaining the specific patterns of neural networks.[4] Previously, glial cells were thought to only physically support neurons in the brain. (Thus the Greek reference to *glia*, meaning "glue.") This new research is highlighting the fact that glial cells are critical for improving brain function.

The terms *neuroplasticity* or *brain plasticity* are not new ones, but were coined in 1948 by Jerzy Konorski, a Polish neurophysiologist, in his book, *Conditioned Reflexes and Neuron Organization* (Cambridge University Press, 1948). Around the same time, in Montreal, Quebec, psychologist Donald Hebb was also writing about his theories of neural

---

3. T. Fellin, "Communication between neurons and astrocytes: relevance to the modulation of synaptic and network activity," *Journal of Neurochemistry* 108, no.3 (2009), 533–544.
4. M.M. Halassa and P.G. Haydon, "Integrated brain circuits: astrocytic networks modulate neuronal activity and behaviour," *Annual Review of Physiology* 72 (2010), 335–355.

plasticity. In 1949 he introduced the concept in his book, *The Organization of Behavior: A Neuropsychological Theory* (Lawrence Erlbaum Associates, 2002). Hebb has been described as the father of neuropsychology and neural networks.

The concept of the brain's neural functions as being malleable is much older, having been acknowledged in the early 1890s by William James, an American psychologist and philosopher (*Principles of Psychology*, Cosimo Classics, 2007) and by Santiago Ramón y Cajal, a Spanish histologist, physician, pathologist, and Nobel laureate (*New Ideas on the Structure of the Nervous System in Man and Vertebrates*, MIT Press, 1990). In fact, Dr. Mark Rosenzweig notes in *Neural Plasticity and Memory: From Genes to Brain Imaging* (Federico Bermúdez-Rattoni, ed., CRC Press, 2007) that in 1783, Michele Vicenzo Malacarne, a Piedmontese anatomist, studied the influence of mental exercise on neural growth. Malacarne found that trained animals such as dogs and birds had more folds in their cerebellums than untrained ones. Research in neuroplasticity has been going on for well over two hundred years.

Norman Doidge, in his bestselling book about neuroplasticity, *The Brain That Changes Itself* (New York: Viking Press, 2007), coined the term "the plastic paradox." That is, the brain has the ability to change itself in both positive and negative ways. Neuroplasticity does not necessarily mean that the change that is occurring is for the benefit of that individual or society. For example, some forms of behaviour can become extremely debilitating, such as that seen in obsessive-compulsive disorders (OCDs). For educators who work with children with disabilities, "the plastic paradox" can hinder their ability to see new possibilities. For decades, their ideas have been firmly set that children who struggle with cognitive functioning weaknesses will continue to struggle throughout their lives. The children's caregivers must give them all the support they need to ensure they make it through school. *Learned helplessness* is the term used in the fields of education and psychology to describe many children with learning difficulties. In fact, this learned helplessness does not have to be the case.

Brain School asks politicians, educational administrators, psychologists, psychiatrists, family doctors, educators, parents, and others involved in education to be open to the idea that cognitive functioning can improve and the brain can change. Many educators are not even aware of brain plasticity. In education, the establishment's common understanding is that the brain is more or less fixed; that is what many of them learned at college or university. Perhaps they have not read the latest information on brain plasticity and neuroscience. As a result, they keep practising the same instructional remediation methods for children with learning disabilities as though they are the only options available.

I was much the same; it was not easy for me to accept that the brain is plastic. I clearly recall classroom discussions about the brain during my undergraduate education in psychology and then in my graduate program in special education. The brain was fixed, unchangeable, hard-wired like a computer. My professors were critical, almost mockingly so, of so-called radical scientists discussing the brain's ability to change. They acknowledged that there are some formative years of brain development in early infancy, but that was it. This was my training and background. In fact, I co-wrote handbooks and produced educational videos advising parents and their children with learning disabilities to accept their cognitive weaknesses and view them in a positive light.

Barbara Arrowsmith Young has been working with brain plasticity for thirty years. Yet some educators disregard her program due to their inability or refusal to conceptualize what she is doing. These educators are so focused on improving skills such as spelling, reading, and writing that they fail to see it is the brain's current cognitive functioning that affects these behaviours. As well, they do not see that children who fail in school are often dealing with more significant issues with reasoning, memory, auditory processing, visual-perceptual processing, visual-motor integration, and social-perception problems—all cognitive functioning weaknesses—and that these cognitive functions can be improved. Yet Arrowsmith Young has persisted and her results outstandingly speak for themselves. She is the first neuroplastician with operating schools and licensed programs in the field of education in North America.

This is not to deny that many wonderful minds in education and psychology have provided major insights into learning disabilities and attention disorders. Nevertheless, the notions that the brain can change itself and that cognitive intervention methods can be designed to improve cognitive functioning are revolutionary to many education experts, who refuse to depart from their own entrenched neural pathways. When a dramatic change of thought is presented they become uneasy and often dismissive, preferring to stick to old ways of doing things.

The inaugural International Mind, Brain, and Education Society (IMBES) conference took place in Fort Worth, Texas, in November 2007. IMBES encourages collaboration between all fields relevant to the connection between the mind, the brain, and education. The IMBES website states:

> The mission of the International Mind, Brain, and Education Society (IMBES) is to facilitate cross-cultural collaboration in biology, education, and the cognitive and developmental sciences. Science and practice will benefit from rich, bi-directional interaction. As research contributes to usable knowledge for education, practice can help to define promising research directions and contribute to the refinement of testable hypotheses.

Two of the society's advisors are Howard Gardner, author of *Frames of Mind: Theory of Multiple Intelligences* (Basic Books, 2004), and Kurt Fisher, who is the Charles Bigelow professor of human development and psychology and director of the Mind, Brain, and Education Program at the Harvard Graduate School of Education. I attended this conference, along with several of my colleagues from Eaton Arrowsmith School, taking in numerous lectures on neuroscience and education. A common issue was raised in all the lectures: the neuroscientists were frustrated with their universities' education departments for their reluctance to explore the benefits of their research. In essence, there was a significant gap between educational practice and the proven theories of neuroscience research. This gap existed because educators were either not seeing the relevance of neuroscience's findings or they were too set in their ways in how education should work—the plastic paradox. This has been Barbara Arrowsmith Young's reality over the past three decades.

By 2004, I had become interested in educational neuroplasticity.

Prior to this, my assessment company, Eaton Learning Centre,[5] had just completed three updated psycho-educational assessments of several Vancouver children whose parents, finding a lack of resources in Vancouver, had enrolled their children in Toronto's Arrowsmith School. The results surprised and impressed me. For the first time, I observed notable intellectual and cognitive improvements in my clients, children with learning disabilities. I had previously seen *achievement* improvements but never such dramatic improvements in *cognitive functioning*. I also realized that such changes in cognitive functioning were likely to have an enormous impact on these children's future success.

My findings excited me enough to visit Barbara Arrowsmith Young and her Arrowsmith School in Toronto, Ontario, in December 2004. Upon my return to Vancouver, I conducted an updated psycho-educational assessment on Andrew, one of Arrowsmith School's students whom I had previously tested. Andrew's reassessment results were so impressive that they were the catalyst for my decision to start the Eaton Arrowsmith School in Vancouver, British Columbia.

There is no magic or quick fix for improving cognitive functioning. It is difficult and tiring work for the child with learning and attention disabilities; it takes resilience and diligence to improve. Neuroplasticity does not occur without significant active engagement over a lengthy period. Not surprisingly, some critics use this as a way to dismiss this work. They say, "Why would you make children with learning disabilities work so hard? They are already struggling enough."

Optimal cognitive functioning remediation for a severe learning disability, and in some cases an accompanying attention disorder, can take three to four years in a full-time school environment, which will be shown in the stories in Part II. Some of our most remarkable children persistently and repeatedly worked on cognitive exercises in order to achieve their

5. For clarity, the Eaton Learning Centre is used as the name of my assessment company throughout this book. In fact, the name evolved from Eaton Educational Consultants to Eaton Coull Learning Group, and finally to Eaton Learning Centre. The Eaton Learning Centre closed operations in 2008 as we wanted to fully focus on cognitive remediation at Eaton Arrowsmith School.

noteworthy accomplishments and become honours students after transition to mainstream classrooms. The Arrowsmith Program's belief is that nothing is wrong with hard or tiring work if it has an important purpose. This is how many great minds developed breakthroughs in engineering, physics, chemistry, architecture, literature, music, mathematics, medicine, and other disciplines. They spent hours going over ideas and theories. Similar to the body's physical training, in order for the brain to become efficient at a particular task or behaviour, it must practise it repeatedly. Children with learning disabilities and attention disorders must stimulate and strengthen their brains' ability to learn with repeated cognitive exercises in order to overcome their neurological weaknesses.

Above all, *Brain School* is for those people concerned about children with learning issues, social problems, and underperformance at school. You will read about children and watch their progression from despair to hope to achievement in cognitive functioning. You will see educational psychometrics that will encourage you and provide you with increased awareness. The children in this book have attended Eaton Arrowsmith School and succeeded under its professional teaching staff. Their stories were assembled from assessments, school records, teachers' comments, and parent interviews. Neuroscience research is discussed, showing how it is connected to the Arrowsmith Program and why the program is so effective.

In analyzing the children's cognitive functioning, two different formats of assessments are described in this book: psycho-educational assessments and Arrowsmith assessments. The psycho-educational assessment is administered under the guidance of a registered psychologist and team of educational assessors, most often to determine if a child has a learning disability and to recommend the types of assistance needed at school. It is also used in public and private schools to aid in the writing of individual education plans or programs for children at school.

The psycho-educational assessment includes measures of intelligence, cognitive functioning, and achievement levels in reading, writing, spelling, and math. At times, it is completed prior to the children starting at Eaton Arrowsmith School. This assessment enables us to analyze improvements in cognitive functioning, as the children are given an updated assessment after the completion of their Arrowsmith Program. It also provides impartiality: we can see before-and-after cognitive improvements on an assessment not directly connected to the Arrowsmith Program itself or Eaton Arrowsmith School.

The other format is the Arrowsmith assessment, created by Barbara Arrowsmith Young, which analyzes nineteen areas[6] of cognitive functioning. The purpose of this assessment is to determine the level of severity of each of these nineteen cognitive functions in order to individually design a child's Arrowsmith remediation program. (For a detailed list and description of the nineteen cognitive functions and their common features, see Appendix A.) The Arrowsmith assessment is re-administered yearly to assess the progress of each child, evaluate whether the child requires an additional year in the program, and re-evaluate the child's Arrowsmith remediation program design for the following school year (if the child does require an additional year).

Throughout this book, reference is made to both psycho-educational assessments and Arrowsmith assessments. The results from the updated psycho-educational assessments provide remarkable evidence of how the Arrowsmith Program affects children's lives. It is also interesting to observe that the Arrowsmith assessment often highlights the same cognitive functioning weaknesses as a psycho-educational assessment does. However, it is clear that the Arrowsmith assessment offers a broader understanding of each child's cognitive functioning abilities. At Eaton Arrowsmith School, our goal is to help parents and their children with learning and attention disabilities to find rescue, hope, and achievement. Along the way, if we are able to generate wide support for educational neuroplasticity, if we are able to increase awareness of Barbara Arrowsmith Young and her unique program, and if we can help interest schools across North America—especially K to 12—all this will help to foster our goal.

---

6. Over the last thirty years, Arrowsmith Young has identified nineteen important cognitive functions that have an impact on academic and social learning. She has designed cognitive remediation programs or exercises for each of these nineteen cognitive functions.

Brain School is for:

- Parents of children with learning disabilities including dyslexia, attention deficit hyperactivity disorder (ADHD), and other disorders
- Young adults and adults with learning disabilities
- Educators, particularly those involved in special education
- Members of school boards
- Counsellors working in schools
- Neuroscientists, MDs, psychiatrists, psychologists, and therapists
- People interested in the potential of the brain to change

When it comes to children with learning difficulties, we are all responsible. A key to helping these children is to improve cognitive functioning and bring school success and a happier life within their grasp.

I thank you for your interest in *Brain School* and your desire to keep your mind open to the world of new possibilities neuroplasticity holds.[7]

—Howard Eaton, Ed.M.
Vancouver, B.C., Canada
www.eatonarrowsmithschool.com

7. People sometimes rightly ask if I myself have completed the Arrowsmith Program. While my dyslexia affected my reading, writing, and spelling at the school level, these achievement disabilities were largely overcome by five years of Orton-Gillingham tutoring and continued repetitive reading and writing throughout my education, right up to M.Ed. work. Through attention to reading, spelling, and writing tasks, I have become fairly proficient in these areas of achievement. My cognitive weakness with auditory processing still affects listening comprehension or following oral language tasks (e.g., listening to lectures or audio books). As well, learning a second language is next to impossible for me. However, these cognitive weaknesses do not affect my work or career; in addition, I surround myself with people with cognitive functioning talents that are not part of my cognitive skill-set. If my work were to be affected by my cognitive weaknesses, I would certainly not hesitate to study areas of the Arrowsmith Program designed to improve these cognitive functions.

Part I

The Journey

1

The Boy They Called Persistent

Energy and persistence conquer all things.

—BENJAMIN FRANKLIN

The Enigma of Dyslexia

I was fortunate. It seems a strange statement to apply to a person with dyslexia.[8] My Grade 1 teacher at Maple Grove Elementary School in Vancouver had happened to read an article in *Scientific American* magazine on dyslexia. The article started her thinking about my poor school performance. The term *dyslexic* applied to me, she thought. The field of learning disabilities (LD) was in its infancy in North America. In the 1970s and '80s, most children like me were commonly labelled stupid, slow, dumb, even retarded. Almost everyone used those labels—friends, teachers, and sadly, parents. In reality, most children with dyslexia were never diagnosed. In my case, luck intervened early in life.

8. Dyslexia is a language-based learning disability often affecting reading, writing, listening, and speaking. In medical terminology, *dys* means "abnormal," "impaired," "difficult," or "bad," and *lexia* pertains to words. Thus, someone with dyslexia has difficulty with words in some aspect of language communication. Most often dyslexia is used to identify children with reading disabilities. The word *dyslexia* is now used by parents and educators to describe many forms of learning disabilities, bringing confusion to the field.

My own road to special education and psycho-educational assessing was improbable. My Grade 1 teacher, Ms. Podivinikoff (a confusing tangle of letters for a child with dyslexia to pronounce, let alone write), had asked my parents to meet with her. She explained that I might be dyslexic and that although I drew complex, elaborate pictures more typical of older children, I had difficulty reading and I spelled poorly. She also explained that I couldn't read the sight words (whole words written on flash cards). I found it impossible to hold an entire word in my brain and then attach a sequence of sounds to it to form a pronounceable word. Yet she was sure I was bright. Ms. Podivinikoff recommended testing me for dyslexia.

Like other parents, my mother and father had no idea what dyslexia meant. Was it a disease? Was it permanent? Could I make it through school? Was college a consideration? There was some family history with dyslexia. My father has a younger brother whom the school system failed in Grades 1, 6, and 9. He graduated from high school at twenty-one years of age, and it affected his entire adult life. Certainly it impaired his self-confidence. Dad also told me about a great uncle on his father's side who was labelled retarded by the school system in the 1850s, but who went on to become a highly successful businessman, confusing his critics.

My parents knew I was different. They told me I wrote backwards, sometimes from right to left. They would hold my writing up to a mirror and read it that way. Like other parents, they read children's books to me and tried to help me recognize letters and words. They helped me practise spelling. Nothing worked.

In Grades 1 through 4, I developed strategies to disguise my learning dysfunctions. I asked my parents to read my school stories to me, and because I had a strong memory, I would memorize the stories *word for word*. The next day at school, when it was my turn to read, I looked at the pictures on a page and recited the words from memory. I got through Grades 1 and 2 with this strategy. After all, the books had pictures, so I had prompts in the form of visual cues. This worked less well in Grade 3 because readers had fewer pictures.

Diagnosis: Dyslexia

In 1972, by Grade 3, my parents reached out for help. They called Dr. Carl

Kline, a child and adolescent psychiatrist who had recently arrived from Chicago. Dr. Kline happened to be an expert on dyslexia—more good fortune. An appointment was made and off I went at the age of eight to be tested for dyslexia. I worked with Dr. Kline's wife, Carolyn, for several days, during which time I was given batteries of tests assessing my intelligence and levels of school achievement. Several weeks later, my parents were called in and told, "Howie is a bright boy—he tests in the top 10 percent of IQ, but he has severe developmental dyslexia. That is why he's struggling to read. It's not easy for him to pick up sound/symbol associations of the English language. He will need special tutoring to learn to read and spell, and it could take years."

There was some good news. I had exceptional visual-spatial abilities. My weakness was in auditory processing of speech sounds and overall ability to follow and recall speech. I would pronounce *reading* as "readin" and *arithmetic* as "rithmetic." Dr. Kline recommended both speech-language therapy and Orton-Gillingham tutoring. Orton-Gillingham tutoring is a method of teaching sound/symbol associations, spelling rules, syllable division, and other components of the English language to children with dyslexia.[9]

I went from the classroom to the janitor's closet. Orton-Gillingham tutoring was set up for me in a custodian's closet at Maple Grove Elementary. A tutor came daily and took me out of my regular classroom. This was, of course, highly embarrassing. A janitor's closet! My stupidity was advertised schoolwide.

I suffered emotionally. I was mercilessly teased as "the boy who couldn't read." Classmates would form a circle and dance around me, taunting in sing-song voices, "Howie can't read." I would fight back by picking the biggest boy and hitting him. A teacher always stopped us, but I usually suffered the brunt for trying to defend myself, after which I was sent to the principal's office and then sent home. My parents were flummoxed.

---

9. The Orton-Gillingham remediation method for reading, spelling, and written expression has been used for many decades to improve children's achievement skills. This is especially the case for children diagnosed with dyslexia. Although the methodology benefits all children at the early elementary levels, it often is not used in the regular classroom.

I started wearing rebellious clothes: red trousers, wide belts, purple shirts, and offbeat shoes. My wild outfits were meant to bolster my ego, but as I reflect on it, things only worsened. I was teased and bullied by older students and often chased home, which fortunately was just three blocks from school. I became a fast runner.

I had classroom performance problems, but one in particular made me furious. After writing a list of short sentences on the blackboard, the teacher instructed us to copy them into our writing books. I would look at the board, then look down and copy the first sentence into my writing book. After that, I would look up again and write the next sentence; this went on for several sentences. Suddenly I would realize that I had written the same sentence repeatedly. In a rage, I would take my pencil and scribble all over my work, asking myself, "What's wrong with me?" This was a recurring problem.

If life has any blessing, it is to give children a particular talent. Mine was sports, and I used this to gain respect at elementary school. I was bigger than other boys my age and I could throw a baseball with either hand, kick a soccer ball with either foot, and run like the wind. In sports, other kids wanted me on their teams. Sports made school bearable.

By Grade 5, the situation had become intolerable. My progress in reading was very slow due to the severity of my dyslexia. None of my usual tricks worked for reading aloud in class. My cues were gone: Grade 5 readers had almost no pictures. I was still receiving Orton-Gillingham tutoring in the janitor's closet, and my classmates endlessly ridiculed me. School was a constant humiliation. I clearly remember the day when I decided to drop out. I got home from school one day and approached my father, declaring, "Dad I'm quitting school. I hate it. I hate it so much that I think of jumping off the Lions Gate Bridge." Ignoring me, he said, "Okay, but if you don't finish school, what will you do when you are older?" I looked him squarely in the face and said, "I'm going to be a professional hockey player. They make a lot of money, don't they?" Both of my parents listened to me, were empathetic, and with their permission I dropped out of Grade 5. I was home-schooled for the remainder of the school year.

Following this, I was reassessed by Dr. Kline (who eventually became a professor at the University of British Columbia). He again met with my parents and strongly recommended the Kildonan School, a school for children with severe dyslexia. My parents were taken aback when he explained that it was a boarding school located in Bucks County, Pennsylvania, in the United States. It was 1975, and few resources were available on dyslexia anywhere in the world.

I, too, was upset. The United States! It seemed a million miles away from our home on Canada's Pacific coast. I was in tears. There was no way I was going to that school. The last thing I wanted was to live at a boarding school two thousand miles from home for two years. I was miserable. Life seemed a persecution. But I was just ten years old and my opinion wasn't what mattered. That September, I was sent to boarding school.

Kildonan School

I attended the Kildonan School from 1975 to 1977, and it turned me around. By the time I graduated, I was at grade level in reading. My written expression and particularly spelling were still weak, but more importantly, I had regained my self-esteem. I remained dyslexic but I had tools to assist me.

Kildonan is synonymous with Diana Hanbury King, one of two founders of the school. Since my years at the school, she has deservedly received many awards for her distinguished contributions to children with language-based learning disabilities, specifically dyslexia.

The Kildonan School was formerly a four-hundred-acre farm, and its setting was magnificent. I fondly remember taking walks through the forest and down to a stream that ran through the school property. The classrooms were renovated farm buildings that had housed livestock prior to the school's founding. In the years I attended, it was a private school for boys. We lived in dormitories. My dorm room slept a total of twenty students who shared bathrooms and showers. A dorm counsellor had his room adjacent to ours, just in case we tried to sneak out at night.

The school's focus was on remediating the reading, writing, and spelling difficulties of children with dyslexia through the use of the Orton-Gillingham method. Today, most other phonetic-based remediation programs have their origins with Orton-Gillingham; the method's tutorials integrate spelling rules, syllabication, and the teaching of Latin and Greek prefixes, root words, and suffixes. While at Kildonan I received two years of intensive Orton-Gillingham tutorials, which combined with my previous three years with an Orton-Gillingham-trained tutor in Vancouver. This one-on-one tutoring was done five days a week for sixty-minute sessions. My reading, spelling, and writing began to advance as a result of this intensive intervention. The school also provided academic instruction in English, math, social studies, and science.

Class sizes were small, which ensured appropriate instruction and feedback. The student–teacher ratio was often just five to one, allowing real focus and attention on each student. Kildonan teachers were remarkably talented and frequently brought instruction alive with trips to museums and through the use of video and film.

The school offered equestrian riding, which did much to improve the self-confidence of initially jittery riders. We rode almost daily, and I learned to handle a horse with expertise. Jumping competitions were arranged, and evening gallops through the Bucks County woods were thrilling events. In winter, we took weekly ski trips to the Appalachian Mountains, which most of the boys loved. We couldn't wait to get out of a regular school day and enjoy those mountains. We learned about independence and hard work. The Kildonan environment encouraged us to be successful students.

Homesickness was a common occurrence, but the staff did a good job of keeping our minds busy and our bodies exercising. This helped keep our thoughts off our families and focused on our self-improvement. During my time there, I had some bad news. My dog died in an accident, one of my grandfathers died, and my parents separated, so I faced important personal changes. Mrs. King and my teachers provided excellent counselling.

After two years, I was ready to transition back into a regular education environment—with accommodations. With my confidence rebuilt, I saw myself as a successful student. I could read and write and I trusted teachers once again. There were no negatives about this experience; the Kildonan School was a wonderful place with gifted teachers who instilled hope and self-esteem in students with dyslexia.

After high school, however, I had no plans for university, nor was college a consideration. The truth was that I still disliked school. Nobody seemed to truly understand my learning difficulties. Though I got B grades in my last two years of high school, the thought of more school was anathema to me.

University Years

Not pleased about having a son staying at home unemployed, my father intervened, and with his business connections discovered that the University of Southern California might consider a late application from me. I applied, took the Scholastic Aptitude Test (SAT) with poor results, met the admissions director at USC, and got in—late—in September 1982. Without question, my father's connections in business at the time helped me considerably.

I lasted two months at USC before dropping out. I was behind in my reading and could not write an essay. I did not seek help or tell my professors; I had not yet become a passionate advocate for my dyslexia and just wanted it to go away. I left USC and moved back to Vancouver, where my mother was living. I started working as a dishwasher, trying to figure out what to do next in my life.

I supported myself with odd jobs—dishwashing, a short-order chef, gopher work at construction sites, and painting houses—anything to make a living. In 1984, after a couple of years of this, I decided to make another attempt at university, so I enrolled at the University of British Columbia in Asian Studies. I was fascinated with Asian history, and Vancouver was the gateway to China and Japan. Interestingly, as someone with dyslexia, I failed to analyze the course requirements for an Asian Studies degree, which included a second-language element. Given my dyslexia, one would think this would have hit my consciousness and turned on a mental caution light. Oddly, no self-reflection occurred.

Three months into my first year I was failing all my classes; the university's second-language requirement was the main reason. I spent hour upon hour trying to learn Mandarin, hours that did not leave enough time for other courses. I failed all of my term-end exams. In fact, in my Mandarin final, I sat in the back of the auditorium (I decided to show up because I didn't want my friends to think I had quit or didn't know my material) and doodled in my examination book until everyone had finished and left the room. After the exam, I apologized to the professor for not completing a single question. "Don't worry," he said. "There is the oral section, and that might make a difference for you." I left knowing I had failed that class as well.

My marks arrived during the winter holidays. Somewhat ironically, I had failed all my courses except one: Mandarin. But it was a mercy pass, not one based on academic achievement. The report also notified me that I had to discontinue my studies at UBC for one year and then reapply for acceptance. This was the second time I had failed. Deeply disappointed, I decided to give up on post-secondary education.

Persistent is a term that people use to describe me, for better or worse. Truth be told, my girlfriend and future wife, Karen, inspired me by example to try again. Also, her mother, Henriette, gave me several motivational talks. Karen was in an undergraduate honours physics program at Stanford University, and her academic success influenced my academic aspirations. A year after failing so miserably, I reapplied to UBC and was accepted back for the next fall term. This time, however, I did things differently: I became an ardent self-advocate. I told professors about my dyslexia, I asked for longer exam times, and I requested oral exams. This was difficult because I didn't want any of my peers to discover my secret. As well, the university's policy for a Bachelor of Arts degree required two years of a second language, so I needed an exemption.

I asked Dr. Carl Kline for a letter addressed to the Faculty of Arts. The letter disclosed my dyslexia, explained how learning a second language was difficult for me, and asked for a language exemption. It was hand-delivered to the Faculty of Arts to place in my records. Even Harvard University grants this exemption. Without the stress of learning a second language, increasing my hours of study to fill up my weekdays and weekends, and increasing my self-awareness on how to deal with my dyslexia, my marks improved steadily. For example, I developed a strategy of rereading my textbooks four times over, using different highlighters, which gradually improved my comprehension and retention. I also rewrote notes several times, as the repetition seemed to help store this information in my memory. Additionally, I learned how to take multiple-choice exams by study strategies outlined in study skills handbooks. By my last year at UBC, I was earning As and Bs in all my courses, so I applied to graduate schools for a master's degree in special education. I wanted to work in the field of learning disabilities and help children who had dyslexia and related issues.

Then, in March 1990 of my graduating year, I received a letter from the Faculty of Arts stating I could not graduate unless I completed the university's language requirement. I was asked to finish the second half of my Mandarin course. The letter was a shocking blow: I had always understood that my foreign language exemption had been granted. The next day I met with my academic advisor, who simply said, "There is nothing I can do—it's the policy." What made the policy even more puzzling was that I had already been accepted into graduate school at Boston University. Its graduate program had not required a second language on my application because of my dyslexia.

I began an ardent program of self-advocacy. I realized that if I was ever going to graduate with a B.A. in psychology, I had to speak out against this discriminatory policy. I went to the *Vancouver Sun*, Vancouver's largest newspaper, determined to find a reporter who would write about my situation. I could scarcely believe my audacity as I entered the elevator of the Vancouver Sun office building. After waiting for about thirty minutes, I was met by a reporter who listened to my story, why I felt the university was discriminating against me, and how major universities like Harvard had language exemptions. Following the interview, the reporter asked for a photograph. Only at that moment did I fully realize this was actually going to be in the newspaper.

The *Vancouver Sun* story appeared the next day—second page, front section in bold headlines, "Dyslexic Fights UBC." Unexpectedly, I received a call from the Canadian Broadcasting Corporation (CBC) for an on-air radio segment. I thought this would coerce the university into changing its second-language policy. But to my dismay, there was no reaction.

Next, I wrote to the Faculty of Arts, requesting that they change their policy and allow me to graduate. Two weeks later I received a response from the director, who stated that they would give me two years to try to complete the Mandarin language course. That was their solution? By this time I was more than a little distraught. I had a 3.64 grade-point average out of 4. And I had already been accepted by Boston University for its master's degree program in education! However, Boston U still required my B.A. I was outraged.

I decided to go straight to the president's office and demand a language exemption—and not accept "no" for an answer. The car was in full choke all the way to UBC and so was I. After I drove to the Student Union Building, I called several news stations at the SUB payphone to let them know what I was doing. Still furious, I walked from the SUB straight to the president's office where, shaking, I addressed the receptionist. "I want to speak to the president. I'm that dyslexic student. You might have heard about me?" She had not. I continued, "I want to speak to the president. I am not leaving this office until I get my language exemption and my B.A." By this time I was in tears. She asked me to sit down on a sofa near her desk while she went to talk to the vice-president. The president, Dr. David Strangway, was in Victoria. So I sat and waited.

After several hours, Dr. Birch, the vice-president and provost, approached and greeted me. He invited me into his office and sat down behind his desk. For the next hour I told him my story and why I felt it was discriminating to demand that someone with dyslexia learn a second language. My last two-year grade-point average was 3.64. I had been accepted by Boston University for graduate school. He listened, took notes, and when I was done, said, "Based on your current academic record and because you've have taken a Russian Literature course [in English], we will grant you your B.A. degree in psychology." We didn't speak for fully thirty seconds, and finally I thanked him. That was it—I had my B.A. in psychology. He explained that during the time I was waiting to meet with him, he had conducted several meetings with Faculty of Arts department heads. He also said that he would be creating a committee to look into developing a second-language exemption policy. I was delighted with this news, and equally as important, I'd learned the power of self-advocacy.

Boston University was a life-changing experience. I enrolled in a two-year master's program in special education. My professors all knew about my dyslexia and welcomed me in to their program. I had done poorly on my GRE (the Graduate Records Examination is used by universities to select top graduates for their graduate programs), but that deficiency was offset by my relatively high GPA. My professors especially admired the fact that I had confronted UBC and won my case.

Success finally came in graduate school, where I earned an A average. I was completely engrossed in my studies and fascinated with the history of learning disabilities and methods to assist children with dyslexia. The focus was on finding ways to "accommodate" learning differences, how to assess for learning disabilities, and working on programs to teach reading, writing, and math. There was no discussion about neuroplasticity, changing the brain itself. We were taught that at a young age the brain is fixed and learning disabilities are lifelong, and for the most part this teaching persists in education today. My own experiences with dyslexia seemed to bear it out. Later, I would discover that this is not necessarily so, but I joyfully graduated from Boston University in the spring of 1992 with a master's degree in special education—Howard Eaton, Ed.M. It had been a long, torturous road for the boy who couldn't read.

Truro, Cape Cod

From Boston University I at last went to the front lines of special education. Truro, Cape Cod, became the home of my first job. I worked in the districts of Truro and Provincetown for three years, helping develop reading programs for children with learning disabilities. I also co-taught classes with elementary school teachers for children with high levels of reading disorders. I loved teaching. It was terrific, formative work for me because I learned firsthand how difficult it is, in terms of both mental and physical fatigue. As well, I learned how important it is for administrators and teachers to work effectively together toward common goals. In Truro and Provincetown I began to deeply appreciate the parents of children with learning disabilities, who live with an unceasing mixture of pain and hope and frustration and commitment. I draw on all of those experiences today.

The school principal in Truro asked me to introduce more phonics into the classroom. My biggest challenge was that the teachers weren't trained to teach phonics. (At that time in the United States, most teacher colleges had dismissed phonics as a method of teaching reading.) I found myself dealing with children with reading disorders and teachers not trained to help them. This is still the case in some classrooms today. In order to improve the situation, I spent my time bringing in experts on phonics, purchasing materials, and teaching—using accommodations—children with reading issues.

Gradually, I began to realize that learning disabilities such as dyslexia are not just about reading and spelling. I also began to see that many different kinds of learning disabilities exist beyond those related to reading problems. These children also had severe cognitive functioning weaknesses affecting other areas of academic performance, including memory problems, slow information-processing abilities, taking longer to understand concepts, poor motor output abilities, weak social skills, and poor organization and planning abilities. I had read about this during my graduate program at Boston University but didn't fully appreciate the impact of these cognitive functioning weaknesses until directly teaching children with learning disabilities. Although I questioned the ways in which we accommodated learning disabilities, I continued working earnestly with parents, students, and other teachers, knowing I was still helping to some degree.

Parents strived to help their children. They were familiar with the symptoms but did not know how to classify the deficits. They would visit with me in my classrooms and pour out their grief, grasping at any straws of hope. They knew their children were smart and despaired that school for them was such a struggle. What should they do? Did a learning disorder have to be a lifelong sentence? Parents worked, hoped, and prayed for success for their children.

My approach for helping children with these problems continued to be guided by a learned belief that the brain is fixed. I provided accommodations or learning strategies or, in the most difficult cases, modified their programs to make the content easier to learn, and I let them move on to the next grade. I granted extra time on tests, use of spell-checkers, and use of computers for written output. I made sure calculators were available and gave them learning assistance to help solidify the understanding of concepts taught in class. In those days, that was the strategy: bypass the cognitive functioning weaknesses because the issues were lifelong. And that strategy is still in use in most of our schools today. Does it work? Yes, it is helping children with learning disabilities significantly. Undoubtedly, increasing numbers of students with learning disabilities are graduating from high schools today because of the policy of accommodating these cognitive functioning weaknesses. This is all good news. I was delighted to be helping children with learning disabilities, making sure they got accommodations and extra remediation in reading, writing, or math, depending on the individual case.

Front Lines – Vancouver, B.C.

In the summer of 1994, my wife and I moved back to Vancouver, British Columbia, after the birth of our first child. We wanted to be near our parents and friends. As well, we loved Vancouver, a marvellous city in a beautiful province. I worked for the Fraser Academy, a private school for children with dyslexia or language-based learning disabilities, as an Orton-Gillingham tutor and math teacher. I spent one year there before starting my own psycho-educational assessment and tutoring business, Eaton Learning Centre (ELC).

I enjoyed running my own business. We conducted psycho-educational assessments designed to diagnose learning disabilities and taught children with dyslexia how to read and spell. Through the company's comprehensive psycho-educational assessments and in-depth discussions of the results of these tests, staff members helped children, teens, and adults gain a better understanding of their unique learning profiles. We worked closely with a registered psychologist and other educational assessors. We also included keyboarding classes for children with *dysgraphia*, a deficiency in a person's ability to write, regardless of his or her ability to read.

On behalf of parents and their children with learning disabilities, we visited schools and worked with teachers and administrators. We focused on accommodation methodologies and the use of assistive technology such as computers, calculators, talking dictionaries, and voice-to-text software.

At this time, my colleague Leslie Coull and I developed a series of educational videos and written material on self-advocacy for children with learning and attention disabilities. Research was showing it was important that children with these disabilities understood their unique strengths and weaknesses. As well, they needed to be capable of speaking up for themselves and defending those strengths and weaknesses. Leslie and I travelled throughout Canada and the United States promoting the importance of self-advocacy training.

I wrote my first book, a small one entitled *Self-Advocacy*, for high school students with learning disabilities who, just as I had, wanted to transition from high school to university or college. Leslie Coull and I also developed transition skills for elementary and high school students.

Also in 1994, I had the first glimmer of how neuroscience would influence my future when I came across the work of the founder of the All Kinds of Minds Institute, Dr. Mel Levine, and his book *Educational Care: A System for Understanding and Helping Children with Learning Problems at Home and in School* (Educators' Publishing Service, Inc., 1994). This organization believes there are neurological reasons for children struggling in school. It was the first effort I had seen that connected neuroscience with education. I became fascinated with the institute's work on helping teachers and parents understand the neurodevelopmental profiles of children with learning difficulties. Yet the focus of All Kinds of Minds was and is still to find ways to accommodate or bypass the child's cognitive functioning weaknesses.

My world view of learning disabilities and attention disorders essentially was about assessment for labelling and funding purposes. It was about accommodations and use of technology to bypass cognitive functioning weaknesses. It was about teaching children and young adults to be advocates for themselves by helping them understand their cognitive functioning strengths and weaknesses. It was about finding achievement remediation methods to improve reading, spelling, math, and written expression. In addition, I belonged to several professional groups that focused on these issues. Throughout this period, I continued to believe the brain was more or less fixed from childhood on.

It was often difficult, repetitive work, but I believed I was making a difference. I felt I was putting my knowledge to good use, helping children and families improve their lives in a positive way. This was my life's work, and I felt good about it.

My efforts in this vein would continue until July 2000, when I met and began working with Andrew and his family. My paradigm of how the human mind functions was about to undergo a radical change.

2

"My Boy Is *Not* Slow"

It is possible to treat learning disabilities by identifying and strengthening cognitive functions.

—BARBARA ARROWSMITH YOUNG

Determined Parents

They were told Andrew had considerable problems. What Andrew's mother, Nancy, clearly heard was, "Your child is not capable," though those words were not used. That was the analysis of the school board psychologist who had measured Andrew's vocabulary, word reasoning, and general knowledge. The psychologist also reported that Andrew's verbal abilities (vocabulary), visual reasoning (solving puzzles), and overall IQ were very weak. To back up her analysis, the psychologist said Andrew ranked low—below the 5th percentile (out of a top rating of 100) in many areas of intellectual functioning, and in a few at or below the 1st percentile. Nancy admitted she did not understand everything she was told—only that her son's achievement skills were well below grade level, which she already knew. The worst part of what she was told, she said, was that "this is the way it is and don't expect too much."

Nancy was first surprised and dismayed, then angry. She also realized that if she accepted the school board psychologist's conclusions,

Andrew's educational prospects were poor. He might not graduate from high school, and university was a faint hope. But Nancy rallied, insisting that the psycho-educational assessment profile was not the Andrew she knew. Something was wrong. She decided to fight back, defend her son, and struggle for a better outcome.

"I formally objected to the school board," Nancy said in an interview. "I wrote a letter to them and said the psychologist wasn't qualified to make such statements." Others in the medical community supported her. "That was when the school board became very aggressive with me."

The school board's special education department gave Nancy's letter to its lawyer, who warned her that she would be sued for slander or worse if she continued her allegations. Not one to be intimidated, Nancy, with her parents' resources, hired a lawyer and began to fight back. Nevertheless, she was terrified, wondering what she was getting into. Above all, however, she felt she was right: Andrew did not have low intelligence, and Nancy did not want her child's psycho-educational assessment results on his permanent record. But the board refused to rescind the psychologist's report, and Andrew's psycho-educational assessment remained a permanent record. Nancy described her fight with the school board as a losing battle. She decided not to pursue a lawsuit and to move on. The bureaucracy was more powerful. Nothing good would come of a lawsuit.

Nancy decided to get a second opinion. Through neighbourhood connections and friends of friends, Nancy had learned of Eaton Learning Centre and my work in special education with learning disabilities and assessments, particularly in psycho-educational assessments.[10]

---

10. There is often no specific pattern to how various types of assessments are conducted on children with learning difficulties. The psycho-educational assessment is used to identify issues regarding intelligence, cognitive ability, and achievement skills. It can be used to label learning disabilities or other learning challenges. The speech-language assessment is used to intensively analyze receptive and expressive language abilities from sound discrimination to the processing of stories, although some psycho-educational assessments can look into language processing and expression as well. The occupational therapist's assessment is used to analyze gross and fine motor abilities of children, and to assess any sensory processing problems (tactile, olfactory, auditory sensitivities). The issue for parents is synthesizing all this information and finding time to schedule various interventions recommended by these professionals. Parents can often feel at a loss as to how to manage these important recommendations.

I met Andrew for the first time late in July 2000, when he was eight years and nine months of age. Nancy had called me, and we agreed she would bring Andrew to my office for further testing. Different psycho-educational tests would be used that might help more clearly identify which of Andrew's cognitive functions were strengths and which ones might be weaknesses. I would not redo the same tests; there were other standard measures of cognitive ability to use. After Nancy's call, I was reminded of the overriding stress borne by parents of children with learning disabilities.

Although I didn't know it at the time, Nancy and Andrew had initiated my journey into educational neuroplasticity and neuroscience. But like many others, I initially resisted change; I had not yet accepted brain plasticity. I had spent the last ten years developing self-advocacy programs for students with learning and attention disabilities, testing children and adults for disabilities, and consulting with schools regarding education remediation programs. I spent many hours volunteering for dyslexia and learning disability associations. In fact, in Vancouver, my involvement with dyslexia organizations was my primary focus professionally. For the past six years, I had worked closely with not only the Fraser Academy but with two other schools for children with dyslexia in the Vancouver area, Kenneth Gordon School and James Cameron School.

This work in psycho-educational assessment had convinced me that learning and attention difficulties were caused by numerous cognitive functioning weaknesses. I knew that when we tested a child for dyslexia at our office, ways could be found to improve their reading, writing, and spelling skills. Various programs are available such as Orton-Gillingham, Lindamood-Bell, and the Wilson Reading Program, to name a few. The client could be referred to a tutor or company that could provide the necessary assistance. For math-based learning disabilities, math tutors could be engaged. But even with these remediation programs, progress could be limited based on the severity and/or number of cognitive functioning weaknesses that led to the achievement problems. For example, as an Orton-Gillingham tutor, I found that some children progress rapidly while others struggle to make half a year of progress in two years. Other children might make it to grade-level reading levels, but their cognitive functioning weaknesses in visual processing speed, auditory working memory, or reasoning often make learning in school extremely problematic. They simply can't keep up with the workload because they need more time to process information.

I could also recommend technology and accommodations. A child with weak motor control and output (printing and copying ability) could use a computer or a scribe. If the child read slowly, even after reading tutoring, extra time for exams could be given. If math calculations were a concern, a calculator could be used on quizzes or tests. If attention or listening comprehension were weak areas, the child could have a note-taker in class or use a small digital recorder. If written expression was weak, voice-to-text computer software could be used. All of these accommodations and assistive technology were available.

Andrew's Psycho-Educational Assessment

The first time I assessed Andrew, I used my traditional approach—a psycho-educational assessment. Andrew stuck close to his mother's side, nervous, looking me over. I welcomed them both into my home, mostly trying to establish communication with Andrew. He was a polite child who enjoyed participating in discussions when asked questions. In terms of outward appearances, he appeared to be a normal-functioning eight-year-old. Andrew was sociable and appeared to have a good attitude and quite a bit of self-confidence. He certainly did not appear intellectually deficient. His mother gave me the documentation she had gathered from the school board assessment and other paperwork I had asked her to complete. I explained that I would work with Andrew during the morning hours and see how much energy he had left to continue after lunch. If needed, we would continue the assessment the next day.

Andrew and I headed upstairs to my office. He showed a keen interest in the various objects in my office, and enjoyed peering out my window at the scenic vista of Howe Sound.

Andrew was particularly difficult to test because of his great problems with attention control. He was highly impulsive, hyperactive, and easily distracted. He couldn't sit still for more than five minutes. Noise interfered with his ability to pay attention to me and my instructions, and he continually moved around the room. Concentration was not an easy task. Andrew wasn't rude or disrespectful. His cognitive functioning weaknesses caused him to be incapable of focusing on what he was asked to do. In frustration, I could have demanded that he sit down and remain still, but that would have been damaging to his self-esteem. The eight-year-old boy simply couldn't help himself—he wasn't able to control his behaviour.

Andrew had serious issues. The early test results showed that he took much longer than his peers to read, write, and copy information. He could not process numbers, hold them for a matter of seconds, and repeat them back to me. Andrew could decode simple words like *he, it, so, me, I, we,* and *us,* but it took him a great deal of time to get through consonant-vowel-consonant combinations like *dog, cat, hat, pot,* and *fin.*

Were the boy's hyperactivity and inattentiveness the primary problems? Or was his slow cognitive processing caused by anxieties about learning? Were his anxieties affecting his attention span? Perhaps Andrew just tuned out in a learning environment. His mother had said that he tuned out in class, distracting and annoying others. In those instances—and they were frequent—teachers and classmates found him irritating and disruptive, frustrating their own efforts at focusing. In cases like Andrew's, it is difficult to know which comes first, the disruptive behaviour or the dysfunction. Did his learning dysfunctions result from attention disorders or from other primary cognitive dysfunctions that manifest as attention disorders? In my experience, if a child cannot listen to instructions because of auditory processing weaknesses, the child shows problems focusing. The resulting anxiety from not being able to keep up with peers further interferes with focus.

Together, his mother and I examined Andrew's results. He did not have borderline intelligence in our psycho-educational assessment. He scored within the average range for nonverbal intelligence on an assessment that did not require timing. He also scored within the average range on measures of one-word expressive and receptive language, though at the low end of average. As well, some of his language comprehension scores were also average, though again at the low end of average. In my opinion, not all of Andrew's scores on measures of intelligence, language, and comprehension were at borderline level, nor did they indicate some form of severe intellectual delay. Table 1 shows some of Andrew's low cognitive functioning scores as well as his nonverbal intelligence score.

TABLE 1. ANDREW'S INITIAL PSYCHO-EDUCATIONAL ASSESSMENT RESULTS

Psycho-Educational Assessment Measure	**Description**	**Before Arrowsmith Program**
Visual-Motor Integration (Beery-Buktenica Developmental Test of Visual-Motor Integration —BEERY)	A measure of fine motor skills, visual perception, and hand-eye coordination.	10th %ile
Processing Speed (Wechsler Intelligence Scale for Children—Third Edition—WISC-III)	Ability to scan and copy visual symbols under timed conditions.	12th %ile
Auditory Processing (Woodcock-Johnson Tests of Cognitive Ability—Revised—WJ-R)	Ability to analyze and synthesize speech sounds. Critical cognitive ability for reading and spelling development.	1st %ile
Verbal Comprehension IQ (Wechsler Intelligence Scale for Children—Third Edition)	Knowledge of word meanings and relationships. Ability to understand social rules and norms. Mental math problem solving.	4th %ile
Sound Blending (Woodcock-Johnson Tests of Cognitive Ability—Revised)	Ability to blend sounds into words.	1st %ile
Fluid Reasoning (Woodcock-Johnson Tests of Cognitive Ability—Revised)	A measure of fluid intelligence. Ability to recognize patterns and/or relationships.	4th %ile
Nonverbal Intelligence (Test of Nonverbal Intelligence—Third Edition—TONI-3)	A measure of fluid intelligence. Ability to recognize visual patterns and relationships.	32nd %ile

Note: The average performance range on psycho-educational assessments is considered to fall between the 25th and 75th %ile ranking.

Andrew had profound cognitive functioning weaknesses, as seen in the table above. This was apparent from his test scores. Eighty-eight percent of his peers could scan and copy visual symbols at a faster speed. He was also slow at processing auditory information. It was painstakingly difficult for him to look at visual designs and then with a pencil replicate the image on a page of paper. His results clearly indicated that he took much longer than his peers to process, analyze, and output information. When Andrew was asked to listen to instructions, scan visual images on paper, and then give quick verbal responses, he barely kept pace.

I recommended that Nancy and Andrew's father, Mike, enrol Andrew in one of the only private schools in Vancouver with a program for children with language-based learning disabilities such as dyslexia. However, I knew Andrew had more severe cognitive issues that went beyond just language processing, and the school was not designed to remediate these specific cognitive deficits. Many schools designed for children with language-based learning disabilities across North America accept children with a variety of learning disabilities. In most cases, there are no alternatives. Thus, children with visual-perceptual deficits and reasoning difficulties, for example, often do not receive the necessary remediation to address those specific cognitive functioning weaknesses.

These thoughts occupied my mind when I suggested that Andrew attend the local private school for children with language-based learning disabilities. Nancy had already been thinking about this and agreed it would be the best option. She was familiar with the school and had toured it. As well, she was familiar with several mothers whose children attended the school, and she had heard positive things about it. The decision was made, and Andrew's parents enrolled him in Grade 3 in September of 2000.

"He was quite happy," she later reported. "He liked it. The small classes were great and they had tutoring. But I just really felt it was little more than a way of coping. I didn't feel that there were ever going to be changes with his learning ability. At the time I didn't believe anything would really fundamentally change."

After a year and a half, more than halfway through Grade 4, Nancy withdrew Andrew from the local private school. At that time, she contacted me with the news that Andrew had been enrolled in a school in Toronto called the Arrowsmith School. Nancy noted that Andrew's father, Mike, had heard about the school through a friend and attended an open house. The school focused on neuroplasticity, the premise that neural pathways and patterns are not fixed, but malleable—"plastic." He had been very impressed and felt this program would be an excellent idea for their son. I told Nancy that I knew little about the Arrowsmith Program, and it seemed unlikely there was any empirical evidence to prove that it worked.

"Let me tell you about his last school," she said, ignoring my remark. "What initially attracted us was the extra one-on-one tutoring, and it seemed that it was really our only option for Andrew at that time. But our experience at his school wasn't what I hoped it might be. The children in Andrew's class had a vast array of learning and emotional issues and I became disenchanted with the school. In the end, I concluded they only offered a Band-aid solution to Andrew's learning issues. At this point we started to rethink Arrowsmith." In addition, on a field trip with Andrew's last school, Mike had begun to sense that this was not the right school for his son. Nancy clearly agreed with Mike.

The local private school had been the only option that I knew of for Andrew. To be honest, I did not have much hope for the Arrowsmith School in Toronto. How could Andrew improve cognitive functioning? It was not possible. All my hard-won university and graduate school education had taught me to believe that the brain is more or less fixed, hard-wired. Eventually I lost track of Andrew.

Three years passed. In December 2004, I visited Barbara Arrowsmith Young in Toronto to discuss her program. I had decided to make the visit on the recommendation of Kathy, a mother from Vancouver. Kathy felt a school that could deliver the Arrowsmith Program in Vancouver would be important to establish. In addition, my business partner at the time, Leslie Coull, had visited the Arrowsmith School several years before and had come back fascinated with what the teachers were doing with cognitive remediation. I had been frustrated with the programs available in Vancouver, and I was now very curious about the Arrowsmith Program, so I flew to Toronto with as open a mind as possible.

During our meeting, Arrowsmith Young answered her phone. In an odd twist, it was Nancy. Andrew's three-year term at Arrowsmith was almost finished, and she wanted to discuss her nervousness about Andrew's next steps. The family wanted to return to Vancouver after the Arrowsmith Program ended, but where would he attend school? Was an updated psycho-educational assessment called for? She wanted to be sure Andrew was placed in the right grade and the right school.

"This is your lucky day," Arrowsmith Young told her. "Howard is in town. Actually, we're talking right now about the possibility of an Arrowsmith school in Vancouver."

Nancy was delighted; she could meet with Arrowsmith Young and me together. After a meeting that included Andrew's father, we reached the conclusion that Andrew should do an updated psycho-educational assessment over the winter holidays.[11] ELC would perform the assessment, and we scheduled Andrew for an appointment in Vancouver. Little did I know what I was to discover.

Andrew's Second Analysis

Four weeks later, at the end of December 2004, Nancy flew her son home to Vancouver for the winter holidays and the reassessment. Our registered psychologist conducted the intelligence testing and our educational assessor conducted the achievement measures. The results were then tabulated by the assessor and reviewed by the psychologist.

---

11. Parents of EAS students often seek updated psycho-educational assessments for transition purposes and to determine if cognitive capacity improvements are observable in IQ or Cognitive Ability standardized testing. In most cases, children who have completed their full-time Arrowsmith Program show positive shifts in cognitive and intellectual functioning on standardized testing pre- and post-assessments. It should be noted that psycho-educational assessments do not measure all the cognitive capacity intervention exercises that take place within the Arrowsmith Program, because of their limited number of measurements. As well, if the focus is on improving basic achievement skills at a young age, the child is likely working on improving the cognitive capacities needed for the acquisition of these skills. The first two years of the Arrowsmith Program may show slow achievement gains in basic skills until these cognitive capacities have improved toward the average range of functioning, although it must be noted that each child shows different responses to the Arrowsmith Program itself.

It is important here to recognize the difference between achievement weaknesses and cognitive weaknesses. Children with learning disabilities struggle with reading, writing, and mathematics, which are considered areas of achievement weakness, and achievement testing looks at these abilities. In the field of special education, the focus of remediation has traditionally been on improving children's achievement skills. Each year a child may receive updated achievement testing to analyze whether improvements have been made over the course of a school year. If achievement weaknesses still exist, continued remediation will likely be recommended.

Cognitive weaknesses relate to specific aspects of brain functioning that may hinder school performance. These cognitive weaknesses are the primary cause of a child's frustration at school. In fact, cognitive weaknesses are often the main reason why a child has difficulty with an area of achievement. For example, if a child struggles to efficiently process speech sounds (a cognitive skill), then reading acquisition (an achievement skill) is often negatively affected. The primary goal of the Arrowsmith Program is to improve cognitive weaknesses. In doing so, the child builds the neurological capacities to improve learning outcomes in reading, adding or subtracting numbers in memory, understanding math word problems, following a classroom lecture, improving planning and organizing ability, or reasoning through a science class concept.

The results of Andrew's second psycho-educational assessment astonished me. Remember, I had reviewed and conducted psycho-educational assessments for the last ten years, long enough to have a sense of the usual pattern when an intellectually weak child is retested. Essentially, cognitive functioning results either did not change, or became worse (i.e., their percentile rankings were lower). And my thinking was still somewhat biased to the concept that neurological functioning was fixed, that one cannot improve a weak cognitive functioning area if one has a learning disability.

Andrew's assessment changed the direction of my life's work. It was the proof I needed. Table 2 shows Andrew's cognitive improvements after he completed the Arrowsmith Program.

TABLE 2. ANDREW'S PSYCHO-EDUCATIONAL ASSESSMENT RESULTS BEFORE AND AFTER THE ARROWSMITH PROGRAM

Psycho-Educational Assessment Measure	**Before Arrowsmith Program**	**After Arrowsmith Program**
Visual-Motor Integration: BEERY	10th %ile	55th %ile
Processing Speed: WISC-III, WISC-IV	12th %ile	45th %ile
Phonemic Awareness: WJ-III	1st %ile	28th %ile
Verbal Comprehension IQ: WISC-III, WISC-IV	4th %ile	26th %ile
Auditory Processing: WJ-R *Sound Blending: WJ-III*	1st %ile	32nd %ile
Fluid Reasoning: WJ-R *Concept Formation: WJ-III*	4th %ile	25th %ile
Nonverbal Intelligence: TONI-3	32nd %ile	58th %ile

In three years at Arrowsmith School in Toronto, Andrew had moved his knowledge and use of word meanings from low to within average range.[12] His fluid intelligence[13] had also improved from low to within average range. In terms of other cognitive processing abilities, changes not often observed by ELC had occurred. Andrew's score on his ability to hear blended sounds went from low to the average range; and his score on Phonemic Awareness—the analysis and synthesis of speech sounds—went from low to average. His test of efficiency and accuracy in copying designs improved from low to average. The rate at which he could scan

12. In psycho-educational assessments, grade-level or age-level performance is considered to fall at the 50th %ile ranking. An average score is considered to fall between 25% and 75%. Thus, a score at the 50th %ile on an intelligence measure is considered age-level ability. These percentile rankings differ from what would be considered an average score in other forms of testing.

13. *Fluid intelligence* is the intelligence used to reason and solve new problems that do not require acquired knowledge.

visual symbols went up to average. Finally, his nonverbal intelligence (visual reasoning) had improved, moving from 32nd percentile to above the 50th percentile. His cognitive functioning had changed in positive directions in all areas. What used to be scores in the borderline or low range had moved into the average range of cognitive functioning. This was highly unusual.

Even more promising for Andrew were his achievement scores. He had shown dramatic shifts in reading, writing, spelling, and mathematics. Four years earlier, Andrew had scored at the 1st percentile ranking on the Broad Mathematics score of the Woodcock-Johnson Achievement (WJA) tests. In Grade 3, he had been well below grade level. His calculation skills and problem-solving ability were only at beginning stages of development. On this second assessment, he scored at the 40th percentile on Calculation Skills (average) and at the 45th percentile on Applied Problems. As well, on a measure that was new to the Woodcock-Johnson math fluency test—the ability to do simple one-digit adding and subtracting quickly—he scored at the 86th percentile. That meant he scored better than 86 percent of his peers in his efficiency to do simple arithmetic under timed conditions. This was not imaginable three years earlier. With regard to writing, Andrew earlier had not been able to construct simple sentences. On the second assessment he scored at the 41st percentile on Spelling and at the 53rd percentile on Writing Samples (ability to construct sentences) and at the 29th percentile on Writing Fluency (speed of writing sentences). On the written language test, his Story Construction score was at the 50th percentile. In other words, Andrew was now quite capable of writing a story with a beginning, middle, and end that contained characters, a setting, and theme. As for reading, four years earlier his Broad Reading score on the WJA test had been at the 11th percentile ranking, meaning that 89 percent of his peers in Grade 3 were more efficient in reading ability. Now he scored at the 49th percentile in Reading Fluency (speed of reading). He was moving into the average range for reading as well as for math and written language.

Andrew still had six months of the Arrowsmith Program intervention before he would move back to Vancouver. Thus, it was likely these cognitive and achievement scores would improve further.

I was amazed. Andrew was solving specific cognitive weaknesses and had moved himself to the average range of functioning, albeit on the low-average side. I had seen improvements in achievement, but nothing as spectacular as this. Five years earlier, a school board psychologist had measured Andrew and described him with "borderline intelligence." We all have "aha" moments—this was mine. Skeptic though I had been, I was now ready to acknowledge that the brain could change.

I immediately called Barbara Arrowsmith Young and congratulated her on Andrew's improved cognitive functioning and achievement changes. I told her about his updated psycho-educational assessment results and how impressed I was. They were obviously the successful result of the Arrowsmith Program's cognitive exercises. Arrowsmith Young was delighted, but seemed to feel Andrew's impressive results were normal. She said this happened all the time with her students. I was even more impressed, and we talked more specifically about an Arrowsmith Program in Vancouver.

Two years later, when I interviewed Nancy, I asked her about reactions to Andrew's updated psycho-educational assessment. "I remember you being really impressed with his ability to get math," she said.

"Do you remember the cognitive functioning changes I saw?" I asked. I reiterated my pleasure at Andrew's improved processing speed and reasoning ability. Nancy replied that she felt "really positive" about Andrew's experience in the Arrowsmith Program and about his progress since.

Andrew Moves Back to Vancouver

Andrew spent three years at the Arrowsmith School in Toronto before returning to Vancouver. "He went from the intimate environment of Arrowsmith straight into Elkview Secondary School," said Nancy. "There were over two hundred kids in his Grade 8 class, and he didn't know a single one. I've always been amazed that Andrew never seemed to suffer any lack of self-esteem. He's always been a bit on the shy side, but has always felt good about himself.

"Having said that, Grade 8 started off a bit rocky. Just in case of any transition difficulties, Andrew went into the Learning Assistance Program at Elkview, which is terrific. He had never taken French, but instead received a tutoring period every second day. He started off struggling with science in Grade 8. He received an incomplete on an early report card, but after talking with the teacher, changing his lab partner, and buckling down more, he improved to a B. Andrew had an extra hour of private tutoring every week, and at the end of the year was awarded Most Improved Student of the Year. We were so proud."

"Andrew is hoping to go to a college or university after high school," continued Nancy. "Even though his counsellor suggested that math 11 essentials might be an easier course for him, he's not taking it because it doesn't qualify for university entrance credits. He amazes me with stuff like that. The comment I share with the many people who ask about Arrowsmith is through the analogy of a blind person. Other schools for children with learning disabilities taught Andrew how to walk with a cane, but Arrowsmith restored his vision. I think that says it all."

One year later I received another update from Nancy. Remarkably, Andrew received a B in biology 11, B in chemistry 11, A in earth science 11, A in social studies, and C in principles of mathematics 11. In her e-mail she wrote:

> *Andrew hopes to attend Brock University and take a science degree in oenology and viticulture. Standards are high, and his grades need to be really good. With this goal in mind, he's really applying himself. He made this university decision last winter, and noticed he needed chemistry 12 to get in. He wasn't taking chemistry 11 at the time, so enrolled in an online course. I was reluctant about this, fearing that everything else would suffer, and it would be hard for him to pass. I personally have terrible memories of myself doing chemistry 11. I actually tried to dissuade him from taking it! I phoned his counsellor, as well as the woman who runs the skills centre, and they believed Andrew would be okay. As you can see by his transcript, he pulled off a 74 percent (B) on top of everything else.*

Andrew's mother said, "I could, and did, weep with joy."

A New Vision

Andrew's updated psycho-educational assessment results and Arrowsmith Young's vision were instrumental in my decision to start an Arrowsmith School in Vancouver. Earlier, I had asked Nancy to describe Andrew's initial steps at Arrowsmith. "Our first step was for Andrew to meet with Barbara," said Nancy, "which he did in the fall. Separately, Barbara met with me and Mike, Andrew's father, who lived in Toronto. We discussed Andrew's learning deficits. Barbara said Andrew had 'severe' cognitive dysfunctions, but what amazed both Mike and me was the fact that she *nailed* Andrew. She totally, unequivocally, 'got' Andrew. And she used her assessment to describe what kind of a future he might have if his cognitive dysfunctions went unattended. She made sense of all the nagging concerns we've had over the years regarding Andrew's development. At this point we decided that we couldn't afford *not* to send Andrew to Arrowsmith. This decision took us back to Toronto."

I wondered what kind of information Nancy used to make this big life decision. "It was a leap of faith," she said. "I realize families will change schools, learning methods, provinces—you name it—do almost anything to give their child a chance at success. With Arrowsmith we felt secure that we were giving Andrew the very best tools to carve out his future. Barbara described the successful outcomes of other children with serious cognitive dysfunctions, and she discussed neuroplasticity. Her information bolstered our confidence. In my opinion, we made the best move for our son."

Anecdotal evidence—for example, these children's stories—has a place in educational neuroplasticity. It is powerful because we are able to assess cognitive skill levels. Research has been conducted on the effectiveness of the Arrowsmith Program. For example, a study conducted by Dr. William J. Lancee, head of research at the Department of Psychiatry at Mount Sinai Hospital in Toronto, indicated the cognitive changes made by students in the Arrowsmith Program correlated with specific gains in achievement in reading, writing, and math.[14]

---

14. Dr. William J. Lancee, "Report on an Outcome Evaluation of the Arrowsmith Program for Treating Learning Disabled Students" (November 20, 2005). http://www.arrowsmithschool.org/research.htm.

A study done with the Toronto Catholic District School Board highlighted the independence that students with learning disabilities can achieve after completing the Arrowsmith Program. The data showed that of the sixty-four elementary students studied, 95 percent were receiving resource support during the school day prior to starting the Arrowsmith Program. In fact, thirty-six of these sixty-four students received between four to eight periods a week of resource support and twenty-three received one to two periods a week. Of the 5 percent who did not receive resource support prior to entry in the Arrowsmith Program, all were either waiting for resource support or to be identified as having a learning disability.

After completing the Arrowsmith Program and enrolling at the high school level, only 31% still needed some level of resource support. In other words, 69 percent did not require any resource assistance during the school day and 26 percent needed only one period per day or less. (This included the occasional use of a resource classroom for completing homework and writing exams, which is considered less than one period of support per week.)[15]

The Arrowsmith Program inspires confidence in parents with children with learning disabilities looking for answers that work, answers that lead to better possibilities. The evidence, as shown in the preceding paragraphs, has been building for years that Arrowsmith graduates are able to cope with the regular education system and show improved classroom performance and achievement in subjects and social skills that previously caused them trouble.

The best way to gain a real understanding of Andrew's program is to learn Barbara Arrowsmith Young's story and how she pioneered a unique school for children with learning disabilities.

---

15. Arrowsmith School, "Report on the Arrowsmith Program in the Toronto Catholic District School Board" (January 25, 2007). http://www.arrowsmithschool.org/research.htm.

3

The Woman Who Helped Andrew Build a New Brain

Every great advance in science has issued from a new audacity of imagination.

—JOHN DEWEY, AUTHOR, *THE QUEST FOR CERTAINTY* (1929), AMERICAN EDUCATION REFORMER, PHILOSOPHER, AND PSYCHOLOGIST

The Turtle

Squirrels, Rabbits, and Turtles. These categories ranked the Grade 1 children's reading abilities. Barbara Arrowsmith Young was placed in the Turtles group.

"Unfortunately," she said in our interview, "my teacher was new and she believed that children were willful, that I was willfully doing these things. Once she gave me the strap. She insisted that I had to write over and over again a piece of writing without reversals. My numbers and my letters were reversed, my 9's were 6's, and my *b*'s were *d*'s. No matter how hard I tried, I just couldn't do it. This was interpreted as disobedience. The strapping took place in front of the class with all of the kids watching. It was less painful and more humiliating. I felt helpless. If I could have written properly, I would have, and not because she was going to beat me. And then I also did mirror writing. And writing from right to left, I would smear the work as I was writing. So not only was I writing reversals, making it impossible to read, I smeared the page because my hand sweated. It was the smearing that really upset her. It was awful."

Arrowsmith Young knew Turtles was not the group to be in; it was not the "in" group, though today Arrowsmith Young does not disparage other Turtles. In her mind she was stupid; she could see other children reading words, yet she couldn't. She simply had to look around to see that other kids understood what Turtles meant. Everyone could see who was in the Squirrel group, the ones really excelling, and the Rabbits, who were average. And then there were the Turtles—the slow ones who consequently thought themselves stupid.

In the 1950s and '60s, special education and recognition of learning disabilities and solutions were generally undeveloped or nonexistent. We'll now meet Barbara Arrowsmith Young as she struggled in Grades 1 through 12, university, and graduate school. We'll then learn about her pioneering work in brain plasticity that led to the unique special education program and private school that Andrew attended.

Grades 1 through 12

Barbara Arrowsmith Young was born in Toronto in 1951, the middle child of five, and the only one with learning disabilities. She had areas of brilliance. Her thinking was exceptional and her auditory and visual memory tested in the 99th percentile, but her brilliance coexisted with deficits. Arrowsmith Young's brain was *asymmetrical.*

Dr. Norman Doidge's *New York Times* bestselling book, *The Brain That Changes Itself*, is changing people's beliefs about the brain. Chapter 2, "Building Herself a Better Brain," is about Arrowsmith Young. "This asymmetry left its chaotic handwriting on her body as well," Doidge writes. "Her mother made a joke of it, saying, 'The obstetrician must have yanked you out by your right leg,' which was longer than her left, causing her pelvis to shift. Her right arm never straightened, her right side was larger than her left, her left eye less alert. Her spine was asymmetrical and twisted with scoliosis." Asymmetry affected her early cognitive abilities and school experiences from kindergarten through Grade 8. She endured constant struggle.

Arrowsmith Young is the first to say that she was unhappy at school. Her learning difficulties in elementary and high school were varied and numerous. A psychiatrist, psychoanalyst, and researcher, Dr. Doidge describes Arrowsmith Young's childhood learning profile in detail. He writes, "She had a confusing assortment of serious learning disabilities. The area of the brain devoted to speech, Broca's Area, was not working properly, so she had trouble pronouncing words."

Doidge describes how "She also had a 'kinesthetic' problem." He relates the following story: "One day when Barbara was three she decided to play matador and bull. She was the bull and the car in the driveway was the matador's cape. She charged, thinking she would swerve and avoid it, but she misjudged the space and ran into the car, ripping her head open. Her mother declared she would be surprised if Barbara lived another year."

Doidge writes that "Kinesthetic perception allows us to be aware of where our body or limbs are in space, enabling us to control and coordinate our movements. It also helps us recognize objects by touch." He continues, "But these were not her most debilitating problems. Because the part of her brain that helps to understand the relationship between symbols wasn't functioning normally, she had trouble understanding grammar, math concepts, logic, and cause and effect. She couldn't distinguish between 'the father's brother' and 'the brother's father.' The double negative was impossible for her to decipher. She couldn't read a clock because she couldn't understand the relationship between the hands."

Because she had trouble with logic, Arrowsmith Young could not pick up inconsistencies when listening to smooth talkers, so she was never sure whom to trust. Doidge noted that friendships were difficult, and in my interview with her, she explained this. "I would have just one friend at a time, because language processing was really a challenge. If multiple people were talking, for me to coordinate and understand what this person was saying and what that person was saying, and then trying to connect them—I couldn't do it."

Math presented perplexing issues. "She could memorize math

procedures but couldn't understand math concepts," Doidge says. "She could recall that five times five equals twenty-five but couldn't understand why. Her teachers responded by giving her extra drills."

But there was no such thing as *can't* in Arrowsmith Young's world. She developed a real sense of determination. In my interviews with her, she said, "It was a family mind set. Our parents' approach to a problem was that we have this problem here, so how do we get a solution?" Arrowsmith Young's father was a trained mathematician and physicist who successfully worked for General Electric as an electrical engineer and inventor. When asked how much her father helped her, Arrowsmith Young said, "My dad was working very hard to support a family of five children, so he wasn't around a lot. He left early to go to work, and often came home for dinner, and went back to work or brought work home. He wasn't really present. There was actually a reverse prejudice. He used to say, by which he meant no harm, 'I have only one daughter and four sons, and you've got to really make it.' He meant that in a positive way. He adored me. But I wondered how I was going to make it. 'I have all these problems,' I thought, 'so I'm going to have to work even harder to not let the family down.' That's the way I took it, but that was not his intention. It made me even more driven and my struggles more emotional."

Her teacher-mother was dedicated and had great hopes for her daughter's success in school and life. Yet, like many parents today, neither parent could understand why a child who appeared so bright would struggle in school. But for Arrowsmith Young there was no solution. "Also, in the '50s there were no tutors; tutors didn't exist. There wasn't a word tutor or concept tutor, not in Peterborough, Ontario, not at that time. So, teachers basically told my parents I would never learn properly. My parents were told, 'Get used to it.' However, my parents decided we were going to do something about it, and that is when my mother started creating flash cards—toward the end of Grade 1.

"There were flash cards for reading and math facts. We used flash cards at home every day. Because the school was right across the street, I could come home at lunch and my mother would take twenty minutes and do the flash cards. I became a workaholic. That's what it took to get through Grade 1. I was very determined. It was ruthless, every spare moment."

After school, Arrowsmith Young would work for another hour. They worked on hundreds of flash cards all year.

Arrowsmith Young's mother would hold up flash cards with simple math problems on them. Because the young girl couldn't figure them out, she found a place to sit where the sun made the paper translucent, so she could read the answers on the back. As early as Grade 1, she was working on ways to compensate for her problems.

Arrowsmith Young has an extraordinary memory. Her education was filled with teachers who had no idea what a learning disability was and who would have equated any learning problem with retardation or low intelligence. In many school districts, separate classrooms were designed for students who did not meet the expected outcomes within a regular education classroom. As a result, children with mental retardation, Down's syndrome, autism, and other developmental disorders were integrated with children with learning disabilities. Arrowsmith Young was able to avoid these classrooms because she had an amazing memory for factual information, which in most schools even today is a talent that can earn good grades.

Sadly, all attempts at Arrowsmith Young's remediation failed to address the underlying problem. Remediation simply made her life more agonizing. Yet this girl with severe learning dysfunctions survived school and then went on to create effective remediation programs for children with learning disabilities, all because she had an excellent visual and auditory memory and a strong thinking and problem-solving bent, which, she said, runs in her family. Because she could memorize facts and information, she advanced through school. She would rehearse work sheets until she had the information memorized for tests. Because school was about regurgitation of facts, Arrowsmith Young was able to graduate.

She remained not overly coordinated and passing tests was hit and miss. "I would go into exams in high school," she recalled, "and sometimes I would walk out with 20 percent and sometimes 90 percent, and it wouldn't matter what subject. Most kids come out of an exam and say, 'Well, I know I did really well or I did really badly.' I would say nothing, because I had no idea. When I did do well on a test, some people would say, 'You're just being shy.' I wasn't. I just really didn't know. I just didn't know whether I had done well or poorly.

"My kinesthetic problems hurt test results," Arrowsmith Young added as an afterthought, "which was very significant. I failed typing, which is not conceptual."

She paused and continued. "Also, I was terrible in sports. But not all sports. By Grade 9 I discovered badminton. Not really fast badminton, but gentle badminton. It gave me time—the birdie would be flying through the air and I could figure out the position, so if I had the time I could compensate. Swimming was another matter. I was actually quite good and I became a lifeguard. Swimming would be the main thing that I really did. I didn't fit in with teams and sports."

As Arrowsmith Young progressed through school, demands on her cognitive skills changed, and logical reasoning and cause-and-effect reasoning become a necessity. When these cognitive skills were required in a specific class, her course grade dropped. Her grades were okay, she said—in the 70 percent range—and in those days 70 percent was acceptable to get into university. Her talent for memorization got her through high school and into university. All of the Young children were expected to go to university. "I don't know if it was ever said," Arrowsmith Young recollected, "but the expectation was that you were going to university. It was never a question. It was an unspoken expectation."

University Years

Arrowsmith Young was accepted by the University of Guelph, about an hour's drive from Toronto. Eventually she focused on psychology with a specialty in child development. However, the young woman first thought she would become a nutritionist.

"I started in nutrition at Guelph," she said. "It was one of the premier places for this. It was a four-year degree. First-year sciences were a challenge. I hadn't thought this out very well, because I had organic chemistry, physical chemistry, and physiology—way too many sciences, all of which require conceptual cognitive skills. I got through the first term, passed everything with marks in the 60 percent range, but switched majors.

"I remember getting on the bus, the bus from Toronto to Guelph.

Halfway to Guelph, I was thinking I just had to get off. I didn't, but I just felt a panic. My vision was that I would get off and stand in the field beside the road and stay there for the rest of my life. I couldn't go forward, I couldn't go backward. Once again I was a failure. I just thought, 'I can't do this,' so I switched to child studies. I justified it to my parents because previously [they] had helped found the Unitarian Church in Peterborough, and I worked in the children's program. So I told them that once I was in the university environment, I realized this is what I was truly interested in—working with children—and I'd had this previous experience.

"It turned out fine," Arrowsmith Young said. "I did enjoy working with children, but that wasn't the reason I switched. I switched because the courses were easier, because it mostly involved memorizing. I began to blossom. I was particularly good in practicums [student teaching or internships] observing children's behaviour. We had a laboratory preschool, so we would sit behind one-way mirrors, observe children, and write up our observations. I really enjoyed that, actually. This was probably the first time that people felt like I had a gift. I enjoyed it and found it quite fascinating; it was like nonverbal problem solving and puzzles, and looking at nonverbal patterns of interactions. They weren't discussing neurology and cognitive functioning then, but Jean Piaget[16] was a preeminent thinker—famous for studying cognitive development and studying children. Once I got into it and started exploring and watching these kids learn differently, it spurred me into going into school psychology, and I really do think underlying that was an attempt to understand what was working for me and what wasn't, and why I was struggling so much.

"So I finished my undergraduate degree and was hired by University of Guelph. I worked there for a year as head teacher in their preschool laboratory. Privately—and this shows my lack of self-esteem—I was convinced, truthfully, that they hired me because I was such a failure. They couldn't allow a graduate to go out and work for somebody else because it would reflect so badly on their program that they had to work on me

16. Jean Piaget (1896–1980) was a Swiss developmental psychologist and philosopher. He developed a theory of cognitive development based on stages that has influenced the thinking and practice of medical doctors, psychologists, psychiatrists, educators, and researchers.

longer, as if they had to keep me in house to do more finishing work so I wouldn't damage their reputation. For most people it would have been an honour.

"By this time I really had become interested in learning, and why people couldn't learn. The book *Why Johnny Can't Read*[17] was breaking new ground. It was an age of important new material on learning disabilities. I decided to go to graduate school."

Graduate School

Arrowsmith Young attended the Ontario Institute of Studies in Education (OISE) of the University of Toronto. A graduate program, OISE is one of the largest and most innovative teacher education programs in Canada. At OISE, she would become an innovator in special education. While she was there, her own Arrowsmith program was born.

Graduate school presents learning challenges unlike those of undergraduate university programs. No more rote memorization. Now Arrowsmith Young had to use her brain in a different way. Not only did she have to work diligently, read hundreds of pages of graduate text, organize her papers, and synthesize complex information from research articles, but at OISE, she began to build herself a better brain.

Simply put, during her years at OISE, Arrowsmith Young became one of the pioneers of neuroplasticity. Two things deserve particular emphasis. First, she realized she could (and did) develop her own cognitive exercises, relying in part on the work of two famous scientists: neuropsychologist Alexander Luria and psychologist Mark Rosenzweig. Second, using her cognitive exercises, Arrowsmith Young built her brain to strengthen weak cognitive capacities that otherwise would have hindered her in graduate school.

Alexander Luria (1902–1977) was a Soviet neuroscientist and developmental psychologist who gained attention by investigating the brain of an injured soldier. Luria's book, *The Man with a Shattered World: History of a Brain Wound* (Harvard University Press, 1972), opened Arrowsmith

---

17. Rudolf Flesch, *Why Johnny Can't Read: And What You Can Do about It* (New York: Harper, 1955).

Young's mind to the fact that she was not alone with her own learning profile. Luria's description of the brain-injured Russian soldier appeared to match her lifelong learning challenges. After his brain injury, this soldier struggled with understanding cause and effect and was confused with grammar. He struggled with visual-spatial thinking and comprehension. Luria hypothesized that the region of the brain injury in the soldier—a bullet in the left hemisphere where three perceptual regions interconnect: temporal or auditory, parietal or spatial, and occipital or visual images—was responsible for integrating these learning functions. Arrowsmith Young speculated that Luria's analysis might also apply to her, though she did not have a brain injury like the soldier's. For her, it was evidence that her similar learning struggles had a cause—a specific brain weakness.

Mark Rosenzweig (1922–2009) was most recently a professor emeritus at the University of California at Berkeley. He made great contributions in the areas of cognition, brain plasticity, and behaviour. Professor Rosenzweig studied brain change in rats in three environments: one enriched with toys, a normal one, and one with no stimulation at all. His straightforward experiments proved that the more stimulating the environment, the more effective the rats were as learners and the more neurologically complex were their brains. Thus, in rats, it was proof of neuroplasticity; if a rat's brain were stimulated, it would change. Rosenzweig's study also caught Arrowsmith Young's attention. She asked herself, "Why not me?" She figured that if a rat's brain could change by stimulating it, why not create cognitive exercises that would stimulate her own brain?

Arrowsmith Young became her own laboratory rat. She decided to invent cognitive exercises with which to test herself. One of the impaired neurological capacities of the soldier in Luria's book caused him to lose the ability to tell time using an analogue clock. "The first exercise I created was a clocks exercise to test Rosenzweig's conclusions on myself to see if the brain is plastic and can change." She devised this exercise because she thought it might help her overcome two big issues: first, she also had difficulty telling time on an analogue clock, and second, she could not easily relate symbols.

"I [also] read Luria's *Basic Problems in Neurolinguistics*," said

Arrowsmith Young (Berlin: de Gruyter Mouton, 1976). "In one section he described the myriad of difficulties I too had, and he also mentioned that people with lesions to this cortical region had trouble reading a clock. In his book *Higher Cortical Functions in Man* (London: Tavistock Publications, 1966), he makes mention again of reading clocks being related to this area. Further, I was reading Rosenzweig's article, 'Effects of environmental complexity and training on brain chemistry and anatomy,'[18] and this gave me the idea of creating a cognitive exercise to stimulate the cognitive area that I had difficulty with, which involved reading clocks. It was the activity I chose based on my theorizing of what would stimulate this area."

Inspired by Rosenzweig and Luria, Arrowsmith Young created her clocks exercise. She used analogue clocks on flash cards to see if she could train her brain to improve her cognitive functioning.

After repetitive daily training for several months, she began to notice a change. The clocks exercise helped her develop the capacity to grasp logic, see cause and effect, and understand mathematical concepts. For the first time, she did not have to rely on her ability for rote memorization.

Arrowsmith Young was twenty-eight years old. Her husband (since deceased), who had his M.Ed in special education from OISE, was supportive. She spent long days working on this task, creating increasingly complex clocks.

The various clocks had hands drawn on them (later this was computerized). The exercise is used when a child has difficulty with reading comprehension, mathematical reasoning, logical reasoning, reading analogue clocks, understanding cause and effect, and reversals of the letters *b* and *d* or *p* and *q* when reading and writing. Arrowsmith Young wanted a result that would enable her to be able to reason better—for example, to be able to differentiate between "the father's brother" and "the brother's father."

In order to measure success or the lack of it, Arrowsmith Young pretested herself using the Miller's Analogies Test, which measures verbal

18. D. Krech, M.R. Rosenzweig, and E.L. Bennett, "Effects of Environmental Complexity and Training on Brain Chemistry and Anatomy," *J Comp Physiol Psychol* 53 (1960), 509–519.

reasoning, and using a mathematics test. After working with her clock exercises, she retested herself on the same tests. She saw meaningful changes, the most noteworthy of which was that she now was beginning to grasp concepts as they were being explained either in print or in discussion. She no longer had to spend hours poring over material to try to understand it, with little success. She could now do this in real time, which was a major, exciting change.

Arrowsmith Young intuited that an effective cognitive exercise involved *repetition*. Using flash cards, she practised diligently. After about three months, Arrowsmith Young noticed improvement in her understanding of relationships in mathematical reasoning, reading comprehension, and cause and effect. Still, at this point, she had little idea of the innovations she would eventually bring to the field of educational neuroplasticity.

While at graduate school, Arrowsmith Young also developed another cognitive exercise called Kinesthetic Perception. She had not forgotten her injury while playing matador and bull when she was three years old, and she is the first to explain that she was clumsy and uncoordinated, to the point where her left side was almost nonfunctional. When we first talked, she reminded me of what she had also told Doidge: that the left side of her body was constantly bruised, and even the left side of her car was dented. She had been unable to use her left hand for tasks that involved using tools, typing, or even holding a teacup without dropping it.

Common symptoms of kinesthetic cognitive dysfunction include awkwardness of body movement, difficulty with writing tasks including deviation from the line if not visually focused on it or not applying consistent pressure, and difficulty with sports, particularly team sports where more coordination may be required. Arrowsmith Young was intent on solving her clumsiness by changing her neural pathways through these repetitive exercises.

The young woman clearly benefited from both exercises. She could now more easily analyze and process information. Learning with comprehension was less arduous and more efficient. Concepts could be understood faster and with less repetition when reviewing material. She became much less uncoordinated and could effectively use the left side of her body.

By now Arrowsmith Young fully recognized the power of the brain's plasticity. She went on to develop specific cognitive exercises to strengthen other cognitive weaknesses, eventually creating nineteen exercises over the next several years.

Arrowsmith Young considers herself a researcher-inventor. Her father was a researcher and inventor and she believes the propensity came from observing him. She recalls the time he did spend at home, when he would share his inventions, even though as a child she didn't understand them. Arrowsmith Young caught the passion and excitement of creating something practical that didn't already exist. Her father registered over thirty patents; processes in the field of engineering still use his work. When asked where her knowledge of the brain and brain maps came from, Arrowsmith Young explains that she reread Luria exhaustively (her copies of his books are underlined and highlighted in multicoloured ink) as well as journals in the field of neuroscience.

Arrowsmith Young received her master's degree in psychology from OISE. Her degree was granted by the University of Toronto.

A School with a Difference Is Born

In 1980, using her savings, Arrowsmith Young started her first school for children with cognitive dysfunctions, one that would use her cognitive exercises. With her brother and husband, she rented a one-thousand-square-foot space in downtown Toronto. They kept expenses to a bare minimum. She started with eight students aged twelve to eighteen. A YMCA vocational counsellor recommended young adult students struggling with learning disabilities to her. Other students came to her from the regular school system's part-time remedial program. Armed with several of her own cognitive exercises and a small staff of three, including herself, she opened her modest school. Over the years, Arrowsmith Young watched how her students responded and then adapted and developed more cognitive exercises as needed. While helping children with learning disabilities, she was steadily changing the face of special education. Improving cognitive dysfunctions is about repetitive cognitive exercises. After a student completes one level of a cognitive exercise, it increases in complexity and difficulty. Since 1980, thousands of children with serious cognitive dysfunctions have benefited.

Opposition and criticism are part of many new movements, and Arrowsmith Young's school was no exception. From the beginning, it faced strong opposition because the education establishment did not accept neuroplasticity. Even today, a majority of educators resist the fact that the brain can change itself. And most know almost nothing of Barbara Arrowsmith Young. Her school start-up was not easy, but her resilience had already been proven. After all, despite serious learning disabilities, she had survived elementary school, high school, university, and graduate studies.

Educators and scientists who believe in traditional paradigms did not deter Arrowsmith Young. From her own Arrowsmith experiences and assessments, she had learned that children can change their cognitive capacities. After all, hadn't she redesigned her own brain? She applied her newfound abilities to programs that have improved the lives of many children with learning disabilities. She is passionate about her findings and her conviction that the brain can change.

Today, Arrowsmith Young spends countless hours at her desk on the top floor of the Arrowsmith School brownstone building on St. Clair Avenue West. She is often surrounded by hundreds of red program files containing test results of each student in the Arrowsmith Program. On the same floor, program coordinators work with schools across North America implementing the Arrowsmith Program. Students on the first and second floors work on their individual, personalized cognitive programs.

Early on, Arrowsmith Young made the choice to devote her time to developing and refining the cognitive programs she created and to working on systems to deliver the program to other schools, all the while maintaining the integrity of the program to ensure she was serving the needs of the students rather than simply promoting her ideas. Consequently, the Arrowsmith Program has stayed close to home and not received international recognition or widespread application across North America. It may have been necessary for her to proceed in an unrecognized fashion to allow her to improve and develop her program over thirty years. Now her hope, and the hope of many others, is that the Arrowsmith Program will become widely used.

The program is now moving into the United States, particularly in

Jewish day schools. Arrowsmith Programs are also licensed by a number of mostly private schools in North America. These include Catholic, Jewish, Christian, and Montessori, as well as the Eaton Arrowsmith School. As well, charter schools in the United States and the Learning Disabilities Association of Saskatchewan have recently started implementing the program.

Arrowsmith Young is resilient and determined in her work, rarely letting setbacks or rejections of her approach slow her down. She feels frustrated when they occur, but is not deterred and does not let them interfere with her commitment to making her work broadly available to children with learning challenges. She is quiet, reserved, and modest about what she has accomplished over the last thirty years. She likes the peace and comfort of her home and garden. And there is no doubt that the thousands of children whom she has helped have given her the hope and sense of possibilities she needs to continue her remarkable work.

Arrowsmith Young is a kind, considerate, thoughtful woman, who on many occasions has experienced lashes of criticism from other professionals—educators and special education people alike—but she continues her journey undaunted. She has sincere hopes that one day children with learning disabilities across North America will have access to her program. Each passing day, Arrowsmith Young regrets that other children with cognitive dysfunctions have a lifetime of struggle ahead of them. She looks forward to a day when all parents, grandparents, teachers, administrators, psychologists, psychiatrists, and medical doctors will learn about and accept educational neuroplasticity. She knows it will take time. But above all, she knows that children like Andrew can change their brains and flourish.

4

Brain School Opens—with Controversy

As a parent, you feel as if you've finally found a place where every person truly cares, but more importantly, really understands your child and can give you a plan for measurable improvement.

—PARENT, EATON ARROWSMITH SCHOOL

Controversy

Starting Eaton Arrowsmith School in Vancouver was going to be controversial, but at first I did not fully appreciate this fact. I see the glass as half full most of the time. When my colleagues learned that I would be opening a school using the Arrowsmith Program methodology, some were surprised and others upset and confused. I had anticipated some reaction, but not at the level of intensity that ensued. Eaton Learning Centre was removed from the referral lists for psycho-educational assessments by several of the private schools that worked with children with learning disabilities. Previously, we had worked with those schools for over ten years. One director of a private school for children with dyslexia wrote an article in the school's newsletter warning parents of a school that would be using unproven methods of improving cognitive functioning. I was removed, without notice, from an advisory board of the organization overseeing Orton-Gillingham tutors in British Columbia.

It was surprising how quickly some of my colleagues decided to distance themselves from me.

This is neuroplasticity at its worst: the plastic paradox Norman Doidge wrote about. Once an idea is entrenched in the minds of some who work with children with learning disabilities, it can be so strongly rooted that it is impossible to examine and appropriately analyze new ideas. Ironically, my former colleagues' brains were "fixed" on ideas rooted in the concepts of dyslexia and phonics-based instruction—in particular, Orton-Gillingham. Any form of remediation that was not within this conceptual framework was challenged vehemently. The Orton-Gillingham method of improving the reading, spelling, and writing skills of children with dyslexia had been part of the learning disabilities community of Vancouver for over thirty years. It was the first program to which I had been introduced in Grade 2 to help me develop reading skills. For over twenty-five years the program had been the focus of remediation in the three private schools for children with learning disabilities in Vancouver. In 2005, there were close to sixty Orton-Gillingham tutors working in the Vancouver area. This program framed my colleagues' thinking. It framed their lives and was hardwired in their consciousnesses.

The problem, however, is that not all children with learning disabilities are dyslexic and require phonics-based or other reading intervention instruction; not all have reading and spelling problems. Certainly a majority of children with learning disabilities have reading problems. These can range from reading comprehension and word decoding (reading a word unrelated to understanding it) to spelling and reading speed. The Orton-Gillingham community in Vancouver did not fully conceptualize why these children had learning disabilities and why they failed in regular-education classrooms, even after tutoring. This was my main obstacle in developing an understanding of the importance of the Arrowsmith Program. It was not well understood that the primary causes of learning disabilities are specific cognitive functioning weaknesses, many of which are related to reading but also affect other areas of academic attainment.[19] The idea that these cognitive functions can be improved was far from their frame of thinking.

This problem did not affect enrolment. The traditional education community's written and verbal skepticism and criticisms of the Arrowsmith Program did not discourage parents from attending our presentations on the opening of Eaton Arrowsmith School. When we opened our doors for the first day of school in September 2005, we had over fifty students ready to change their lives using the Arrowsmith Program. Why this high level of interest despite the negative remarks from the traditional community? The answer was obvious. The method of remediation for learning disabilities in Vancouver focused on only one category of learning disabilities—dyslexia. But parents who enrolled their children in our school realized it was more than just reading trouble that was resulting in their child suffering at school. They were looking for greater possibilities and answers previously unaddressed.

The Eaton Arrowsmith School program would be modelled exactly after Barbara Arrowsmith Young's school in Toronto. I visited the school for a week and reviewed how its systems were implemented, how its classrooms were designed, and how many staff were employed during the school day. I wanted to know how teachers interacted with students, what level of administration was needed, what each cognitive exercise looked like, and how children reacted to their cognitive exercises. I watched, listened, and took notes.

There was some irony in that prior to learning about the Arrowsmith Program, I had never wanted to run a school. I had mixed feelings at the thought of working as a principal or director of a school. It is not easy running a school, and I had seen some principals and headmasters become disheartened over time. They deal with anger, frustration, happiness, sadness, and joy at such intense levels that it is all too easy to lose energy and motivation. Those who last come to compassionately understand that parents are only searching to have their child's needs addressed in some way. I had been asked to consider running schools, but had always

19. T.P. Alloway, "Working Memory, Not IQ, Predicts Subsequent Learning in Children with Learning Difficulties," *European Journal of Psychological Assessment* 25, no. 20 (2009), 92–98. Working memory is one area of cognitive ability that is receiving significant research. In fact, working memory ability is being observed as more predictive of academic attainment than a full-scale IQ score. Tracy Packiam Alloway's research is highlighting these findings.

refused out of concern for whether I could actually handle this kind of work. But the Arrowsmith program was different. It was a brilliant concept. The benefits this program could give to hundreds of children in the Vancouver area were undeniable, and I was drawn irresistibly to the idea. It just had to happen.

Teacher Training

Arrowsmith Program cognitive teachers are talented, highly trained, and passionate about their work. A long selection process is undertaken to choose just the right individuals for this kind of work. Trying to persuade a child to work on their cognitive functioning weaknesses is both rewarding and challenging. The rewarding part of the job is seeing the child improve his or her cognitive capacities and become capable of doing tasks never dreamed possible prior to Arrowsmith. The challenge is working with students who are stuck on a specific level of mastery, who may have been working on that same level for a month or more. At this point, it is often difficult to persuade a child to persevere, and a teacher needs exceptional patience to help the child believe success is possible.

Barbara Arrowsmith Young is keenly determined to make sure her program is executed appropriately. Each August, cognitive teachers spend long hours in the training programs held in Toronto. Arrowsmith Young's chief education officer, Annette Goodman, has also provided essential guidance in further developing the training modules. Teachers come from all over North America each summer to learn about the Arrowsmith Program and to qualify as cognitive teachers. The excitement runs high during the first few hours of training, before it is quickly realized the volume of knowledge that has to be assimilated in three short weeks.

As teachers progress in the cognitive training, they begin to realize what they were *not* taught in their education programs at universities or colleges. They are often surprised at what they did not know about the human brain and its neurobiological structure. There is both an inspired sense of appreciation for what they are learning and a pervasive sense of trepidation that they won't measure up to Arrowsmith Program instructors' standards. No one wants to fail Barbara Arrowsmith Young.

In addition to all-day training sessions, instructors give several hours of homework every evening. Tears and laughter blend for those weeks in Toronto. Arrowsmith Young is determined that the certified cognitive teachers leave Toronto with the right knowledge base and instructional tools for guiding children with learning disabilities and attention disorders. When the teachers officially become Arrowsmith graduates, there is a true sense of joy in the room.

A Brain School Day

A day at "Brain School" begins like any other day in most schools across North America. The school day consists of eight periods or blocks and runs from 8:30 a.m. to 3:00 p.m. The students spend six periods in their cognitive classroom and two periods in academic subjects—math and English. No other academic subjects are taught. The focus of the school is cognitive remediation.[20]

In the morning, the principal and vice-principal stand outside, greeting about a hundred children by name as they enter the building, located at the University of British Columbia in Vancouver. The children then head up to the second floor and take off their coats and backpacks in the cloakrooms. Photographs of staff adorn the walls, along with plaques recognizing student achievement and display boards full of the students' art and writing. The receptionist greets the children, asking them about their evening and their homework assignments. The atmosphere is hopeful, inspiring, and focused. After a few minutes of talking to one another, the children head to their classrooms—called cognitive classrooms—and get ready to settle in for the day.

In many ways, EAS cognitive classrooms look just like traditional classrooms. Ten to twelve computers are lined up side by side against the wall in each classroom. Desks are lined in rows facing the teachers' desks

20. Other academic subjects such as science and social studies are not taught primarily because children with learning disabilities often do not have adequate cognitive functioning to find success in these subjects. Instead, the goal is to improve cognitive functioning as quickly as possible. Progress in math and English at Eaton Arrowsmith School is shown to be most significant when the children's cognitive functioning necessary for these academic subjects also improves.

positioned in the front of the room. The whiteboard displays the day's activities, including special announcements such as birthdays or goals for the week. Children's names are written on the board in recognition of their achievements of the previous school day. An auditory centre is set up in each classroom, usually with three desks lined up against a wall, each equipped with MP3 players and headphones. Many people might observe this classroom and think it is just like any other. But there are big differences.

Each of the school day's eight blocks is forty minutes in length; thus, six blocks spent in the cognitive classroom equals approximately 240 minutes of a 320-minute school day. Each child works with his or her individualized cognitive program, designed by the Arrowsmith Program in Toronto, after extensive assessment of their strengths and weaknesses. Each student's program is posted on the classroom wall for review at any time. Two blocks take place outside the cognitive classroom, the English and math academic blocks. The children look forward to these two academic blocks, which provide a change of pace during the school day during which they do not to have to be so intensely engaged in repetitive cognitive exercises.

In period 1, each cognitive classroom at Eaton Arrowsmith School has approximately eighteen to twenty-five children. From periods 2 through 8, five to eight students per period leave for their academic classes. Thus, with two teachers per classroom, during most cognitive classroom periods the teacher-student ratio is between one to eight and one to ten. If you were to observe a cognitive classroom, you would see seven students at work doing computer-related cognitive exercises. Another four students would be focused on auditory cognitive exercises, and the remainder would be working at their desks on cognitive exercises that require paper-and-pencil activity. The two teachers would be checking constantly with the students, watching the active engagement levels of each child. *Active engagement is the life force of neuroplasticity.* If children are not engaged in a task, their brains are not optimally learning. Children who are struggling with active engagement are given encouragement and praise. New goals are set for them. The teacher sits near them to influence more engagement in the cognitive exercises.

Let's look at a student named Alissa. She may suddenly say, "I mastered!" The entire class looks at her; she has mastered one of the harder levels of a Symbol Relations exercise. (This cognitive exercise builds reasoning or conceptual understanding.) Everyone cheers for Alissa, and her cognitive teacher notes Alissa's mastery and writes it on the classroom whiteboard. The children then resume with active engagement on their own individual cognitive exercises, hoping they can be the next one to say, "I mastered!"

Each child's program is uniquely tailored to his or her learning needs. After the Arrowsmith assessment, parents meet with staff at Eaton Arrowsmith School. Their child's results are outlined and strengths and weaknesses are explained. Often parents leave these meetings marvelling at how accurate Arrowsmith assessments are in explaining their child's learning profiles. As well, the fact that each of these cognitive weaknesses can then be targeted with a series of cognitive exercises leaves them with a renewed sense of hope. At times the results conflict with parents' previous perceptions of the problem because they may not have fully understood the challenges their child faces in learning. As well, many children use creative compensation techniques to get around their frustrations, and parents may believe their child is more capable of learning than is really the case. Often, in the early grades, what is not perceived as a neurological weakness by a parent can become even more of an issue as a child moves to advanced grades in high school.

At EAS, the six cognitive blocks are filled with exercises for which the child has shown a cognitive functioning weakness. There may be blocks for fine motor, auditory memory, social perception, development of reasoning, and working memory for numbers. As the student masters a cognitive exercise, that exercise is stopped and a new one started on another area of cognitive weakness that needs improvement. By the end of a school day, students at Eaton Arrowsmith School are tired. They have just spent 240 minutes engaging their brains in challenging exercises that promote neuroplasticity, and their English and math classes have also challenged them to use their developing neurological abilities. In total, including homework, a student at Eaton Arrowsmith School will spend between 300 to 330 minutes a day (based on age) working on cognitive exercises.

Students in regular schools are not required to spend such concentrated time in cognitive exercises, active engagement, and repetition. They find ways to lose focus and avoid notice in most public and private schools. This is not the case with the Arrowsmith Program. EAS classes are closely monitored by the cognitive teachers. Furthermore, at the end of each period, children must record in a notebook how much they have completed and their new goals for the next day. There is little opportunity to lose focus and drift. The result is a fine-tuned executive-functioning brain that is capable of long periods of focus. Public school teachers who work with graduates of the Arrowsmith Program are often surprised at how focused Arrowsmith graduates are and how well they complete assignments in a given time.

The children's cognitive exercises are complex—tasks most of their parents could not possibly accomplish. Perhaps you are wondering how a child can do this kind of repetitive work for three and sometimes four years. How can parents persuade their child to return day after day for more of the same exercises? Does the child not become bored? Detailed explanations lie in the case studies in the following chapters.

Extracurricular Activities

While it is certainly true that students at EAS focus intensely on strengthening their cognitive abilities, their days are strongly balanced by a variety of physical activities and other fun projects. In fact, students get more physical activity than the weekly requirements of most public schools. Dr. John Ratey, in his book, *Spark: The Revolutionary New Science of Exercise and the Brain* (Little, Brown and Company, 2008), highlights the importance of physical fitness. His book has inspired the staff at EAS to increase physical fitness opportunities for both students and staff. Daily physical education at EAS consists of forty minutes of outdoor play at the various University of British Columbia athletic fields and residential playgrounds. At different times of the year, the children enjoy supervised soccer, football, basketball, baseball, dodge ball, ultimate (Frisbee), tag, ice hockey, skating, and swimming. Although groups are formed for some of these sports, because EAS is a small school, we do not have enough students to form competitive intramural and extramural teams based on specific grades or ages. EAS does offer track and field as an official school sport in which we compete with other schools throughout the year.

Students can opt to participate in many other extracurricular activities. Staff members offer a morning running club, a morning yoga club, and a noon-hour dance club. The school presents an annual talent show in which many of the children take the opportunity to demonstrate their musical or dance skills. Practice in dance, singing, guitar, piano, and other performance arts takes place for a month leading up to the show.

Extracurricular activities include a variety of field trips including snowboarding, a pumpkin-patch visit, and attending a play or musical. Guest artists are invited to visit the school to teach various techniques in watercolour, collage, painting, drawing, and other art media, and guest speakers from UBC—often brain researchers—discuss their fields of interests and research with students.

Students also participate in a variety of fundraisers, including the Sun Run, the ChildRun for BC Children's Hospital, and the Terry Fox Run. They look forward to not wearing their uniforms on the Jeans Day fundraiser for BC Children's Hospital and on anti-bullying Pink Shirt Day. They have also raised money for Haiti relief efforts and for wells to be drilled in remote areas of India.

Success and Self-Esteem

Prior to attending Eaton Arrowsmith School, our students struggled academically and socially, usually failing some of their classes and dealing with low self-esteem and bullying. The negative impact of this stress on cognitive functioning is being highlighted in current research.[21] In the Arrowsmith Program, students find success. They learn to recognize that they are in control of their own lives. They learn that it is possible

21. Dr. Tracy Vaillancourt, the Canada research chair in Children's Mental Health and Violence Prevention at the University of Ottawa, has been conducting research with her colleagues on the impact of being bullied on cortisol levels in children and corresponding negative consequences on cognitive functioning; T. Vaillancourt, J. Clinton, P. McDougall, L. Schmidt, and S. Hymel, "The Neurobiology of Peer Victimization and Rejection," Shane R. Jimerson, Susan M. Swearer, and Dorothy L. Espelage (eds.), *The International Handbook of School Bullying* (New York: Routledge, 2010), 299–304.

to change their cognitive capacities, and that they are in charge of the change. This feeling of control over their own abilities gives them confidence and a sense of self-worth that is cumulative and feeds on itself. Their newfound sense of self-worth enables them to continue their daily work on the cognitive exercises. There are certainly days they wish they could be doing something else, but what child doesn't struggle with those feelings from time to time? The key to their continuation in the program is their developing self-esteem, their resilience, and their determination. Often, just as importantly, it is also their parents' determination to help their children avoid the learned helplessness model of some special education programs.

The learning disability community in Vancouver has gradually become more receptive to the Arrowsmith Program and the existence of the Eaton Arrowsmith School. There are now 102 graduates of the program in schools across Vancouver. Each year we graduate between twenty to thirty students. They are achievers, proud of themselves, with great self-esteem and plans for their futures, and this news is buzzing positively around Vancouver's LD community.

Part II

The Stories

5

The Awakening Brain

Children develop only as the environment demands development.

—DAVID SHENK, AUTHOR, *THE GENIUS IN ALL OF US*

Davis's First Psycho-Educational Assessment

When Davis was interviewed for this book at the age of sixteen, I asked whether he could recall his earliest memories of his troubles. He remembered preschool.

Surprised, I asked, "Preschool? You actually remember preschool? What do you remember?"

"I didn't have many friends," Davis said, laughing half-heartedly.

"Really—you knew that?"

"I was young and immature and I made a lot of mistakes," he said. "And I just kind of kept making mistakes."

"Socially?" I suggested.

"Yes, socially."

"Did you understand why you were making social mistakes?"

"No, I didn't understand."

"How old were you?"

"Four."

"Tell me what you remember about friends at preschool."

"Well, I only had one friend and I could tell she didn't like me much," he said. "She told me to stop [annoying her] and I wouldn't stop. That was what isolated [me from] a lot of my friends. I didn't know how to stop. In kindergarten it continued, but it wasn't as bad as Grade 1."

I asked Davis whether he could recall a major social incident in primary school. He explained that it wasn't until Grade 5 that a particularly bad incident occurred.

"One of the kids was bullying me in the playground," he said, "so I pushed him down and he bruised his elbow. He was really dramatic about it, and everyone thought that he had broken his elbow. They thought I had broken his arm, and these kids told their parents. Then the parents told the teachers they didn't want their kids playing with me. I was suspended, even though the other guy had been bullying me. *I* got suspended and he didn't get in trouble. Later my parents and I found out that it was only a bruise. I was pretty annoyed."

Davis's problems were recognized early, but his helpful, supportive parents had a heavy burden. Glenn and Simone were both highly respected dentists. They had adopted two children as infants, of which Davis was one. Like other parents, they had high hopes for their children, but Davis had social and learning problems.

He exhibited hearing problems—at least that's what his parents initially thought. By the time Davis was three, they noticed his behaviour was different from that of other children. Glenn described a typical evening as Davis was asked to prepare for bed. "'It's eight o'clock, Davis,' I would say. I would ask him to get into his pajamas, get his toothbrush, and bring back a book to read. But he'd come back with toothpaste, because he'd only got part of it. Or he would come back with his pajamas on but no book."

Simone added, "And he'd look right at you, like he was listening. And then it was like he was defiant too." It was also apparent that Davis did not understand no. At one point a professional told his parents that their son perhaps had oppositional defiance syndrome (ODS), but this was quickly dropped.

Glenn and Simone continued to be surprised by the severity of their son's learning difficulties. Language was a big problem. "Davis was very endearing," said Simone. "A very big child. Size five. The size of a five-year-old at three, but he was speaking his own language. We called it 'Davisese.' He would go up to a person and engage them in conversation and it was like gibberish. No one knew what he was saying, and it wasn't like he was saying words backwards. He used proper intonation but he would stumble, say 'ah...ah' between sentences. He would do these endearing little things and people would look at us with a great sense of angst, because they had no idea what was wrong with him." Eventually, Davis's parents had him tested by experts, including a child psychologist.

Because most medical doctors do not test for weak neurological functions that exhibit as an attention problem, Davis was diagnosed with attention deficit hyperactivity disorder (ADHD). He was unable to listen to and follow directions, and he was impulsive, easily distracted, and could not consistently focus on tasks. A child psychologist noted that despite average skills in a number of cognitive areas, Davis lacked confidence in his fine motor skills such as printing, writing, and drawing. His parents thought these problems would impede his progress in kindergarten, so they hired an occupational therapist to work with him. As noted, Davis also had trouble with speech. From the age of three on, he worked with a speech and language pathologist. This is a testament to so many parents of children with learning disabilities and attention disorders, who struggle heroically trying to help their children expand their possibilities and potential.

Kindergarten went surprisingly well for Davis because of an exceptional teacher who facilitated his learning style. Simone and Glenn also provided him with every possible intervention to improve his learning weaknesses.

Grade 1, on the other hand, was troublesome. Davis was required to work more independently, and he struggled. Still, he was a happy boy in general. He would say to his parents, "I like school. I like the monkey bars, skipping, and drawing pictures." At that time, Davis appeared unaware of the severity of his difficulties. But as problems with his academic work mounted, so too did his problems with social skills.

In October 2000, Davis was seven years old and in Grade 1 when Simone first called me, requesting an appointment for a psycho-educational assessment. At this time, I had not yet started Eaton Arrowsmith School. Davis's school, an elite private school in the area, had referred his family to me.

Davis arrived at my office for his psycho-educational assessment. He was slightly overweight, broad shouldered, with curly brown hair. He was certainly big for his age. He had a round face and he smiled frequently. Davis was curious. He looked at objects in my office, played with them, and if possible took them apart, including my pens, stapler, and hole-punch. He wasn't pleased when, after a while, I cleared my desk in order to keep him focused on his assessment activities. He worked fairly diligently during the remainder of the testing session, although he sometimes became frustrated with his performance. He needed a quick pace and a variety of challenges to stay on task.

His Grade 1 teacher had written: "[Davis] has great difficulty following oral directions, working independently, and, at times, recognizing social boundaries." Davis's parents, however, had seen improvements in his social interactions over the previous few months. Parents are usually hopeful about their children even in the face of despair. They desperately want to see improvements, so they do.

It became apparent that Davis was struggling with conceptual understanding or, in lay terms, reasoning. He scored low on reasoning measures, indicating how difficult it was for him to group specific critical features into categories. His score on the fluid intelligence cluster of the Woodcock-Johnson Tests of Cognitive Ability—Revised was at the 5th percentile compared with his peers. In other words, 95 percent of his peers showed better fluid intelligence capabilities. No wonder he struggled at school. However, he could spell better than 93 percent of them—which isn't necessarily preferable to good reasoning capabilities. As well, his knowledge of verbal concepts—for example, how words might be alike (*fence* and *wall*)—was weak. He could define words at the average range but he could not understand their relationships. He was stronger at using his hands to put together puzzles or objects. This accounted for his love for manipulating objects, disassembling them, and reassembling them.

Davis struggled with social awareness. He was asked to arrange a sequence of story cards so they told a story that would make sense in our social world. The exercise is akin to cutting a comic strip into separate frames, mixing them, and then having to put the story back together in the correct sequence. Davis could not properly reassemble the story cards. He could not consistently see social relationship patterns, which accounted for his social problems. He struggled to see common themes or patterns occurring in his social interaction with peers. For example, if a teacher reprimanded Davis for taking a classmate's baseball cap in class, he had difficulty understanding why he couldn't take the same cap away from his classmate outside at recess. The concept of taking someone's baseball cap as the common problem could not cross contextual boundaries in his brain.

Davis scored low on math problem solving because of his weak reasoning skills. Approximately 84 percent of his peers had better math problem-solving abilities. However, in spelling and word-decoding skills he scored at the 93rd percentile—a very good score. Davis clearly did not have dyslexia as it related to word encoding and decoding. At the Grade 1 level he could read, write, and spell quite effectively. His reading comprehension scores were good because at this level he could rely on his strength of visually matching the answers to the question, which did not require truly understanding what he read. These scores would quickly decline as he became older because of his weakness with understanding relationships in language. As children move through elementary school and into the higher grades, conceptual understanding gets more demanding, more abstract.

From my testing of Davis, I determined he had a conceptual-based or fluid-reasoning learning disability—difficulties forming concepts. As well, he had serious social-perception problems, which is not unusual for children with learning and attention disabilities. These were two distinct but at times interrelated problems. His weakness with conceptual understanding resulted in an inability to easily grasp what people were saying to him in conversation. This also resulted in social problems, where he would respond with something that did not make sense to the listener. To make matters worse, Davis was failing in an academically demanding private school due to his severe reasoning disability. Finally, he also had considerable problems with recalling what people said to him. For example, his ability to recall sentences was at the 24th percentile compared with his peers. It was not going to be easy to explain to his concerned parents the seriousness of Davis's problems.

Three weeks after the initial testing, Simone and Glenn arrived to discuss their son's results. I began by calming their nerves. "Davis has many talents. His strengths are certainly in solving puzzles and putting objects together, and he shows skills that are well within the average range of ability for children his age. This is excellent. For example, he had an average score on some measures of visual or nonverbal intelligence. He's also a great speller.

"However," I went on, "Davis has several certain cognitive weaknesses that impair his learning. He has problems with fluid reasoning or conceptual understanding. He doesn't fully grasp cause-and-effect thinking. And he has trouble seeing relationships between words and ideas." Glenn asked whether his son could reason at all. I assured him that he could, but he couldn't easily distinguish relationships presented in language. For example, when I asked Davis to tell me why two words are alike, he struggled, especially if I used abstract words like love and peace. These were significant problems that, if unsolved, could affect him, probably for the rest of his life. Part of Davis's psycho-educational assessment results before he began the Arrowsmith Program are outlined in table 3:

TABLE 3. DAVIS'S INITIAL PSYCHO-EDUCATIONAL ASSESSMENT RESULTS

Psycho-Educational Assessment Measure	**Description**	**Before Arrowsmith Program**
Visual-Motor Integration (Beery-Buktenica Developmental Test of Visual-Motor Integration —BEERY)	A measure of fine motor skills, visual perception, and hand-eye coordination.	45th %ile
Processing Speed (Wechsler Intelligence Scale for Children—Third Edition—WISC-III)	Ability to scan and copy visual symbols under timed conditions.	12th %ile

Psycho-Educational Assessment Measure	**Description**	**Before Arrowsmith Program**
Auditory Processing (Woodcock-Johnson Tests of Cognitive Ability—Revised—WJ-R)	Ability to analyze and synthesize speech sounds. Critical cognitive ability for reading and spelling development.	38th %ile
Applied Problems (Woodcock-Johnson Tests of Cognitive Ability—Revised)	Ability to analyze and solve math problems.	16th %ile
Fluid Reasoning (Woodcock-Johnson Tests of Cognitive Ability—Revised)	A measure of fluid intelligence. Ability to recognize patterns and/or relationships.	5th %ile
Nonverbal Intelligence (Test of Nonverbal Intelligence—Third Edition—TONI-3)	A measure of fluid intelligence. Ability to recognize visual patterns and relationships.	34th %ile

Note: The average performance range on psycho-educational assessments is considered to fall between the 25th and 75th %ile ranking.

Glenn and Simone asked what kind of intervention was available. At that time, I did not know about educational neuroplasticity, so I recommended some direct teaching of word associations and patterns. These were the strategies in use at the time by teachers and therapists. He could also join some children working with counsellors or psychologists on developing social skills. With these programs, children's capacity to understand social behaviour did not change, but at least they made friends with a few other children. Davis would have to depend on his strong visual memory, and he wouldn't truly comprehend important ideas, concepts, and social behaviour. I noted that other children with Davis's problem did well in school if they already had strong memories. Reading comprehension and math problem solving would likely be a significant problem. I explained how we used conceptual mapping as a way to show children with this difficulty the connections between ideas or concepts. Specifically, this is called *webbing* or *mind-mapping*. These were all the intervention tools we knew of at the time. As Davis's parents prepared to leave the meeting, Glenn said, "We're not sure whether to thank you or not."

"Don't give up hope," I said. This was not our last interaction.

Davis's Arrowsmith Assessment

In April 2005, just after I started the Eaton Arrowsmith School, Simone and Glenn contacted me again, wishing to enrol their son. By this time, he was an adolescent who had developed multiple learning disabilities. Children in this category face more obstacles in coping with school. Davis had trouble dealing with peers, motor output issues for writing and printing, poor attention span, weak memory for information, poor reasoning ability, and difficulties with math problem solving. His reading comprehension skills had dropped dramatically from his Grade 1 assessment. His earlier interventions clearly had not helped his progress. He faced huge obstacles, and so did we. But this time we were far more equipped with solutions.

To develop an individualized program of Arrowsmith cognitive exercises for a child's entry into Eaton Arrowsmith School, an intensive testing of cognitive abilities is required. The Arrowsmith assessment helps identify specific cognitive weaknesses.[22] Not surprisingly, Davis's results showed problems. Of the nineteen cognitive functions that Barbara Arrowsmith Young identified and developed cognitive exercises for, seven of them presented struggles for this child.

The Arrowsmith assessment results showed that Davis had a deficit in the Motor Symbol Sequencing cognitive area, which explained his sloppy handwriting and slow copying speed. He also had speech and listening problems, challenges with remembering what he heard, and difficulty maintaining plans and strategies using language. He had trouble understanding relationships between two or more ideas or concepts. Davis also had difficulty registering and interpreting nonverbal information such as facial expressions and body language; as a result, he couldn't change his behaviour according to the signals people were sending him. Table 4 shows a partial breakdown of Davis's first Arrowsmith assessment results

---

22. The purposes of the psycho-educational assessment are different from those of the Arrowsmith assessment. For detailed information about these differences, please see Appendix B.

completed in May 2005. Six of his seven cognitive weaknesses are identified along with the common features associated with each weakness and degree of dysfunction. These six cognitive deficits are the ones that Davis addressed at Eaton Arrowsmith School.

TABLE 4. DAVIS'S INITIAL ARROWSMITH ASSESSMENT RESULTS

Cognitive Function	Description	Davis's Level of Difficulty
Motor-Symbol Sequencing	Problems associated with printing neatly and copying quickly. Careless errors in math, slow reading speed, inconsistent spelling.	Severe[23]
Symbol Relations	Problems understanding concepts and cause-and-effect reasoning. Logical-reasoning problems.	Moderate
Memory for Information and Instructions	Problems following language or oral information.	Severe to Moderate
Symbolic Thinking	Problems being self-directed and self-organized in learning, limited mental initiative, difficulty keeping attention focused on a task to completion, trouble seeing main point, and limited problem-solving abilities.	Severe
Artifactual Thinking	Problems understanding and interpreting social cues.	Moderate to Mild
Supplementary Motor	Trouble with finger counting, problems learning math facts and holding numbers in his head, poor sense of time management.	Mild to Moderate

23. The Arrowsmith assessment has a twelve-category rating system ranging from very severe to

The impact of these cognitive weaknesses on measures of achievement was disheartening. When Davis started in Grade 7 at EAS, he was at Grade 2 level in reading comprehension; this difficulty had been predicted five years earlier in his first psycho-educational assessment. This is a common pattern with children with concept or reasoning problems: because understanding abstract ideas and concepts becomes a school requirement in the higher grades, achievement scores as they relate to comprehension and reasoning drop over time. Added to this, Davis had an attention deficit disorder likely as a result of these multiple cognitive weaknesses. (This will be discussed more in chapter 7.)

In terms of his strengths, Davis could read words and spell at grade level. But this was offset by other serious problems. At the Grade 7 level, understanding abstract ideas is somewhat more important than word decoding and spelling. Unfortunately, with learning disability remediation programs in schools today, the focus is on reading, and within reading, the focus is on word decoding and spelling skills. Schools often entirely miss problems like Davis's.

The Arrowsmith assessment results indicated that Davis's program would take three to four years to bring all the important areas to average functioning. Another consideration was the fact that Davis was currently using medication for his past attention problems. We recommended that he stay on his medication in order to maintain active engagement in the cognitive exercises; without active engagement he would not make good progress in the program. At EAS we find that 60 percent of children using attention medication can come off their drug upon completion of the program due to strengthened cognitive capacities. We knew it would take a minimum of three years for Davis's cognitive remediation program

above average (see the full spectrum of ratings in Appendix C). The Arrowsmith Program does not measure performances above "above average." The primary goal is not to build superior cognitive capacities, but to move cognitive functioning to an average performance level, which is what a child needs to perform well academically. Barbara Arrowsmith Young has observed that these improved cognitive capacities can continue to build after completion of the Arrowsmith Program. In contrast, in a psycho-educational assessment, a child can receive a percentile ranking in the superior range; e.g., a score at the 95th percentile is considered superior ability compared with a child's peers.

to work before we would see changes in his behaviour. The Symbolic Thinking, Artifactual Thinking, and Symbol Relations cognitive exercises would be critical for his future success. The Symbolic Thinking exercise would improve planning and strategizing, and the Artifactual Thinking exercise would develop social-perception capacities.

Let's take a look at how the Symbol Relations exercise is related to the posterior parietal cortex and prefrontal cortex and other regions of the brain in functional magnetic resonance imaging (fMRI) scans.

Symbol Relations and fMRI

The Arrowsmith Program uses an analogue clock exercise to build cognitive reasoning capacities. Specific neurological pathways and specific cortices are involved in this task. The same pathways that are involved in understanding a clock face are also involved in fluid reasoning, which is the ability to find meaning in confusion—to understand the relationships of various concepts, independent of past experiences. We cannot tell a child with learning disabilities not to worry about learning to read a clock face simply because now we have digital watches. As most elementary school teachers will attest, many children struggle with reading an analogue clock, and the impact on their lives is immense.

In the Symbol Relations exercise, the child is asked to read multi-hand clock faces. It may be difficult to imagine that reading or understanding an analogue clock could considerably improve reasoning, and in turn, that this could improve reading comprehension and mathematical reasoning. How is this possible? The indirect evidence that this is occurring in the brains of children doing the Clocks exercise comes from neuroscientific fMRI studies, which use MRI equipment to detect regional changes in blood flow based on neural activity.

It is important to note that fMRI has only recently been used to create images of the human brain. Since the early 1990s, fMRI has been used by neuroscientists to determine brain activity while subjects perform specific activities. Much remains to be understood about the brain that fMRI studies do not entirely reveal at this writing. Nevertheless, the findings from fMRI studies are leading to new discoveries about how the brain may function and could lead to further insights into neuroplasticity.

In Frankfurt, Germany, at the Departments of Neurology and Neuroradiology of the Klinikum der Johann Wolfgang Goethe Universitat, the areas of the brain used to imagine clocks were identified by researchers. Luigi Trojano and his colleagues were interested in learning what areas of the brain were involved in spatial analysis when no visual stimuli were present. Their findings were published in the May 2000 issue of *Cerebral Cortex*.[24] These researchers studied seven right-handed postgraduate students aged twenty-three to thirty-two. The subjects were asked to imagine two analogue clock faces based on times presented to them verbally by the examiner. As they were doing this visual imaging, their brains were scanned. The study noted: "The most striking results of our two experiments demonstrated that cortical activation (as measured by an increase of the fMRI BOLD signal) during the mental clock test was the most prominent in the posterior parietal lobes of both hemispheres."

The areas of the brain that are most activated during the drawings of clocks were also identified in Kyoto, Japan, at the Department of Neurology and Department of Radiology, Rakuwakai-Otowa Hospital. Dr. Tadashi Ino and his colleagues studied eighteen right-handed volunteers as they drew the hands of a clock while undergoing fMRI. Their findings were published in the journal *Neuroscience Research* in January 2003.[25] They discovered that while the brain utilizes numerous neural pathways for drawing a clock face, the most strongly activated pathway was between the posterior parietal cortex and the dorsal premotor area. The evidence from fMRIs points to the posterior parietal cortex as a primary cortical location for tasks involved in clock faces—whether reading, drawing, or imagining them.

Furthermore, in 2005, the journal *Neuroimage* published a research article on intelligence and what specific neural pathways may be involved

---

24. L. Trojan, Dario Grossi, E.J. Linden, E. Formisano, H. Hacker, E.F. Zanella, R. Goebel, and D. Di Salle, "Matching Two Imagined Clocks: the Functional Anatomy of Spatial Analysis in the Absence of Visual Stimulation," *Cerebral Cortex* 10 (2000), 473–481.
25. T. Ino, T. Asada, J. Ito, T. Kimura, and H. Fukuyama, "Parieto-frontal Networks for Clock Drawing Revealed with fMRI," *Neuroscience Research* 45 (2003), 71–77.

in reasoning.[26] The research was conducted in South Korea at the Seoul National University. Various departments were involved including the School of Biological Sciences and the Department of Biology Education. The Korea Institute of Brain Science and Department of Psychiatry at the Catholic University in Seoul were involved, and Yale University and its Department of Psychology were also part of the study. The lead researcher was Dr. Kun Ho Lee from the School of Biological Sciences at the Seoul National University.

Dr. Lee noted in his study that the parietal and lateral prefrontal cortices have been acknowledged by other researchers as playing a role in fluid reasoning, the control of attention, and working memory. Dr. Lee and his colleagues wanted to discover the brain location for fluid reasoning of intellectually gifted adolescent students. Could they find the brain region or pathway that was responsible for general intelligence? Dr. Lee studied thirty-six gifted children from the National Academy of Gifted Adolescents in Busan, South Korea. The students were given the Wechsler Adult Intelligence Scale—Revised (Korean version) and the Raven's Advanced Progressive Matrices (RAPM), which is a standard test for general fluid intelligence. The control group was composed of students from a local regular high school.

The experimental and control groups were then given fMRI tasks related to reasoning. The students were placed in the fMRI machine and had to perform specific tasks that had ever-increasing levels of reasoning complexity. As they were doing these tasks, the fMRI showed their brain activity, which was recorded by the researchers. What was their conclusion? Dr. Lee and his colleagues wrote: "The main finding of the current study emphasized the role of the posterior parietal region (specifically, bilateral SPL and right IPS [BA 7/40]) among the entire network components of [general intelligence]." The students with the higher levels of intelligence showed greater activation of the posterior parietal regions as the complexity of the reasoning tasks increased. The researchers continued:

---

26. K.H. Lee, Y.Y. Choi, J.R. Gray, S.H. Cho, J. Chae, S. Lee, and K. Kim, "Neural Correlates of Superior Intelligence: Stronger Recruitment of Posterior Parietal Cortex," *Neuroimage* 29 (2005), 578–586.

"In addition, our results demonstrated that the posterior parietal regions including bilateral SPL and right IPS could be the neural correlates for superior general intelligence. These findings would be the early step toward the development of biological measures of [general intelligence] which leads to new perspectives for behavior interventions improving general cognitive ability." In other words, the researchers are stating that if we can find a way to improve the functioning of the posterial parietal region of human beings we can improve their general intelligence. At EAS we have seen that Arrowsmith Young's Clocks exercise has accomplished this.

It is important to note that the prefrontal lobes of these students were also activated. A specific frontal-parietal relationship occurs when the brain has to think, which is a prefrontal or executive function task. Interestingly, as students became more adept at the various levels of reasoning, their prefrontal activity decreased because less thinking was required to complete the reasoning task. In short, reasoning and thinking are clearly different neurological functions, but are dependent on each other. This is not common knowledge in education circles, since the prefrontal lobe is most often noted as the critical brain region for intelligence. The above-noted research points to the critical association between both the prefrontal and posterior parietal lobes.

Davis, Symbol Relations, and Artifactual Thinking

The Symbol Relations exercise, or Clocks, is fascinating to observe. Guests who visit our school often enjoy standing behind a child working with clocks in this cognitive exercise. They are amazed at how rapidly some of the children move through each clock face.

In order for Davis to build his conceptual or fluid-reasoning brain, he would begin with simple analogue clock faces. Prior to learning about the clock's hands, he needed to understand what a clock is and the concepts that are embedded in its face. That is, a clock face has twelve numbers that circle clockwise from one through twelve at the top. To a child, this is an abstract concept. This is only the beginning; eventually, Davis would move to multi-hand clocks and complete them with extraordinary speed. I recall observing Davis at a more advanced stage, working on a multi-hand clock. I tried to keep pace but could not.

The indirect evidence from fMRI studies of individuals drawing or imagining clocks indicates that Davis was doing a mental workout of the posterior parietal cortex. Also, clearly, other brain areas were affected such as the prefrontal cortex and motor cortex. But critical for Davis's fluid-reasoning development was the neuroplasticity of the posterior parietal cortex and associated lobes.

Next, it was important for Davis to address his weak social perception or ability to read and understand nonverbal cues. Previously, Davis had experienced years of social frustration; he was a constant target for bullies, which caused him great pain.

In order to improve cognitive capacities for social perception, Barbara Arrowsmith Young developed a cognitive exercise called Artifactual Thinking that would require students to actively engage areas of the brain related to perceiving nonverbal cues. Davis did not find the exercise easy to begin with. Simone highlighted her son's frustrations with the exercise in an e-mail to his cognitive teacher, Sarah Cohen. "I had a talk with Davis about it and he seems to understand that it is important," she wrote, "but I don't think he gets the application to his own life. So we talked about it. By the end of the conversation he was attempting to read my body language so I think he is at least thinking about the process."

In one of Davis's first attempts at the exercise, we observed him quietly in the cognitive classroom. In those moments, as he worked on the task, we realized how difficult it must be for this child to interpret nonverbal behaviour in his social environment. The brain processes nonverbal behaviour from social interaction with extraordinary speed, and there is little time to analyze what is happening. Davis's first attempts were challenging, but toward the end of his program, he could perform the assigned tasks with ease. The change was noteworthy. His improved social interactions at school were no coincidence.

Is it possible to build a stronger capacity to reason if one is not born with strength in this neurological area? Is it possible to make fluid reasoning more efficient? Can social perception be improved through cognitive exercises? Can a child improve his or her capacity to read nonverbal social behaviour?

Almost thirty years ago, Barbara Arrowsmith Young discovered this is all indeed possible. Dr. Lee and his colleagues raised these questions about reasoning development in 2006, but the Arrowsmith Program, largely overlooked by the education community, had been proving them possible for years. Davis's progress showed how he continued to improve his fluid reasoning and social perception.

Inconsistency in performance describes Davis's first year at EAS. Sarah Cohen reported that when she first met this twelve-year-old, he was anxious and unsure of everyone. He couldn't understand why people reacted to him negatively, and he lacked confidence in almost every area. Distressed, he often said, "I can't do this. I don't know what's happening."

Davis already had been through difficult school situations and was cautious about establishing new friends at Eaton Arrowsmith School. He was not used to the active engagement required in the Arrowsmith Program, and it took him some time to adjust to the new requirements for success with the cognitive exercises. His teachers steadily gave him the necessary encouragement to stay engaged in the cognitive exercises, and they also supported social interaction by getting him involved with the class in group activities at lunch and during field trips. Davis still required some coaching in relating to his peers effectively, and the cognitive exercises enhanced the coaching.

The occasional mistake occurred. For example, Sarah Cohen called Davis's father because Davis had thrown a squeeze ball (used to help with focusing) at another student in class. One of his problems was impulsiveness and not thinking through outcomes of social behaviour. Sarah told Glenn that she and Davis talked after school about the appropriate use of squeeze balls, explaining why it was confiscated. Sarah also discussed Davis's other antisocial behaviours such as annoying other children by not listening to their "no" signals until he was bullied, and Glenn supported her. It was a volatile year for Davis, his teachers, his parents, and EAS administration. Nevertheless, many positive changes took place in his cognitive abilities in the first three to six months of the program. By the end of the year, he was communicating at home in positive ways and working on his daily routines. Simone and Glenn noticed a marked improvement in his ability to stay connected in conversations and to more accurately interpret verbal information in discussions with them and with his friends.

All EAS students are reassessed at the end of each school year. Davis's second year started with a new assessment of his neurological functioning. His updated assessment results were impressive:

- His reading comprehension improved from Grade 2 to Grade 8 level. This was a dramatic improvement. The Symbol Relations exercise had produced an extraordinary effect in only ten months. The staff at EAS were astonished at this improvement, even with their combined decades of experience in the field of learning disabilities.
- His reasoning score on the Munzert Reasoning Test improved from the 52nd percentile to the 99th percentile—an enormous achievement.
- His copying speed went from the 30th percentile to the 70th percentile on the Copying Text Test.
- His reading speed improved from Grade 4 to Grade 6 level.

Davis was still working on other cognitive dysfunctions. His new program designed by Arrowsmith in Toronto would address those specific needs.

Davis's Continued Improvement

Cognitive teachers like Sarah Cohen and another EAS teacher, Mark Watson, are the lifeblood of the Eaton Arrowsmith School. When I interviewed Davis, I asked him how important he felt the cognitive teachers were to his progress. He said, "They always pushed me along whenever I was having a problem. And if I was frustrated, they understood and they would let me take a break. After that, I would work way better. I felt better and they could tell the difference. But if I was frustrated, they understood that I just couldn't go further. They would back off a little. When they knew I had pushed my limits, they would just say 'good work, take a break, and then come back and try your best again.'"

At the start of his second year, Davis still had some social difficulties. Not only did he struggle to visually perceive the social event accurately, but he also found it difficult to remember what was said. He still needed improvement in Artifactual Thinking and Memory for Information and Instructions in order to cross over successfully to real-life events. Happily, by the end of his second year, his cognitive functioning in these areas had moved closer to the average range.

Today, Davis talks freely about his improvement with social skills, saying, "Before, I would simply just assume things. But now I *think*. Like, if someone doesn't show up at my party, previously I would think that they just didn't like me. But now, I'll think that maybe their bus stopped, or got stuck, or they got caught in traffic. Now I wait and see if they show up. I wait until I talk to them, maybe tomorrow or the next day. I don't just freak out and start yelling at them. I just ask, 'Why didn't you show up yesterday?'"

At the end of the second year, the Arrowsmith School in Toronto reviewed Davis's profile to help determine what kind of progress he had made. (Each school using the Arrowsmith Program sends its own Arrowsmith assessment data to the laboratory school in Toronto, which monitors each student carefully and designs ongoing specific programs for implementation.) In reviewing Davis's progress, the Toronto school noted he had made good progress in his cognitive exercises over the last two years. The lab school has gathered thirty years' worth of data from thousands of students to be able to now determine what is considered good or slow progress for each cognitive exercise.

Davis was now at average to above average in Symbol Relations and at average in Supplementary Motor Skills (ability to perform mental numerical operations such as making change and learning multiplication tables). The most important elements remaining that were not yet rated average were Motor-Symbol Sequencing, Symbolic Thinking, Artifactual Thinking, and Memory for Information and Instructions. We combined the Toronto lab's analysis with our classroom experience and observations and reported everything to Davis's parents.

When Davis started a third year at Eaton Arrowsmith School, we were confident he would be able to complete the remainder of the important cognitive exercises, all of which would be critical to his future success. His programmed cognitive exercises focused on building his conceptual reasoning, cause-and-effect thinking, ability to use language to plan and organize strategies, and social perception. By mid-year, both Davis's social and academic weaknesses were no longer significant. He was a different person. His ratings in these new areas had moved up to the average range.

As principal, I watched these changes over three years with interest. Mark Watson, now vice-principal of EAS, met with Davis on February 26, 2008. Mark kept notes of his observations, writing that Davis had wondered aloud about larger issues such as the meaning of life and whether this world is real or just a game. Davis also had questions about the field of science and the concept of death. In other words, Davis was thinking at highly abstract, conceptual levels. As psychologist Jean Piaget might have said, he had moved to the Formal Operational stage of cognitive development. Mark also noted in an e-mail to me that

- Davis is now picking up social cues and is functioning very well socially, even establishing new relationships with peers.
- Davis's reasoning has improved substantially by using the cognitive Symbol Relations exercise.
- His attention has improved substantially. Arrowsmith has helped with this in all of the exercises.
- Symbolic Thinking (problem solving, planning, and strategizing) and Artifactual Thinking (nonverbal interpretation) also improved.
- Davis's self-esteem has increased so much that he looks different physically.
- Davis can understand the "big picture" better in terms of his life and cause and effect for his actions. This is due to many things including his significant reasoning improvements.[27]

With seven months remaining in Davis's third year, his parents requested an updated psycho-educational assessment, a requirement at

27. Parents investigating the Arrowsmith Program often ask if these improvements are not simply a result of the child's having aged three or more years. In fact, this is not the case with children with learning disabilities. Instead, problems with reasoning remain lifelong without intervention such as Arrowsmith. Adults with learning disabilities suffer many problems in employment and social relationships. Teachers unfamiliar with neuroplasticity tend to use the term *developmental problems* to reassure parents that things will improve as their child gets older, but this does not often happen.

the private school they wished to enrol him in. The results were striking. His nonverbal intelligence had improved from low to superior. Visual reasoning (visual-perceptual thinking) went from average to gifted. His score on fluid intelligence or Concept Formation went from very low to average. His visual-motor coordination went from average to superior.

In listening comprehension, Davis was now at high average, whereas in his initial Arrowsmith assessment he had been weak. His cognitive ability for problem solving went from low average to average range. His reading comprehension was also in the average range. Without question, these were important, life-changing alterations in both cognitive change and achievement ability. On table 5, it can be seen how Davis's scores on measures of intelligence, auditory processing, and visual-motor integration went up substantially after the Arrowsmith Program.

TABLE 5. DAVIS'S UPDATED PSYCHO-EDUCATIONAL ASSESSMENT RESULTS

Psycho-Educational Assessment Measure	**Before Arrowsmith Program**	**After Arrowsmith Program**
Visual-Motor Integration: BEERY	45th %ile	92nd %ile
Processing Speed: WISC-III (before) and WISC-IV (after)	12th %ile	34th %ile
Auditory Processing: WJ-R (before) Phonemic Awareness: WJ-III (after)	38th %ile	85th %ile
Applied Problems: WJ-R (before) and WJ-III (after)	16th %ile	31st %ile
Fluid Reasoning: WJ-R (before) Concept Formation: WJ-III (after)	5th %ile	64th %ile
Nonverbal Intelligence: TONI-3	34th %ile	91st %ile

Note: The average performance range on psycho-educational assessments is considered to fall between the 25th and 75th %ile ranking.

The Arrowsmith Program, through cognitive remediation exercises, had helped Davis acquire the ability to conceptualize and reason at levels previously not imagined. As well, he now had the ability to recall oral information, to copy information quickly and efficiently with pen and paper, to "read" social interaction and facial cues, and to effectively plan and strategize. Teachers who knew him in 2005 were astounded that the student who graduated in June of 2008 was the same person. His updated psycho-educational assessment was so positive that he could not be diagnosed with a learning disability. In fact, Davis was now showing the Gifted learning profile, another area in special education. He was gifted in Perceptual Reasoning (IQ 122, 93rd percentile, Wechsler Intelligence Scale for Children—IV), a talent he had prior to the Arrowsmith Program. But while he was at Arrowsmith, Davis moved into the superior range of functioning, and thus into the gifted domain.

Life after Eaton Arrowsmith

Post-EAS, Davis tried to get into a private school. He was both eager and nervous about trying a boarding school environment, living away from home, and learning to be independent. He visited a local private school on Vancouver Island and impressed the admissions office, but due to his previous learning disability and attention problems, they were skeptical he could succeed. He was asked for writing samples, not an area of strength for him, so his performance was not stellar. He still needed to be taught the skills of essay writing. Still, the admissions director liked the teenager and was hoping the headmaster would consider him. I wrote the following letter supporting his application:

> *I appreciate your consideration of Davis's admission at your school.*
>
> *There is no doubt that Davis is a visual-spatial genius. This form of genius is not often recognized in the world of education, which I believe is very unfortunate as our world is in a paradigm shift that favours this type of mindset. One just has to look at the world of computers, science, and technology to understand how critical it is to foster these types of minds in the educational environment.*

Davis is also a wonderful person. He has great compassion for others, is honest, thoughtful, and passionate about his intellectual interests. He scored in the average range on measures of reading comprehension and even written expression (as observed on the Woodcock-Johnson Tests of Achievement). He struggles with writing stories, as he is developing this skill and it is a new one for him. A quote from In the Mind's Eye *by Thomas G. West (1991) states how valuable these visual-spatial minds are: "Many of the problems of greatest importance in the modern world are ones of vast complexity, like understanding large-scale atmospheric or ecological systems.... Some of these complex system problems may be most successfully addressed by certain gifted visual thinkers, using visually based analytic methods and employing increasingly sophisticated computer graphics technologies, similar to those now used in scientific visualization."*

I give full support for Davis's admission to your school. You would not only be providing inspiration and hope to a student who has seldom been rewarded for his mind, but also enriching the student body with an individual who can show others extraordinary ability.

Davis was not accepted. It was frustrating for everyone. The school instead recommended that he apply to the Gow School in South Wales, New York, a program for children with learning disabilities, despite the fact that they had been assured Davis no longer had a learning disability. They had also been informed that he could now succeed in a competitive private school because of his increased cognitive capacities, but this was difficult for them to accept. Neuroplasticity is still not well understood in mainstream education.

Davis's parents applied to the Gow School, but it rejected him too, because—in an ironic twist—he did not have a learning disability. Eventually, I recommended a small boarding school in Nova Scotia, Canada. It had a good academic program and it provided Davis with the boarding school option. This would be a great school environment for any student. It could be a very good transition school for him, since most of its graduates move on to colleges or universities. Simone and Glenn applied, and

Davis was accepted. He was thrilled about going to a private boarding school.

When Davis graduated from Eaton Arrowsmith School, he was more ready than ever for his private boarding school education, but people were sorry to see him leave. Sarah Cohen said, "Because he had to leave one week before the EAS graduation ceremony, the school held a mini-ceremony for him in our classroom, and students in our class were crying because they were going to miss him so much. Everyone in our class wrote in a card for him, and many noted what changes they had seen in him. Most of the students said that in this third year they had come to see him as a friend. One student whom he butted heads with for almost all three years even wrote that he had seen Davis relax, trust people, and learn to dedicate himself to his schoolwork."

The results from Davis's last Arrowsmith assessment in May 2008, shown in table 6, highlighted his improvements in key cognitive functions.

TABLE 6. DAVIS'S FINAL ARROWSMITH ASSESSMENT RESULTS

Cognitive Function	Description	Davis's Level of Difficulty
Motor-Symbol Sequencing	Problems associated with printing neatly and copying quickly. Careless errors in math, slow reading speed, inconsistent spelling.	Moderate
Symbol Relations	Problems understanding concepts and cause-and-effect reasoning. Logical-reasoning problems.	Average to Above-Average
Memory for Information and Instructions	Problems following language or oral information.	Mild to Moderate

Cognitive Function	Description	Davis's Level of Difficulty
Symbolic Thinking	Problems being self-directed and self-organized in learning, limited mental initiative, difficulty keeping attention focused on a task to completion, trouble seeing main point, and limited problem-solving abilities.	Average
Artifactual Thinking	Problems understanding and interpreting social cues.	Average to Mild

In July 2009, I received Davis's report card from his boarding school. He had received the following marks and comments from his Grade 10 teachers:

- English – 83%. The term ended with a study of Ernest Hemingway's classic *The Old Man and the Sea*. "Great job on your long-term assignments and solid test performance. Keep it all going." Davis received a 5 on Interacts Positively with Classmates. A score of 5 indicates "consistently."
- Science – 81%. "Davis did an excellent job presenting the Current Event. He was also well prepared for his exam."
- History – 89%. "Davis, you worked well on your exam review and managed to finish the term with a good mark."
- Math – 75%. "Davis has had a great end to his first term. He worked hard at completing his exam booklet and had it done before the due date."
- Finally, his academic advisor wrote, "Davis's organization and quality of work produced always meets expectations. His ability to manage his time is also quite impressive."

The idea that the brain can change, that reasoning and social perception can improve, has been proven repeatedly by the Arrowsmith Program over the last thirty years. What neuroscience is showing, though indirectly at this time, is that Barbara Arrowsmith Young's Clocks cognitive exercise is likely developing a critical neural structure of the brain involved in fluid reasoning in the posterior parietal lobe, the gateway to higher levels of intelligence. Research on social perception is continually developing.

As principal of Eaton Arrowsmith School since 2005, I have seen these cognitive changes through observations of children's behaviour. Children diagnosed with reasoning and social-perception problems as part of their learning disability profile can benefit remarkably from this program. Unfortunately, most children do not receive the kinds of opportunities the Arrowsmith Program provides, and they struggle all their lives trying to adapt to their employment and social environments. Davis's mind was awakened to a world of academic and social possibilities that he could not previously understand. It took three hard years of building cognitive functions, but Davis succeeded.

The Girl Who Read to Avoid Socializing

The more powerful force in the brain's architecture is arguably the need to navigate the social world, not the need to get A's.

—DR. DANIEL GOLEMAN, PSYCHOLOGIST AND AUTHOR, *SOCIAL INTELLIGENCE*

Madeline at Preschool

Madeline's mother, Janice, sat in my office at Eaton Arrowsmith School, reflecting on her daughter's early difficulties.

"I would just see that she couldn't quite grasp what the other kids were doing socially. She was four years old at the time. She also had trouble following instructions. Once, when her sister, Chloë, was closer to two, I said to them both, 'go upstairs and brush your teeth and comb your hair and put your pajamas on.'"

Looking emotional, Janice went on, "Madeline would still be trying to process the first instruction while Chloë, who was younger by two years, would have finished all three instructions. So even then I could really see Madeline processed information slowly."

Janice tried all sorts of strategies to help her four-year-old daughter remember instructions. "I would do things like draw the pictures of putting her socks on in the morning, and putting her skirt on. We put the pictures on her bathroom mirror, so she could see it. When she was older

I also typed out the things she had to do for the day, like, 'After you put your uniform on, come down the stairs.'"

In 1997, when she was four, Madeline attended Alderson Preschool in Vancouver, British Columbia. It was one of the best preschools in the city. Madeline learned to read early; it was an area of academic strength for her. Alderson used early phonetic instruction to assist children in developing strong reading and spelling skills. Madeline picked up the phonetic code easily and was soon one of the top readers in the preschool. "We read to her a lot," Janice said, "and the program at Alderson was a really good one. They taught phonics and broke down words."

Madeline was never considered to have a behaviour problem at school. Her teachers' concern was quite the opposite: she would not interact with other children. Janice noted that her daughter's teachers would say, "Madeline never joins in with the kids. She stares off into space if we give her a direction."

Janice became very involved with Alderson Preschool. This gave her the opportunities to help her daughter with social interactions, but only to a limited extent. "She was a sweet, sweet child. She was a bright girl. She was always with these other bright kids whose parents had them doing everything, and everything was done quickly. This was difficult for Madeline, and I think she was judged a bit. Luckily for us, she's a sweet child and so likeable, and I was so involved with Alderson that we found a way to make the two years there work. But it really was my being involved with the school."

Janice and her husband, Sanjay, were so concerned that they decided to have Madeline tested. Dr. Teresa Banner, a registered psychologist, met Madeline when she was four years old and attending Alderson. By this time the teaching staff at Alderson had also identified Madeline as having weak social skills. She would respond to other children only with simple yes or no answers. Gradually, she made some improvements—she could hold a conversation with peers, but it had to have been initiated by them. However, even with the social difficulties, she enjoyed preschool and talked about her activities and the other children that attended her program. She was also interested in making friends.

Dr. Banner noted in her assessment that Madeline showed appropriate attachment to her mother. "She discussed topics with appropriate emotion and she discussed various emotions within herself and others. She showed good eye contact, responded to questions, laughed, and initiated conversation and play. Madeline talked about her activities and discussed with much excitement some interactions with other children at her preschool. She talked about playing with her sister at home." Dr. Banner then noticed something unusual. She wrote, "During the play assessment, Madeline showed little representational play, and often asked questions about her play such as 'What should this be?' and 'What do you think these people are doing?' She also asked a number of 'why' questions during play. Her spontaneous play was fairly concrete but Madeline generally had difficulty knowing what to do in play, although she clearly had an interest in play and wanted to interact."

Dr. Banner tested Madeline's intelligence using the Wechsler Preschool and Primary Scale of Intelligence (WPPSI). The testing supported Janice's observations that her daughter was bright. Madeline scored at the high average range on her verbal skills such as vocabulary and word-association knowledge. She was also above average in the development of her reading skills. Because of Madeline's age, Dr. Banner did not wish to label her current social difficulties as a disorder. She noted that while Madeline did show ". . . evidence of poor development of social skills with average intellectual abilities . . . she does not appear to meet the criteria for a diagnosis of a disorder of social development."

Just over a year later, Madeline's family physician was still concerned and referred her to Dr. Aaron Rothberg, a psychologist from BC Children's Hospital, for further evaluation. Madeline's parents still reported long-standing problems with their daughter's ability to follow directions or instructions and with her lack of interaction with peers at school.

Dr. Rothberg reported that Madeline was "alert, active, and a very curious child. Eye contact was reasonable. Socially, she presented as a somewhat younger child, not completely aware of interpersonal boundaries as might be expected from a child of her age, but I felt overall, her social interactions were not outside of normal limits." He did note that "In some types of auditory-verbal tasks, Madeline seemed to quickly forget parts of the question or instruction. In those types of tasks that gave her difficulty, she quickly became withdrawn and very resistant to continuing the task."

Madeline received intelligence testing for a second time. She still showed good verbal intelligence, but her verbal IQ score had declined by sixteen points. Previously, it had been in the high-average range, and now it was in the middle of the average range. Dr. Rothberg noted that Madeline's difficulties with processing directions or instructions could have played a role in her lower verbal IQ score. He noted that "virtually all of the word problems had to be repeated, sometimes two or three times. Madeline's questions made it clear that she very quickly forgot portions of the problem." Overall, Dr. Rothberg was not entirely clear why Madeline's verbal IQ had dropped, though he stated that dramatic changes in intellectual performance can occur when children are given tests at a preschool age. Dr. Rothberg also recommended regular therapy for Madeline if she continued to show signs of social anxiety. Because Madeline was intelligent and sensitive, he said, her social problems would be harder for her to cope with.

Kindergarten and Grade 1

Janice and Sanjay had to decide where Madeline should start elementary school. The psychologists had each reported that Madeline struggled with processing oral instructions and directions, along with her struggle with social skills. Meanwhile, Madeline's peers at Alderson Preschool were heading off to some of the most academically rigorous private schools in Vancouver. "We didn't consider applying to the private schools for her," said Janice. "I thought that if she couldn't process [at Alderson], she wouldn't be able to do that [at a private school]."

Janice and Sanjay decided to look at a public school in their neighbourhood, where Madeline could start kindergarten. Janice went to the school with the information from the psychologist. Without continual supervision, Madeline's parents thought she just might wander out of the playground and get lost—she would not hear the teacher calling. Madeline also needed some kind of assistant to help her with social interactions. Janice met with the school staff, who told her that no help could be provided. "Madeline could read and do everything so well that they decided they could not provide her with assistance," said Janice. "I told them she wouldn't find her way to the washroom and back if she didn't have an assistant." Janice eventually found herself at the school board talking to a special education panel. "I had to sit there and say, 'Look, she may score well and she may be a good reader, but I can tell you that even her own grandmother can't babysit her, knowing that she is not going to follow instructions.'"

After these meetings, Janice finally got the special education panel to agree to a certain amount of support per day for Madeline. Janice said, "It was a very small percentage of the day. By the time I was done, the teachers were frustrated with us because they said she didn't look like she needed anything. They felt other children need more help with their reading and writing problems." The focus for the school system in regards to remediation and assistance was on reading, writing, and math achievement and not oral language processing or social skill development. "I was trying to tell them," Janice noted, "that she does well in reading and writing, as long as I'm doing it with her at home. The minute you put her in front of that teacher, she's not going to have any idea. She'll come home and I'll do it with her."

Madeline struggled through kindergarten. Even ballet class outside of school was unsuccessful. "She went to ballet class once, at age six, and the teacher phoned me from the community centre and said, 'She can't be in this class. She doesn't follow what the other kids are doing.' I thought, 'This is a community centre for six-year-olds?'"

Eventually, in 1999, Janice and Sanjay decided to place Madeline in a school for children with dyslexia. The school accepted her based on her difficulties following oral language. Many of the children at this private school struggled with developing reading skills, but this clearly was not Madeline's problem neurologically; she was in fact a good reader at the time. With few other options available, Madeline was enrolled. At least she would get small-class instruction with teachers who understood learning problems in children. Janice and Sanjay felt this private school would provide the educational care and understanding that other schools could not.

Madeline's first year at the school for children with dyslexia was relatively successful. "She was often happy. That first year was pretty good. Here was a little six-year-old teaching the older boys with dyslexia how to read. Socially, the thing that kept her there for Grade 1 was Kara, her best friend. Some days the boys overwhelmed her and she would just withdraw. She became frightened at their jokes and teasing—she just didn't get it. Also, she couldn't read other people's expressions."

I asked Janice if any of the psychologists thought she was autistic. She replied, "They didn't think it was autism. They just weren't sure what it was. Some people thought it might be Asperger's, though she wasn't typical of Asperger's, or of anything really. She wasn't typical of ADHD, and she wasn't typical of—well—she wasn't even dyslexic. She didn't seem to fit into anything."

Madeline's friend Kara left the school after Grade 1. Madeline returned, but began to develop excessive worries. Said Janice, "Madeline was shy and she was withdrawn. She wasn't going to put herself out there to be laughed at. She'd get really nervous, and what we started to notice was when I picked her up from school she'd have this nervous tic. I said to myself, 'This is something she's never had.' I would then notice on the weekends it wasn't there." Janice took Madeline to a pediatrician, who told her that Madeline should not return to this school.

Janice stared out of my office window for a long moment, then looked back at me. "So we pulled her out at Christmas and started homeschooling her."

My First Meeting with Madeline

In February 2002, Janice heard about my psycho-educational assessment services at the Eaton Learning Centre through Madeline's last school. Madeline was now in Grade 3, being homeschooled, and Janice and Sanjay were looking at options for Grade 4. Madeline had never been diagnosed with a specific learning disability, and they felt it was best to investigate further with a full psycho-educational assessment. Janice and Sanjay were still searching for answers and solutions.

Madeline's testing took two days. My psycho-educational assessment team, which at the time included assessment manager Sandra Heusel, used traditional psycho-educational tests. These highlighted notable discrepancies in cognitive and achievement abilities that previously were not as obvious, probably because of her young age. Because she was older now, Madeline could be given more items for each subtest, and the tasks were more complicated.

Madeline had shown a strong verbal IQ, and it remained the same. She scored in the top 25 percent for her age group on measures of vocabulary knowledge. She even scored at the top 5 percent of her age group for word-association knowledge (understanding of how words relate to one another conceptually). She clearly had tremendous vocabulary knowledge compared with her peers. Given her strength in all the previous verbal IQ subtests, it was expected that she would score well on the Comprehension subtest. This is a measure of a child's awareness of social rules and norms. Madeline was asked questions about various social norms, and she was expected to respond with thought-out answers. It quickly became clear that she could not provide answers to many common social norms and rules.

Madeline also struggled on several measures of visual-perceptual ability. She had shown a dramatic drop in visual-perceptual IQ in just two and a half years. Her ability to assemble puzzle pieces or objects had dropped from superior to low—a huge drop. She struggled to look at an incomplete picture of a common object and identify it, and she also had difficulty with the Picture Arrangement subtest. This subtest measured Madeline's ability, using a shuffled group of story cards, to structure a sequence of events that would make logical sense. Madeline couldn't perform this task. Similarly, if she saw two children playing together and then saw another child joining in with frustration on his face, she did not have the ability to determine what was taking place. Her brain did not have the capacity to synthesize all the visual information, look for visual cues, analyze facial expressions, and then come up with a possible scenario to solve the problem. When overwhelmed with sensory information, most of us tend to shut down and walk away from the situation. In Madeline's case, she would not engage in social play that involved groups of children, most likely because her brain could not make sense of what was happening.

In most areas, Madeline's achievement skills were very good. Results from the Woodcock-Johnson Tests of Achievement showed grade-level or above word-decoding and spelling skills. Madeline's reading speed was also at grade level. Her math problem solving was grade level, as was her reading comprehension. She also showed good writing samples, demonstrating the ability to construct grammatically correct sentences. Madeline's weaknesses in achievement were with writing fluency and math fluency, which meant she took longer to get ideas down on paper and to solve basic math facts. She scored at the 8th percentile on writing fluency and at the 18th percentile on math fluency. Certainly this would make public school problematic, and she would likely struggle to keep pace with in-class writing tasks.

Psycho-educational testing does not always provide accurate information. This was clear on the Oral Language cluster score on the Woodcock-Johnson. For years her parents and her psychologists had identified problems with Madeline's oral language processing of instructions and directions. Yet in our assessment of Madeline, she scored at the 70th percentile on Oral Language ability. There appeared to be no problem. On one of the subtests of the Oral Language cluster called Understanding Directions, Madeline scored at the 66th percentile—with age-level ability being the 50th percentile. It might be assumed that she had average ability to understand directions, but a problem was inherent in this subtest. Madeline was first asked to scan a picture that contained items or objects. She was first given time to scan the picture, and then she listened to a tape providing instructions that asked her to point to various objects in the picture in specific sequences. The task was not purely auditory, but included a visual component. This likely improved Madeline's ability to process the instructions, thereby providing a false conclusion that she was good at following oral directions. The assessor must carefully analyze all the cognitive tasks required for measuring a specific cognitive ability.

The overall finding of the psycho-educational assessment was that Madeline did have an identifiable learning disability. Because of the discrepancy between her verbal IQ and her measure of writing fluency, she could be labelled as having a Written Expression Learning Disability. Another cognitive weakness highlighted in this assessment related to the previous concern about an attention problem: Madeline showed signs of an attention deficit disorder. She was disorganized, would lose things, and did not seem to pay attention to instructions. The question was, why? Was this due to other cognitive weaknesses? At this point we didn't know.

Madeline needed a small class size, repetition, and structure to help her with organization and planning. Assistive technology such as a laptop was recommended, along with self-advocacy training. We felt that the more she knew about her strengths and weaknesses, the more insightful she could be with her own learning.

Madeline was enrolled at a different school with programs for children with language-based learning disabilities. This was one of the only options where she would receive small-group instruction, personalized writing support, and could make use of assistive technology and teaching strategies. Even though the school was designed to support reading and spelling remediation, at which Madeline was highly adept, it still provided the necessary classroom support that she so badly required. Janice noted, "They were hesitant, originally, about whether it was the right program for her, saying, 'You know, we're small, and we really do focus more on dyslexic kids.'" This is a common problem faced by both parents and professionals working with children of various learning disabilities. The private schools across North America for learning disabilities are often focused on remediating dyslexia by teaching phonics, and the other learning challenges that come with learning disabilities are not adequately addressed. For example, the underlying cognitive weaknesses that result in reasoning, social perception, memory, receptive and expressive language, written output, and mathematics difficulties are not remediated.

But this was the best that the field of learning disabilities could offer in terms of remediation—or so I thought in 2002, before I became aware of Barbara Arrowsmith Young and the Arrowsmith Program.

Madeline Begins the Arrowsmith Program

Madeline continued to struggle with group interactions at school. She was better with interacting with one child at a time. Janice noted, "[In groups] she would completely withdraw because she couldn't follow what the conversation was or the game. She'd walk away. She'd go pick up her book as soon as she got to school. She always read her book because that way the other kids couldn't see that she couldn't get it socially or follow conversations. It's not that she wanted to go to her book. She's very clear about that now." Madeline was also struggling with her sister. Chloë found school easy and Madeline was likely resenting this fact. Janice said, "She would lash out at Chloë, and that's not Madeline's nature. She'd yell at her, or even sometimes even hit her, and it's so not Madeline's personality. Chloë could just get it and this poor kid didn't."

From 2002 to 2004 the Eaton Learning Centre continued to conduct psycho-educational assessments. Many ELC clients had no idea that by January 2005 I had begun the process of starting an Arrowsmith Program in Vancouver. In September 2005, Eaton Arrowsmith School's first year of operation was underway. Meanwhile, Madeline's parents had heard about the opening of Eaton Arrowsmith School through Kathy, the Vancouver mother who had been instrumental in getting the Arrowsmith Program started in Vancouver, encouraging me to consider the new ideas on neuroplasticity and to talk to Barbara Arrowsmith Young.

The fact that neuroplasticity was a revolutionary concept didn't bother Janice and Sanjay. They were encouraged that their daughter would have a chance to improve her life. In a meeting several weeks later, we discussed the Arrowsmith Program interview screening, which determined that Madeline was appropriate for the program. After enrolment, she completed a full Arrowsmith assessment, after which specific cognitive exercises were developed for her. Based on the results of this assessment, the Arrowsmith School in Toronto estimated her program would take three years to complete. Table 7 shows Madeline's personalized program, with emphasis on the neurological functions she had the most difficulty with.

TABLE 7. MADELINE'S INITIAL ARROWSMITH ASSESSMENT RESULTS

Cognitive Function	Description	Madeline's Level of Difficulty
Motor-Symbol Sequencing	Problems associated with printing neatly and copying quickly. Careless errors in math, slow reading speed, inconsistent spelling.	Moderate to Severe
Symbol Relations	Problems understanding concepts and cause-and-effect reasoning. Logical-reasoning problems.	Moderate
Memory for Information and Instructions	Problems following language or oral information.	Moderate
Symbolic Thinking	Problems being self-directed and self-organized in learning, limited mental initiative, difficulty keeping attention focused on a task to completion, trouble seeing main point, and limited problem-solving abilities.	Moderate to Severe
Artifactual Thinking	Problems understanding and interpreting social cues.	Moderate to Severe

The Arrowsmith assessment reports brought further insight into Madeline's learning profile. I was interested in how closely the Arrowsmith assessments matched the cognitive weaknesses apparent in Madeline's 2002 psycho-educational assessment. The Arrowsmith assessment clearly identified each of the cognitive weaknesses Madeline had exhibited at school. The 2002 psycho-educational assessment had also identified some of these issues, but had missed the difficulties with following oral directions and instructions. In addition, her ability to develop and maintain plans and strategies through the use of language (Symbolic Thinking) was not previously assessed, and the new assessment helped explain her problems with organization and planning. In reality, psycho-educational assessments are almost solely used in schools today to find out which students require learning assistance due to weak reading, writing, spelling, and math skills. Much less often, they are used to determine the underlying cognitive weaknesses that result in school-related failure.

More importantly, Arrowsmith assessment tools are then matched with specific cognitive exercises, something a psycho-educational assessment cannot do. Another critical factor is that the Arrowsmith assessment can identify multiple cognitive weaknesses that can affect an area of achievement (e.g., reading comprehension) or academic functioning (e.g., taking notes from the board while listening to the instructor requires numerous cognitive abilities). The Arrowsmith assessment can identify problems with visual-motor copying, listening comprehension, reasoning, and use of language to organize and plan, all of which can affect a child's ability to take notes effectively in a classroom. The Arrowsmith assessment also examines factors that can influence social skills. Children are assessed for listening comprehension, object recognition, and social perception. If one or more of these cognitive abilities are weak, the result is often social-skill deficits.

Throughout my undergraduate and graduate training, none of my professors had Barbara Arrowsmith Young's insights in matching neurological weaknesses with cognitive remediation. Here, for the first time in Vancouver, was a program that could work with Madeline's learning profile, the first ever comprehensive program to support cognitive remediation for children with different kinds of learning disabilities.

Madeline was nervous on her first day of school, but knowing some of the other children mitigated her apprehension. The new school vibrated with general excitement as eager staff members prepared to implement the Arrowsmith Program and change lives. Sandra Heusel, who had been my assessment manager with Eaton Learning Centre, had now become one of our new cognitive teachers. She would be co-teaching Madeline, along with a former student of mine, Kristin Harbut. Kristin, also a talented individual, had been enrolled in one of my courses on learning disabilities at the University of British Columbia.

Sandra and Kristin made an exceptional team of cognitive teachers.

Sandra remembered Madeline well from administering her psycho-educational testing four years earlier. She recalled, "Madeline was twelve years old [when she entered] my cognitive class. Aside from having become older, taller, and much more interested in fashion, not much had changed about Madeline. During the first four months of the first year with Kristin and me, she was very disorganized. After every period one of us would have to remind her that we were moving on and help her put away her materials from the current period and take out her things for the next period. If we didn't help her, Madeline would sit in the same place all day. She was constantly losing things and was not putting very much effort into her exercises—they didn't interest her. Interest for Madeline is everything. She is a very bright girl. When she finds something she is passionate about she gives it her all. She even tried to make our uniform fashionable, wearing 'cool' earrings and high heels. Her interest was sparked by fashion and makeup. She loves it!"

In school, Madeline took to the Symbol Relations exercise—understanding the relationships among two or more ideas or concepts—and wanted to do it every period. She was the first person in the class and one of the first in the school to master the exercise by reaching the above-average range. The impact on her reading comprehension and reasoning abilities was immediate. By the end of her first year, she had improved her reasoning capabilities from the 34th percentile ranking to the 86th percentile. Her reading comprehension had improved from Grade 6 to Grade 8 level.

The Memory for Information and Instructions cognitive exercise was not easy for Madeline. Her weakness in this area of cognitive functioning had been identified by her parents at a young age, and then by psychologists during preschool. In this area, her score fell at the moderate range; it needed to move to the average range over the next three years. This exercise requires a significant attention span and can be frustrating to complete.

Socially, Madeline continued to struggle until the spring of her first year at Eaton Arrowsmith School. Prior to that spring, she preferred to eat her lunch by herself, away from others, and read a book. We encouraged others to ask her to join, and we helped set up situations where she could be socially successful. In the spring, Madeline began the Artifactual Thinking cognitive exercise, and the effect was again almost immediate: by the last term of her first year Madeline began to share music with the other girls and was having more fun. Her improved reasoning and social perception was giving her the ability to make sense of facial expressions, social routines, and a language to describe her emotions and those of others in her group.

By the spring reporting period of Madeline's first year, Sandra and Kristin were able to write in Madeline's cognitive progress report: "We have begun to notice that Madeline's ability to organize herself is improving, and we are happy to see that her transitional times have shortened. Along with shortened transitional times, we have seen Madeline's active engagement and determination to master increase. Madeline is showing time management in her Memory for Information and Instructions exercise. Socially, this has been a great period for Madeline as she has become an integral part of a new grouping of friends. We are pleased to see her taking part in being social during the appropriate times."

Artifactual Thinking

This cognitive exercise is ingenious and the benefits are dramatic. The need for a cognitive exercise that can improve social skills cannot be understated. Statistics on how many children with learning disabilities have social-skills problems vary from 33 percent[28] to 75 percent.[29] In either case, the number is high and the need for appropriate intervention is critical. Without intervention, social deficits can lead to unemployment, psychiatric disorders such as depression, and other health problems.

The Artifactual Thinking exercise enables children to understand their own emotional responses to a variety of social events. Their brains are trained to look for appropriate social cues and to begin to understand both simple and more complex facial expressions. Some children con-

---

28. J. Lerner and F. Kline, *Learning Disabilities and Related Disorders: Characteristics and Teaching Strategies*, 10th ed. (Houghton Mifflin Company: New York, 2006), 521.
29. N. Bauminger, H. Edelsztein, and J. Morash, "Social Information Processing and Emotional Understanding in Children with LD," *Journal of Learning Disabilities* 38 (2005), 45–61.

tinue working on Artifactual Thinking for one or two years, depending on the initial severity.

Research conducted by Nirit Bauminger, Hany Schorr Edelsztein, and Janice Morash at Bar-Ilan University, Israel, provides interesting insights into how the Artifactual Thinking cognitive exercise works on neurological weaknesses exhibited by children with learning disabilities. The researchers studied one hundred children in Grades 4 to 6 attending two large elementary schools. Fifty children with learning disabilities were matched with fifty children without LD. Of the fifty with LD, thirty-five were boys and fourteen were girls. The researchers sought to understand the differences in the social information processing skills and emotional understanding of the two groups.

To assess differences in social information processing, the researchers presented the children with five short auditory social vignettes. They asked the children questions based on what they had heard. They looked for the children's abilities to:

- Encode social cues (remember what they heard)
- Interpret social cues (determine what the problem was)
- Clarify goals (if you were in the same situation, what would you have done?)
- Search for possible social responses (what ways could the subject of the vignette have dealt with this situation?)
- Make a response decision (which solution would you choose?)
- Demonstrate a suitable enactment process (show what action should be taken)

To assess emotional understanding between the two groups of children, the researchers studied both emotional recognition and knowledge. To compare emotional recognition, the researchers used both stories and pictures. To examine emotional knowledge, they used the Kusche Affective Interview. This interview analyzes a child's emotional knowledge by assessing five emotions: happiness, loneliness, embarrassment, pride, and guilt. The assessments look at complex emotions that children with or without LD have to interpret in life. The researchers wanted to find the similarities and differences between the two groups of children in their abilities to understand complex, mixed, and hidden emotions.

The researchers discovered that children with LD have significant problems in understanding complex emotions. For example, they noted that children with LD have difficulty understanding that two conflicting emotions like love and hate can be simultaneously experienced. The researchers also stated:

> Our findings revealed an inconsistent profile of social information processing among children with LD. On the one hand, these children encoded social cues less well than their NLD [non-learning-disordered] group peers; the LD group children recalled less information and tended to add more irrelevant information while processing social situations. On the other hand, their ability to identify the problem and to interpret the situation as positive or negative resembled that of the NLD group, although the NLD group evidenced better attributions to the situation's social context. Furthermore, children with LD suggested fewer social solutions to problems than did the NLD group peers . . . children with LD revealed a less appropriate response decision, elicited fewer social goals, and were less likely to link their elicited goals and response decisions.[30]

In this study, the researchers noted that children with LD clearly had a broad range of social deficits. Most importantly, these children struggled to understand, recognize, or interpret complex social emotions such as embarrassment, pride, guilt, and loneliness. The understanding of these complex social emotions depended on social context and the perspectives of the individuals engaged in the interaction. In social environments, the children with LD relied heavily on quickly analyzing nonverbal cues and looking at multiple facial expressions, especially during group interactions. These children did significantly better when less complex emotions such as happiness or sadness were analyzed. Here again, they differed in the range of solutions they could provide to take action in specific social situations.

---

30. Ibid., 56.

The researchers from Israel discovered that children with LD do indeed experience complex social emotions. They speculated that the problem for these children is that they struggle to reflect on their own emotional experiences. This is because they fail to develop social-emotional scripts, or if they do, the scripts are not developed normally. The Artifactual Thinking cognitive exercise provides children with LD the opportunity to strengthen the area responsible for these skills. Over time, they begin to make sense of their social world and become more comfortable engaging with both peers and adults.

Madeline's Progress

By the spring of her first year at Eaton Arrowsmith, Madeline had made great improvements in reading comprehension, reasoning, reading speed, and copying speed, as shown in table 8. This was a good start to the Arrowsmith Program.

TABLE 8. MADELINE'S PROGRESS AFTER ONE YEAR OF ARROWSMITH

Arrowsmith Assessment Achievement Measure	**Start of Arrowsmith Program**	**After Year 1 in Arrowsmith Program**
Reading Comprehension (Monroe Sherman Test of Achievement)	Grade 6.5 Level	Grade 8.0 Level
Reading Speed (Monroe Sherman Test of Achievement)	Grade 6.8 Level	Grade 8.9 Level
Copying Text (Monroe Sherman Test of Achievement)	20th %ile	50th %ile
Reasoning (Munzert Reasoning Test)	30th %ile	86th %ile

Note: The average performance range is considered to fall between the 25th and 75th %ile ranking.

Madeline needed more time working on Symbolic Thinking to improve her organization and planning skills. Sandra Heusel noted, "While Madeline was always polite and obedient at school, I know she and her mom had a bit of a tough time at home. When she was not interested in a cognitive exercise and/or did not see the point, Madeline at times resisted coming to school. Then her mother would have to push. Not fun."

It can be difficult for parents to wait for these changes to take place. Often parents want immediate results, without which they may be skeptical that the program is working. They may look for any slight change to validate their decision. In fact, parents need to exercise a great deal of patience as their child works through the Arrowsmith Program. In some cases, dramatic improvements in reading comprehension and reading speed can be observed within three to six months. These swift changes often provide a sense of security to parents. Other cognitive abilities, however, can take more time depending on the severity of the weaknesses prior to the start of their program. For example, if a child has weak social skills due to a combination of severe cognitive weaknesses, it could take up to a year of cognitive remediation to begin seeing improvements in social engagement and understanding. The child may have severe deficits with reasoning, listening, and interpreting nonverbal information. Each of these cognitive abilities ultimately has to be moved to the average range of ability, and it can take three years of work to see the full benefit of the program. Parents who have shown this patience are often the most appreciative of the benefits of the program.

Janice and Sanjay's decision to bring Madeline back for a second year was simple. It had to happen. "Madeline didn't want to do the cognitive homework in the evening," said Janice. "We would be insistent. It was a struggle. [In other ways] it was one of our greatest years. That first year, she gave up her book and made friends. She did this without me. I didn't know these kids. That showed me that something was happening. The other thing was that I never worried about her. I never worried about her safety. It was the first time I could honestly say that. She was never frightened here."

For Madeline, the decision to come back for a second year was more difficult. Janice noted, however, that "Madeline felt good about certain things, and eventually she was able to convince herself to go back because her buddies were all going back."

Madeline's second year proved even more beneficial, but this would not be evident until the end of the year. This is often the case as the child begins to improve more and more cognitive weaknesses. Jason Cruickshank and Chris Watson (not related to Mark Watson) were Madeline's cognitive teachers for her second school year. Jason recalled, "I remember teaching math to Madeline last year. [She had] no organizational skills to speak of, her binder was exploding with loose papers, she was never prepared with a pencil or calculator, but always did reasonably well on tests. Nor could she explain how she arrived at a particular answer—she just knew what the answer was. It was clear she was very bright."

The second year started much the same as year one ended: messy binders, disorganized locker, and need of constant reminders for what she should be doing each new period. A typical reply was, "Oh, why can't I just listen to my iPod?" The Artifactual and Symbolic Thinking cognitive exercises were the most difficult for her, requiring an enormous amount of focus. We had ongoing motivational discussions with Madeline and her mother about the importance of the cognitive exercises. It was a constant struggle with no easy solutions. The year continued with ups and downs.

Later in her second year, we had a breakthrough. We attached a reward of concert tickets with Madeline's goals; we set high goals, and she achieved them, including getting to attend her concert. It was at this point we all—including Madeline—realized this bright girl was indeed capable of engaging long enough in her exercises to be successful. She was proud of herself and made it through the rest of the year without much resistance to her teachers' encouragement to do her work.

Madeline was enjoying social interaction with her friends, performing well in school (with no extra support), and showing more focus and determination to accomplish a task. She was changing. She worked independently, got her thoughts down on paper, and understood instructions. She had a new confidence in herself and she continued to make new friends.

The achievement results from her second year at Eaton Arrowsmith School were also positive, as seen in table 9.

Table 9. Madeline's achievement progress after two years of Arrowsmith

Arrowsmith Assessment Achievement Measure	**After Year 1 in Arrowsmith Program**	**After Year 2 in Arrowsmith Program**
Reading Comprehension (Monroe Sherman Test of Achievement)	Grade 8.0 Level	Grade 9.3 Level
Reading Speed (Monroe Sherman Test of Achievement)	Grade 8.9 Level	Grade 10.0 Level
Copying Text (Monroe Sherman Test of Achievement)	50th %ile	80th %ile
Reasoning (Munzert Reasoning Test)	86th %ile	98th %ile

Note: The average performance range is considered to fall between the 25th and 75th %ile ranking.

More importantly, she had made significant cognitive improvements with Artifactual and Symbolic Thinking, which was helping her with understanding social interactions and with keeping herself organized. Her parents and the school's staff were elated. None of her cognitive functions now fell in the severe range of difficulty. Table 10 shows Madeline's Arrowsmith assessment results at the end of her second year.

Table 10. Madeline's Arrowsmith assessment results after two years

Cognitive Function	**Description**	**Madeline's Level of Difficulty**
Motor-Symbol Sequencing	Problems associated with printing neatly and copying quickly. Careless errors in math, slow reading speed, inconsistent spelling.	Moderate to Mild

Cognitive Function	**Description**	**Madeline's Level of Difficulty**
Symbol Relations	Problems understanding concepts and cause-and-effect reasoning. Logical-reasoning problems.	Average
Memory for Information and Instructions	Problems following language or oral information.	Moderate
Symbolic Thinking	Problems being self-directed and self-organized in learning, limited mental initiative, difficulty keeping attention focused on a task to completion, trouble seeing main point, and limited problem-solving abilities.	Mild to Moderate
Artifactual Thinking	Problems understanding and interpreting social cues.	Moderate to Mild

Madeline wanted to go back into the regular school system, and she committed to completing the rest of her cognitive exercises in the after-school part-time program. Janice and Sanjay would have gladly enrolled her for the third year at EAS, but they just couldn't persuade Madeline. Even after she was shown the achievement scores she had attained over the past two years, she could not be moved. She was determined to try to succeed at a private school in Vancouver. Given that she had done well over the last two years in the Arrowsmith Program and that she was going to commit to the part-time program, there was a reasonable chance she could continue to perform well at a full-curriculum school.

Madeline Goes out on Her Own

After finishing two years in the full-time Arrowsmith Program, in September 2007 Madeline transferred to Rawlings Academy, a private school in Vancouver. In the part-time after-school Arrowsmith Program, she still had Memory for Information and Instructions to complete along with several other cognitive exercises.

When I corresponded with Janice later that year, she reported that Madeline was doing very well, both academically and socially. She had friends at school. She was getting Bs in most of her classes, and the family was pleased. As well, support services and learning assistance were not needed. Madeline was doing all of this on her own. At Arrowsmith, we were delighted.

In June 2008, EAS cognitive teacher Jason Cruickshank received an e-mail from Janice and relayed the news to me: "Madeline's mom told me she got an overall 78 percent on Rawlings' International Baccalaureate program with no extra assistance."

Janice and Sanjay then decided to look at Wickham Hall, an all-girls private school in Vancouver with high academic standards and an IB program. This was the school Madeline had always wanted to attend, and she was accepted based on her entrance exam scores. Soon after, I asked Janice how things were going socially. She smiled and said, "Great! Socially, there is a difference. Maybe it's the group of girls that feel good about themselves."

Madeline also worked hard at her studies. I asked Janice what a typical week looked like for her daughter at one of the top private schools for girls in the country. "She gets home at 3:30," she said, "and literally works right through until her homework is done—sometimes until ten, eleven, or twelve o'clock. Every subject gives her homework. Even subjects like Information Technology give her tax spreadsheets for an individual's tax return."

Recently, Janice sent me Madeline's most recent report card. She had just finished Grade 10 at Wickham Hall. She received a B in English, A in social studies, B in science, and C in mathematics. She had not had any learning assistance or tutoring. This was the same school Janice and Sanjay had only dreamed of applying to after their daughter's preschool years at Alderson. This was the girl who, upon entering Eaton Arrowsmith School, was terribly disorganized and often at a loss to remember which task she was to perform. This was the girl who, at breaks and lunch, would retreat from her peers and read alone, silently, afraid to socialize. Her Grade 10 report card noted:

Independent Studies 10: During her independent study block, Madeline has been able to complete academic assignments, study for tests, and work on maintaining an organized binder and agenda. She works diligently and makes good use of her time.

Planning 10: Madeline had a successful term. She was consistently prepared and hard-working, and she contributed thoughtfully to class discussions. She has produced good work.

Physical Education 10: Madeline demonstrated a willingness to learn and actively participated in class. She frequently demonstrated initiative and was a good group contributor.

Social Studies 10: Madeline is to be commended for an excellent term; her assignments and tests were well prepared.

My interview with Janice for this book lasted over an hour. I asked her how quickly she had made the initial decision to have Madeline attend Eaton Arrowsmith School. She smiled and responded, "We were on the phone to you and then out to the school in minutes. The second I heard that the school was starting, I never looked back again." Janice glanced down and then out the window. "I wished it had been there earlier. Because we would have done it from the beginning [of Madeline's education]."

In August 2009, Madeline was brought back to Eaton Arrowsmith School to undergo a complete reassessment of her cognitive abilities two years after completing the Arrowsmith Program. Barbara Arrowsmith Young has noted that she observes further improvements in cognitive abilities in the years after the cognitive exercise program is completed. The Arrowsmith Program builds a foundation of neurological ability that then can be further developed with stimulation from other academic activities. She has made the argument to other educators that children continue to show gains in cognitive ability once the program is over.

Barbara's observations were confirmed by Madeline's results. Her cognitive profile had improved in a number of areas since she had graduated from the full-time Arrowsmith Program.[31] Keep in mind that Madeline worked on several cognitive exercises in the part-time program for two

31. It is important to note that Madeline's achievement scores at graduation from Eaton Arrowsmith School were at or above grade-level expectations because of specific cognitive improvements in reasoning and visual processing speed. In addition, other cognitive abilities improved and directly influenced achievement acquisition levels.

further years. Table 11 shows her improvements from the Woodcock-Johnson Tests of Cognitive Abilities—III:

TABLE 11. MADELINE'S WOODCOCK-JOHNSON RESULTS AFTER ARROWSMITH

Psycho-Educational Assessment Measure from Woodcock-Johnson Tests of Cognitive Ability—III	Description	Upon Completing Arrowsmith Program (2007)	Two Years after Arrowsmith Program (2009)
Thinking Ability *-Long-term retrieval* *-Visual-spatial thinking* *-Auditory processing* *-Fluid reasoning*	A sampling of different thinking processes that might be used when information cannot be processed automatically.	34th %ile	85th %ile
Cognitive Efficiency	Ability of the cognitive system to process information automatically.	32nd %ile	81st %ile
Phonemic Awareness	Ability to analyze and synthesize speech sounds.	43rd %ile	95th %ile
Working Memory	Ability to hold information in immediate awareness while manipulating that information.	74th %ile	97th %ile
Oral Language	Ability to follow directions and recall story details.	23rd %ile	41st %ile

Note: The average performance range on psycho-educational assessments is considered to fall between the 25th and 75th %ile ranking.

Madeline continues to thrive at her private school. She has come a long way from a child confused about her social and academic world. She received Bs and As in her academic subjects during the 2009–2010 school year. Madeline started Grade 12 in September 2010 with her thoughts on a university education.

7

The Valedictorian

New neurons can bloom; gray matter can become thicker. Neuroplasticity makes it possible.

—SHARON BEGLEY, AUTHOR, *TRAIN YOUR MIND, CHANGE YOUR BRAIN*

Adoption from Peru

Samantha was born in Peru on September 4th, 1992, amid political unrest and government instability. Her adoptive parents, Connie and Greg, flew to Peru to formalize her adoption and that of her brother, Kevin. Connie and Greg heard the sounds of frequent bombing in the evenings, and they were aware that villagers and political figures alike were being killed at alarming rates. It was October 1992, and Samantha was one month old, Kevin just seven weeks older. Samantha seemed malnourished and appeared to be in pain. She had been fed only condensed milk and tea, and she wasn't very healthy.

Rumours of evil foreigners adopting Peruvian babies for organ transplants or even to be used as servants were rampant, and this made it even more difficult to secure the two children's adoption. The purging of the judicial system and the reorganization of government stalled the process, but eventually Connie, Greg, and the two babies were able to make their way home to Vancouver, Canada.

Back at home, Connie and Greg gave all they could to their newly adopted daughter and son. They introduced them to baby formula and Samantha's health improved. Connie and Greg kept in touch with Samantha's biological mother, providing her with updates on her development. Connie did not notice any significant problems in Samantha's early development; she was a beautiful baby who Connie said seemed to have an old soul.

In my interview with Connie, she said, "Growing up, Samantha really seemed fine. She learned to walk at a normal age, and she talked and was interested in art and stories and toys, so there wasn't really anything in the early years that twigged me." She paused and said, "When I look back at her pictures though, of babyhood and up to three years old, she has this confused look on her face. And I never noticed it." Connie recalled, "I have this little ballet picture of her and she is kind of staring off in the distance with this confused look."

For Connie, the realization that there might be a learning problem came when she asked Samantha to identify letters in storybooks she was reading aloud to her children. "I read *Freddy Fox* by Ronald J. Meyer and *Princess Prunella and the Purple Peanut* by Margaret Atwood to Samantha," her mother said. "She couldn't tell an *f* or a *p* from any other letters. She began to hate those books as she knew I would ask her to identify letters. She just couldn't do it." Samantha's brother, Kevin, only seven weeks older, was able to identify letters, and this raised the first concern for Connie.

Both parents wanted their children to develop an awareness of their Peruvian culture, which included the idea of teaching them Spanish at a young age. When a Spanish teacher was hired to work with the two young children at home, Connie and Greg also noticed problems with Samantha's ability with language.

"The teacher kept telling me how lazy Samantha was," said Connie. "Now I can see that Samantha just wasn't able to cope with it." Samantha was struggling with letter awareness and processing oral language.

Kindergarten

In September 1997, Connie and Greg enrolled their two five-year-olds in kindergarten. This was the beginning of Samantha's considerable learning challenges. Not too long after starting kindergarten, the teacher asked for a meeting with Connie. Connie said, "She told me she felt Samantha was delayed. She recommended learning resource help." Connie and Greg decided to hold Samantha back one year to give her a chance to develop her abilities, although this was not the recommendation of the teacher or school. The family was also moving to another location in the city, so Samantha could start her second year of kindergarten at another school. Kevin was not held back, and this was the beginning of Samantha's feelings of inadequacy when compared with her brother. "I thought it would be easier for her if she was held back, and now I realize it had nothing to do with it," Connie said sadly.

The second year of kindergarten proved equally difficult for Samantha. She struggled to understand numeracy and to develop letter and sound awareness. At this point Connie began to request testing from the school district.

"We started with the public school system, requesting an assessment. They told me they wouldn't give a psycho-educational assessment until she was in Grade 1. So I said, 'Okay. Let's move her to grade one. She's supposed to be in grade one anyway.' But we had already registered her in kindergarten, so she had to stay there. They wouldn't test her until the next year."

In order to speed up the process, Connie and Greg hired a private psychologist to do the testing that summer; Samantha was six years old and due to begin Grade 1 in September. The psychologist, Dr. Perry Sinclair, came to their home and tested Samantha there; Connie felt this would be better than testing at a clinic. Dr. Sinclair provided the following observation in his report: "Samantha was cooperative and friendly throughout the assessment process. While she was able to concentrate and focus on testing activities, she was often very restless and constantly in motion. She had great difficulty at times remaining seated and was often quite impulsive in her response style. She is a very verbal child, and constantly talked either to herself while processing the various test items, or to the examiner. Her enthusiasm and sense of humour were evident at all times."

Dr. Sinclair conducted measures of intelligence, cognitive ability, and achievement. He met with Connie after the testing was completed and the report was written. "Dr. Sinclair sat down with me and said, 'Samantha has low IQ.'" Connie listened and thought, "Okay, that's fine. I can handle it. I can deal with that now that I know what I am dealing with." I asked Connie if she felt that the low IQ issue was to remain with Samantha the rest of her life. Connie said, "I really didn't think that far ahead. I just thought about how we could help her to be happy in life."

Dr. Sinclair identified serious language problems in Samantha. On the Verbal Intelligence Score of IQ on the Wechsler Intelligence Scale for Children (WISC-III) she fell in the "slow learner" category. Samantha was also below age level in reading. Her word decoding skills fell at the 3rd percentile compared with her peers.

Connie and Greg did not recall the fact that Dr. Sinclair had also identified average abilities in intelligence—we discovered this later. Samantha's score on the WISC-III test placed her visual intelligence at the average range. Dr. Sinclair noted, "Processing complex visual information by forming spatial images of part-whole relationships and/or by manipulating the parts to solve novel problems without using words is an area of strength for Samantha. She is considerably less effective at comprehending verbal information and using her verbal abilities to solve new problems."

The Barlow Academy and Public School

Dr. Sinclair recommended that Samantha attend the Barlow Academy, a school for children with language-based learning disabilities such as dyslexia. "He suggested that she sit in the front of the class," Connie continued. "He said that she'd probably not be able to function in a public school setting, that she would benefit from a situation like the Barlow Academy. But she almost didn't get in because of her low IQ scores. I called Barlow and asked if they would please consider her for admissions. They decided to accept her for Grade 1."

Barlow Academy was helpful to Samantha. She completed Grades 1 and 2 at the school, and Connie and Greg then decided to enrol her in public school once again.

Connie described the reason for this transition. "We pulled her out of Barlow Academy and put her back into public school for Grade 3 because I thought it would be nice for her. Lots of kids from the neighbourhood street were going to the school. I knew the teacher. Kevin had had the teacher, who was a special education person. I talked to [this teacher] about Samantha and he seemed to want to help her. And at the time, there were a whole bunch of boys at Barlow Academy, and we felt this way she could make some girlfriends."

The result of this transition was, in short, "a disaster. Around November," said Connie, "I found her crying in her bed each night, frustrated at her inability to understand what was going on in class. I had to speak to the teachers just to make sure that any remaining threads of self-esteem she had stayed intact. I pulled her out of school a few days a week and put her in drama and art classes to get through the year. She could not tell time and still had no sense of numbers."

Her father added, "She just couldn't comprehend the clock no matter how many times we taught about what each hand says."

Of course, Connie and Greg were concerned for Samantha's self-esteem. It was evident that Samantha felt stupid. Her brother, at almost the same age, had progressed much further in his cognitive learning. Said Greg, "Her brother started using the word stupid—I don't know exactly when it was. He'd throw out a few phrases like, 'Oh, you stupid, you can't get this.' I could just see it kind of hit her like an axe." Greg paused and added, "And then she started to believe it more." So Samantha ended up back at Barlow Academy to begin Grade 4.

Samantha's Psycho-Educational Assessment

I first met Samantha and her family at this time, in November 2002. Samantha was ten years old, and Connie and Greg wanted her retested because they had begun to question the low IQ statement of the previous psychologist. Interestingly, in cases like this parents often recall the negative findings of these meetings and forget any positive results. What remained in Samantha's parents' minds were the statements, "Samantha is a slow learner" and "Samantha has low IQ," though at the time Dr. Sinclair was referring only to Samantha's verbal intelligence. And if a parent *only* hears a psychologist say, "slow learner," what would that parent assume the child's potential is? Almost anything else the psychologist may say on the positive side of neurological ability will be forgotten.

Connie and Greg heard about my psycho-educational assessment services from a friend. At the time, I was conducting assessments with several psychologists. When Samantha and her mother arrived at the assessment office, Connie began by describing her daughter as a very creative individual who loved art. She also noted that Samantha's piano teacher, who had spent the last five months with her, described her as possessing a gift. Samantha also enjoyed soccer, badminton, skiing, and swimming. I learned more about Samantha as the interview progressed and the assessment was conducted.

The results highlighted a discrepancy between her verbal and visual intelligence. Her visual intelligence remained in the average range of ability, but her verbal intelligence was no longer in the borderline range; it was now in the low average range. It is important to note why Samantha's verbal intelligence on the WISC-III fell in this range. Samantha had average vocabulary abilities. She scored well into the average range on measures of expressive vocabulary. She was able to define words orally to the examiner, and was quite capable of telling how words related to each other conceptually (e.g., how a pencil is like a pen—both are writing instruments). But one issue for Samantha was a weakness with recall of factual information (e.g., facts about history, geography, and science). She also struggled to perform mental math, finding it nearly impossible to solve math problems in her mind. These two weaknesses on the verbal IQ scale lowered her IQ into the low average range.

Samantha had other areas of neurological and achievement weakness. Table 12 outlines some of the major cognitive functioning weaknesses on her 2002 psycho-educational assessment:

TABLE 12. SAMANTHA'S INITIAL PSYCHO-EDUCATIONAL ASSESSMENT RESULTS

Psycho-Educational Assessment Measure	**Description**	**Before Arrowsmith Program**
Cognitive Efficiency (Woodcock-Johnson Tests of Cognitive Ability—Third Edition—WJ-III)	Ability of the cognitive system to process information automatically.	6th %ile
Coding Subtest (Wechsler Intelligence Scale for Children—Third Edition—WISC-III, and Fourth Edition—WISC-IV)	Ability to scan and copy visual symbols under timed conditions.	25th %ile
Thinking Ability (Woodcock-Johnson Tests of Cognitive Ability—Revised—WJ-R)	A sampling of different thinking processes (Visual-Auditory Learning, Spatial Relations, Sound Blending, Concept Formation) that may be used when information cannot be processed automatically.	56th %ile
Working Memory (WJ-III)	Ability to hold information in immediate awareness while manipulating that information.	17th %ile
Visual-Auditory Learning (WJ-III)	A measure of long-term retrieval/ memory.	3rd %ile
Nonverbal Intelligence (Test of Nonverbal Intelligence—Third Edition—TONI-3)	A measure of fluid intelligence. Ability to recognize visual patterns and relationships.	32nd %ile

Note: The average performance range on psycho-educational assessments is considered to fall between the 25th and 75th %ile ranking.

It was evident that Samantha struggled with cognitive efficiency, working memory, long-term memory, and speed of visual-motor copying. In fact, she was capable of drawing designs perfectly from memory; she was a good artist. Her problems were speed of copying information and getting her own ideas in writing. On the coding subtest of the WISC-III, a measure of visual-motor copying speed, she scored at the 25th percentile. On the Woodcock-Johnson Tests of Achievement—III (WJ-III) she scored at the 17th percentile on writing fluency, meaning approximately 83 percent of her peers could get ideas down on paper at a faster speed. Her overall math ability was well below grade-level expectations; she struggled with calculations and problem solving. Her reading comprehension was also weak compared with her peers; approximately 89 percent were better than Samantha.

In a follow-up meeting with Connie and Greg, I noted these hills and valleys in Samantha's profile. I talked about her many neurological strengths, suggesting she could move into Grade 5, rather than stay in Grade 4, which was one year below her appropriate age level. She was attending a school for children with language-based learning disabilities and getting the appropriate reading and math achievement remediation, so it made no sense to keep her below her correct grade level. In January of 2003 she was transferred to Grade 5.

In our later interview, Connie's eyes filled with tears as she said, "I think this was a real turning point for her, and a turning point for me to realize that all this time I thought she was not very smart and in fact she was. I felt dreadful. Because I—because I thought, well, maybe all through this time I've been treating her like she was somebody with a low IQ. And maybe she was picking up on that. It was a big turning point for her to march into that Grade 5 classroom. It seemed the kids in that class thought, 'Wow! What are you doing here?' It really was a big confidence booster for her."

Samantha stayed at Barlow Academy for Grades 5, 6, and 7. Then, in Grade 7, she began to experience bullying. Connie noted, "Bullying is so common at that age. It was not just because she was at Barlow Academy. Girls can be tough on each other." Connie continued, "She began to be ostracized for whatever reason. She would try to join a group, and they would physically turn their backs on her. They would tell her they were having a party and that she was not invited." This was difficult for Connie and Greg to take because Samantha was a friendly child who would help these girls and listen when they wanted someone to talk to.

Samantha started cutting herself as a result of this bullying. "Cutting," or self-mutilation, is not uncommon in schools today, with one study reporting a 13.9% frequency rate with adolescents.[32] A form of self-harm or self-injury that develops when self-esteem is low, it is more common in girls than in boys. It is also often a sign of emotional difficulties. Connie agreed. "It was a real cry for help. We spent that year in the psychologist's office dealing with cutting. Samantha wasn't very happy and the bullying was continuing. I was very thankful for Barlow Academy for holding her self-esteem together [academically]," Connie said, "but we knew we had to get her out of that situation."

Samantha's Arrowsmith Assessment Results

Connie had heard about the Arrowsmith Program many years earlier. "My family is all in Toronto and we go back every summer to the cottage. My family knew that Samantha had a learning disability, so one of my cousins sent me all the information she could find about the Arrowsmith Program. I actually grew up on St. Clair Avenue where the school is—I know the house it's located in." Connie smiled. "I think my family was hoping we would move back to Toronto for the Arrowsmith Program."

Greg and Connie also knew of my first case study, Andrew, and his parents, Nancy and Mike. Said Connie, "I heard updates about Andrew through the grapevine, that he was doing pretty well there."

Connie attended one of my first information sessions about the new Eaton Arrowsmith School. Both Connie and Greg were interested in the concept of improving neurological functioning. Like others, they felt this was a better idea than simply keeping skill levels up in order to get through high school. They had seen children with learning disabilities receive accommodations and learning support through high school, but end up with serious problems afterward.

Connie and Greg did their homework, learning how the Arrowsmith Program targets various cognitive weaknesses that result in learning dysfunctions and then creates a program of cognitive exercises designed to remediate those weaknesses. They learned that the brain uses many

---

32. S. Ross and N. Heath, "A Study of the Frequency of Self-mutilation in a Community Sample of Adolescents," *Journal of Youth and Adolescence* 31, no. 1 (2002), 67–77.

areas to acquire reading and math skills, and weaknesses in any of these neurological functions can cause specific types of learning disabilities such as reading speed problems, mental math calculation difficulties, or reasoning problems that affect reading comprehension and math problem solving. Connie and Greg liked Arrowsmith's diagnostic approach because it is a brain-based remediation. They decided to give it a try.

Samantha's Arrowsmith assessment highlighted numerous cognitive deficits. The assessment is comprehensive and frequently picks up additional concerns not often identified by a six-hour psycho-educational assessment. Like many children with learning disabilities, she had multiple challenges that did not neatly fit into one descriptive diagnosis such as dyslexia or written expression disability. Table 13 highlights the most significant cognitive functioning weaknesses from the Arrowsmith assessment in May 2005.

TABLE 13. SAMANTHA'S INITIAL ARROWSMITH ASSESSMENT RESULTS

Cognitive Function	Description	Samantha's Level of Difficulty
Motor-Symbol Sequencing	Problems associated with printing neatly and copying quickly. Careless errors in math, slow reading speed, inconsistent spelling.	Severe to Moderate
Symbol Relations	Problems understanding concepts and cause-and-effect reasoning. Logical-reasoning problems.	Moderate
Memory for Information and Instructions	Trouble remembering oral instruction, difficulty following lectures or extended conversations.	Moderate to Severe
Broca's Speech Pronunciation	Mispronouncing words, avoiding using words, speaking in incomplete sentences.	Severe to Moderate
Artifactual Thinking	Problems understanding and interpreting social cues.	Mild to Moderate

Cognitive Function	Description	Samantha's Level of Difficulty
Symbolic Thinking	Problems being self-directed and self-organized in learning, limited mental initiative, difficulty keeping attention focused on a task to completion, trouble seeing main point, and limited problem-solving abilities.	Mild to Moderate
Supplementary Motor	Trouble with finger counting, problems learning math facts and holding numbers in her head, poor sense of time management.	Moderate to Severe

At this stage, Samantha had regressed. She lacked confidence, was nervous, and struggled socially. She was quiet and avoided recognition for any accomplishment in front of her peers. She needed remediation. In particular, it became clear why mathematics was so problematic: she could not hold or sequence numbers in her head. She scored in the moderate to severe range on the Supplementary Motor test, which gauges how well a child can manipulate numerical information. In addition, she showed weak reasoning and conceptual thinking ability on the Symbol Relations measure. This would affect her reading comprehension and math problem solving. Her score in this area fell in the moderate range, thus requiring cognitive remediation. Finally, her difficulty with copying speed and copying accuracy shown on the Motor-Symbol Sequencing measure was evident during testing, with her score in the severe to moderate category. This weakness would result in problems writing math symbols on paper and could lead to careless errors in calculations.

If Samantha was to improve in mathematics, these cognitive weaknesses would have to be addressed first. Even small-group instruction at Barlow Academy could not help her understand math concepts. This was not due to poor instruction, but to the severity of Samantha's cognitive weaknesses related to mathematics. Often, teachers working with children with learning disabilities feel that good instruction, small class sizes, and use of *manipulatives*[33] should be enough to teach any child mathematics. However, this is rarely the case; too often a child simply memorizes the information for the test and then forgets it weeks later. This is because of cognitive weaknesses related to math acquisition that are never remediated.

Despite years of Orton-Gillingham tutorials, Samantha was also behind in reading. Again, this weakness is related to cognitive dysfunctions, not to bad tutoring or a poor reading remediation program. For example, if a child cannot scan symbols rapidly, her reading speed will be slow even with the best phonetic-based reading remediation method. The child first needs to develop faster visual-motor scanning ability and symbol recognition. Reading comprehension can also be affected. Samantha was in Grade 8, but her reading comprehension was at Grade 5 level. Her cognitive weakness in conceptual thinking kept her reading comprehension score below grade level. For example, it was hard for her to remember one concept in a paragraph while introduced to a second, third, or fourth concept in the same paragraph. Thus, she lost the meaning of the paragraph and struggled as she attempted to integrate all the ideas it contained.

Samantha also presented attention problems. This was not a severe handicap, but it would affect her ability to stay organized and plan efficiently. Her score on Symbolic Thinking, which measures the ability to use language to organize and plan effectively, fell in the mild to moderate range of difficulty. Samantha still needed to work on this area of the brain.

Most importantly, the test results highlighted why Samantha's verbal intelligence scores fell in the low range. On almost all measures of language ability, from sound analysis to listening comprehension, Samantha scored in the severe range of difficulty. Dr. Sinclair had discovered this in 1999, and in the six years since, these cognitive weaknesses had remained weak. No cognitive remediation program had been available

33. Mathematic manipulatives are items used to help children understand math concepts, for example, concrete objects such as coloured rods, geometric shapes, base-ten blocks, or real clocks.

at that time for Samantha. In short, she had been finding ways, with help from her teachers, to survive in school with her cognitive weaknesses by using learning strategies and accommodations. If Samantha was going to have any success at school, her brain's language domains would require cognitive remediation. She would need to work on these neurological areas for at least three to four years.

The Barlow Academy—which focused on language-based learning disabilities—had provided the necessary strategies and accommodations so Samantha's cognitive weaknesses would not result in school failure. The Arrowsmith Program would instead uncover each cognitive weakness and, using particular cognitive exercises, remediate them over a period of thirty to forty months of intervention.

Three Years at Eaton Arrowsmith School

Samantha worked hard on her cognitive program. Only two months after she began, her cognitive teachers, Mark Watson and Sarah Cohen, e-mailed her mother. "We are extremely impressed with the quality and amount of work that Samantha is completing in class," they wrote. "She is a very determined student and this is what is required to excel in our program."

Her mother replied, "Samantha has always worked hard to keep up, and now that she can see that the Arrowsmith Program is helping, she is really motivated! Samantha eventually wants to attend a regular school with her friends, so she always does her cognitive homework. On some Saturday mornings, I have to tell her to stop. One day she worked for approximately three hours on an English assignment about Rosa Parks. I don't think her English teacher expected that kind of time commitment, but Samantha wasn't quitting until it was done. She read voraciously and I was constantly at the library looking for books I thought she'd like. She truly amazes me, and with her work ethic, [I am now convinced] she'll have no problem down the road."

There were other gains. When Samantha received her first Arrowsmith assessment update, her mother wrote, "We were thrilled with Samantha's progress—no surprises. It was wonderful to see the grin on her face as we went through it with her. I just wanted you to know what a changed daughter I have this year. Samantha is gaining confidence. She feels supported in her class by both [her teachers] and her classmates."

Connie's message continued, noting that Samantha now was able to focus on her work and not her concerns about social problems. She was laughing and standing taller. "Samantha could never do her times tables, even the 4 × tables, which embarrassed her. But last week, she thought about the equation 4 × 7, and the answer came. But when she said it aloud, it got mixed up again. I realized that [thinking the answer and saying it], two simple and seemingly similar exercises, involve different parts of the brain to do the calculation. First, she has to do the calculation in her head, and second, she has to say it aloud, requiring different cognitive abilities. She realizes she's taking the steps to get there and is excited about what's next."

In a later interview, Connie mentioned another incident that highlighted improvements in neurological functioning related to sequencing. "We were always watching for changes the first little while and didn't see too much until one day, driving home around Christmas of the first year at EAS, and she asked me about the months of the year. She said, 'January is written as 1 and December is written as 12. That means there are twelve months in the year, right?' I hadn't realized at that point that she hadn't even known this, but when I said, 'Yes, that's right,' Samantha's eyes lit up as though a small piece of the puzzle was starting to fit into place. It was a small thing, but so huge to us. She was realizing that things could come together for her. It was one of those 'aha' moments."

By the middle of her first year, Samantha was talking more and showing confidence with her peers. She was doing well with her cognitive exercises, advancing in all areas. Sarah Cohen contacted Connie again, updating her on Samantha's progress.

Sarah wrote, "I just had to let you know how amazing it is to see Samantha initiating more conversations with Mark [Watson, Sarah's co-teacher] and me. She even gets a bit cheeky with other students in a totally fun way. This is evidence of her growing confidence. Today at lunchtime she sat beside my desk, asked me about my first jobs, and told me about starting work at her dad's store. She is really a much braver young woman than we saw walk in here in September. She continues to work very hard and raises the bar for her peers in terms of expectations. We also had a class discussion yesterday about the organization of lunchtime activities, and Samantha had her hand up and contributed several times, a first for her in our classroom. She is liked by all of her peers and her teachers."

Samantha's end-of-year tests indicated notable progress. That summer she read numerous books. Connie reflected, "Before the Arrowsmith Program, Samantha liked to read, but she couldn't get the main idea. I think she liked the *thought* of reading. This summer she read a couple of really thick books. She was really into them. I would ask her what they were about, and now she could tell me."

By the end of her second year, Samantha had moved her weaknesses with expressive language into the mild range. This was due to her improvement on the Broca's Speech Pronunciation cognitive exercise. Now she was more confident in talking to others, and she rarely struggled to pronounce words. Her reading comprehension was nearing grade-level expectations, and her reasoning had jumped to the 93rd percentile on the Munzert Reasoning Test. She no longer had problems with copying text speed as she was now higher than the 90th percentile in ability, and her reading speed was nearing the Grade 10 level.

Samantha's father also observed her increased expressive language abilities. Greg said, "I noticed changes during the second year of the Arrowsmith Program. I could finally understand her—much better. She mumbled much less. There is no doubt about it, because I could communicate with her much better." Greg continued, "You see, I used to drive her to school. She would always listen to her music with earphones, never talking to me. I would encourage her to unplug and talk with me, but for a long time—nothing. I'd be talking and nothing was coming back. Then I noticed I was starting to get some interaction. She started speaking better, and her confidence level changed."

Connie also mentioned that a close friend of Samantha's turned to her one day while they were walking down the street and said, "You talk more now."

I asked Connie and Greg in what ways they had noticed that her confidence level had changed. Connie laughed. "I remember one night we were sitting at the kitchen table. Kevin [her brother] was bugging her again. This always drove Samantha crazy. In the past, she didn't know how to handle him. On this occasion she had a bun or sandwich in her hand. Facing him, she said, 'You need to stop bugging me because it really is not fair. I don't like it when you do that and it's really not necessary.' She then held up her sandwich and whacked him with it. And everybody just kind of thought, 'Whoa!' She started walking out of the kitchen and then turned back at him and threw the sandwich across the room at him. She said, 'I told you to stop, now stop!' She then carried on with whatever she'd been doing before dinner."

I asked if that incident had changed their sibling relationship. Connie said, "I think so." Greg added, "Now he knew he wasn't getting away with anything anymore."

One and a half years were left in her three-year program, but Samantha didn't want to complete it. Midway through her second year at Eaton Arrowsmith School, she informed us that she wanted to return to public school, despite her previous experience with bullying in a regular school environment.

This is not an uncommon response from students having completed one or two years of the Arrowsmith Program. A great sense of confidence can build up with the successes they experience at EAS. Also, being in a "special" school can be embarrassing for them as they don't want to be associated with a disability. Furthermore, Arrowsmith is a difficult program that requires persistence and resilience. Students do not always want to face the daily repetition of the cognitive exercises; they may feel that their peers in the regular school system have things easier. Neuroplasticity requires constant repetition, with a high level of focus and sequential levels to master. There is no easy way to change the brain. Yet frightening statistics on unemployment and lower educational accomplishments are clear regarding those with learning disabilities. Not improving cognitive functioning can mean considerable problems later in life. Unfortunately, some students at this age are not fully aware of the ramifications of not improving their cognitive abilities.

Samantha was already at the Grade 10 level for her age at Eaton Arrowsmith School. I talked with her, learning that one of her main concerns was not having to repeat Grade 10 at her public high school. Samantha had repeated kindergarten and the impact this had had on her emotionally was evident. She was insistent about not repeating any grades. In British Columbia, graduation requirements (specific courses to receive a high school diploma) begin in Grade 10. Because students in Grades 10 through 12 at EAS take only math and English, they miss most of those requirements; they do not take social studies, sciences, or any other required or elective courses. In these cases, they often elect not to follow the regular graduation path, but to take their General Education Development (GED) tests after completing our program, which allows them access to post-secondary studies.

Samantha was determined to begin Grade 11 with her peers and not have to take Grade 10 courses. I suggested the option of taking distance-education courses in order to complete regular Grade 10 requirements while also finishing the Arrowsmith Program. The distance-education program offered by the Ministry of Education would allow Samantha, while still enrolled at EAS, to study her core subjects at a Vancouver high school that offered British Columbia Grade 10 certified courses. She could substitute EAS English and math classes with this distance-education program, as well as work with a private tutor at our school, and she could consider taking an additional course in the summer, which would enable her to begin Grade 11 at her public school. This elaborate plan would require a great deal of work, but Samantha was up for the challenge.

In September 2007, Samantha started her third and last year at Eaton Arrowsmith School. She had a full cognitive remediation program plus difficult distance-education courses in math, English, and science. Early into the school year, her mother noted that Samantha's language abilities were improving each week. She contacted Sarah Cohen and Kathryn Fullerton (an EAS academic teacher), giving them surprising information about Samantha's improved Spanish abilities.

"Samantha was fluent in Spanish and English until she was six," said her mother. "When it became apparent that she was having difficulty in school, we decided not to stress a second language for her. But last night when we were driving home she said she was getting all these Spanish words she hadn't thought of for a long time coming back into her head and then proceeded to tell me some of the words. Maybe Arrowsmith has just jumpstarted a part of her brain that stores second languages. Anyway, I thought you might be interested in that little nugget." Everyone was delighted at this news.

Then trouble surfaced. The distance-education program was putting a strain on Samantha, and it was showing up in her behaviour and ability to deal with stress. I discussed this with her mother. Solutions were considered and corrective actions were taken. She was given more time in the day to work on her distance-education courses. Samantha caught up and stayed committed; she would complete the program. Her mother noted that easing up on Samantha's written work and doing more of it orally was helping. Samantha's December 2007 grades were reasonable: science: 78 percent; English: 76 percent; math: 56 percent (although her math assignments were in the 80s and 90s).[34] If she was going to keep up, Samantha knew she would have to balance spring break with a little relaxation time and a great deal of study time.

Samantha was doing her best to balance both the Arrowsmith Program and the distance-education courses. The easier path would have been to first finish the Arrowsmith Program and then begin public school in Grade 10. Yet she was driven to get the work done, although she struggled at times to get through the course load. Her progress within the Arrowsmith Program remained constant.

Samantha's Final Arrowsmith and Psycho-Educational Assessments

Samantha was given her final Arrowsmith assessment in May 2008. As shown in table 14, the results were very positive.

---

34. Samantha was learning how to effectively study for and take math exams as she worked through a distance-education format. This resulted in very low exam grades in the first three months of the distance-education course. Given that she did well on her assignments, when exams and assignments were averaged her overall grade was 56 percent.

TABLE 14. SAMANTHA'S FINAL ARROWSMITH ASSESSMENT RESULTS

Cognitive Function	**Description**	**Samantha's Level of Difficulty**
Motor-Symbol Sequencing	Problems associated with printing neatly and copying quickly. Careless errors in math, slow reading speed, inconsistent spelling.	Mild to Average
Symbol Relations	Problems understanding concepts and cause-and-effect reasoning. Logical-reasoning problems.	Average to Above Average
Memory for Information and Instructions	Trouble remembering oral instruction, difficulty following lectures or extended conversations.	Moderate
Broca's Speech Pronunciation	Mispronouncing words, avoiding using words, speaking in incomplete sentences.	Mild
Artifactual Thinking	Problems understanding and interpreting social cues.	Average
Symbolic Thinking	Problems being self-directed and self-organized in learning, limited mental initiative, difficulty keeping attention focused on a task to completion, trouble seeing main point, and limited problem-solving abilities.	Average to Above Average
Supplementary Motor	Trouble with finger counting, problems learning math facts and holding numbers in her head, poor sense of time management.	Mild to Moderate

Samantha's cognitive language weaknesses with speech production (Broca's Speech Pronunciation) and Memory for Information and Instructions had all moved out of the severe range and were closer to the average range of ability. Her conceptual reasoning ability had improved to the average to above-average range, and as a result her reading comprehension was almost at grade level, though it still needed development. Her spelling and word recognition skills were at grade-level expectations. Her math calculation skills had jumped three years in just ten months due to stronger cognitive capacities to understand math concepts and manipulate numerical information. She now needed math content to fill remaining gaps in her knowledge base.

An updated psycho-educational assessment in 2008 also showed positive gains for Samantha. She was a faster reader and could get her thoughts down on paper at a level considered average for her peer group. She also had a more efficient brain, enabling her to process information both visually and aurally at a far greater speed than when she was first assessed prior to the Arrowsmith Program. Both her thinking and reasoning had improved significantly. Table 15 shows these gains.

TABLE 15. SAMANTHA'S UPDATED PSYCHO-EDUCATIONAL ASSESSMENT RESULTS

Psycho-Educational Assessment Measure	**Before Arrowsmith Program**	**After Arrowsmith Program**
Cognitive Efficiency—WJ-III	6th %ile	65th %ile
Coding Subtest—WISC-III to WISC-IV	25th %ile	95th %ile
Thinking Ability—WJ-III	56th %ile	91st %ile
Working Memory—WJ-III	17th %ile	51st %ile
Visual-Auditory Learning—WJ-III	3rd %ile	67th %ile
Nonverbal Intelligence—TONI-3	32nd %ile	94th %ile

Note: The average performance range on psycho-educational assessments is considered to fall between the 25th and 75th %ile ranking.

Another critical cognitive functioning improvement for Samantha was with working memory. Working memory relates to the brain's ability to hold and manipulate information immediately or within brief periods of time. For example, making mental math calculations requires working memory capacity. As numbers are added or subtracted mentally, the child needs to hold numerical information in her mind. As well, sounding out letters to form words has a working memory requirement. If the child cannot hold in working memory the first sound for a word she is trying to decode, pronouncing words can be extremely frustrating. During printing, the child is also accessing working memory functions as she tries to form letters with a pencil. Working memory is often described as a temporary storage facility without which life would be very problematic. Research is highlighting just how important working memory is for writing, reading, and math.[35]

In addition, improvements in working memory capacity are being linked to improvements in school performance and fluid intelligence.[36] Fluid intelligence relates to the ability to solve novel problems, or problems that need to be solved with no access to prior knowledge. For example, learning a new concept in math or science often requires a substantial amount of fluid intelligence (also called matrix reasoning, fluid reasoning, or concept formation on some cognitive assessment measures). The Test of Nonverbal Intelligence—Third Edition (TONI-III) is considered a measure of fluid intelligence. Samantha went from the 32nd percentile in ability (average) to the 94th percentile (superior) after two years in the Arrowsmith Program. Her working memory score (WJ-III) went from the 17th percentile (low average) to the 51st percentile (average). The above-noted research on the working memory and fluid-reasoning

35. T.P. Alloway, "Working Memory, Reading, and Mathematical Skills in Children with Developmental Coordination Disorders," *Journal of Experimental Child Psychology* 96 (2007), 20–36; S.E. Gathercole, T.P. Alloway, C. Willis, and A. Adams, "Working Memory in Children with Reading Disabilities," *Journal of Experimental Child Psychology* 93 (2006), 265–281.

36. T.P. Alloway and R.G. Alloway, "Investigating the Predictive Roles of Working Memory and IQ in Academic Attainment," *Journal of Experimental Child Psychology* 106, no.1 (2010), 20–29; S.M. Jaeggi, M. Buschkuehl, J. Jonides, and W.J. Perrig, "Improving Fluid Intelligence with Training on Working Memory," *Proceedings of the National Academy of Sciences* 105, no.19 (2008), 6829–6833.

relationship appears to hold true for Samantha and other case studies discussed in this book.

Samantha's Graduation

For her graduation in June 2008, Samantha was chosen class valedictorian. The entire staff voted for her because of her dedication to both the Arrowsmith Program and her distance-education courses. At the time Samantha was informed of this decision, she was working with her distance-education tutor. She was unsure what it meant. Sarah Cohen explained what a valedictorian was, and why Samantha was chosen. We asked her if she would accept this honour and speak to the graduation class and entire student body at the Chan Centre Auditorium at the University of British Columbia. About one hundred families and their guests would attend. She enthusiastically agreed.

Kathryn Fullerton, Samantha's academic teacher, phoned Connie to tell her the good news. Connie recalled the story, laughing. "When I was told the news over the phone, I burst into tears. Greg was there and said, 'What are you bawling about?' When I told him, he said, 'You'd better teach her what the word *valedictorian* means, because it's a big honour.'" Connie stopped laughing, thinking about that moment, and added, "I was even more excited that she had actually accepted. That really told me that she had the confidence and ability to stand up in front of a group of people and talk. That was *huge* for me."

The graduation ceremony was a wonderful experience. To see thirty graduates of the Arrowsmith Program on stage was a thrill for everyone. Samantha's speech was even more impressive. She presented it with confidence and clarity:

> We all arrived at Eaton Arrowsmith over three years ago. When we came, some of us had difficulty reading. Now we are able to read and we can pick out the main idea. Some of us couldn't tell time. Now we can tell you the time.
>
> When we came to the school some of us had few friends, some of us were lonely, and some of us had been bullied at the schools we had attended. Some of us had even been the bullies. We were unable to read

social cues and we had little confidence in ourselves. With Artifactual Thinking, with our wise teachers, and in the safe environment of EAS, we have learned to make and keep friends. We have learned to stand up for ourselves, and we've learned to be kind and caring to others.

Some of us arrived at Eaton Arrowsmith afraid to speak. Maybe we'd say something stupid. Before, kids had made fun of what we'd said, or how we'd said it. Now it's hard to keep us quiet.

Some of us, like me, have never been able to attend a regular school with any kind of success at all, but now that we are graduating, we look forward to a future with hope and confidence. We will be graduating from high school with our friends. It's a dream I've had for a long time.

It's been hard work over the last few years. At times it's been really boring and not much fun. Sometimes we've been pretty crabby. And it's taken a lot of imagination on the part of our teachers to keep us motivated. It's amazing what a few donuts will do, though.

Sometimes we've needed lots of reminders from our teachers to stay actively engaged and we questioned why we have to do all this repetitive cognitive stuff. They are great at reminding us how it is going to benefit us in the future.

At times I've just wanted to give up, and I know others have felt the same way, but with our encouraging teachers and a strong desire to move on, we've been able to stay on track, get focused, and push through our perceived limits. It's always exciting when someone in our class masters a level. I read in my recent psych-ed assessment report that work ethic and persistence is a better marker of success in life than academic achievement. After being at Eaton Arrowsmith for a few years I think we have it *all* going for us.

To the graduating class, I say:

Create goals and dreams for yourselves and follow them; it doesn't matter if you get exactly what you dreamed for. What matters is that you followed those dreams and goals. You may have to change your dream along the way, or you may even end up in a place beyond your wildest dreams. If you don't have a goal or a dream, you will drift along, never knowing if you got where you really wanted to go. So dream big and go for it! There's nothing to stop us now.

We all have unique gifts so let's make sure to use them.

To those returning to EAS for another a year or two, I recommend that you stay and graduate. I almost left last year and I see now that it would have been a mistake not to finish. A year ago I *would not* have been able to stand up and do this speech...for sure.

I just watched a movie a few weeks ago called *The Great Debaters*. In the movie, the dad, James Farmer Sr., says to his son James Farmer Jr., "Do what you have to do, to do what you want to do." Good advice to all of us.

Thanks to family and friends for all your support and to our outstanding teachers at Eaton Arrowsmith School. Congratulations and best wishes, graduates.

During her final year in the Arrowsmith Program, Samantha finished her Grade 10 distance-education courses through the Ministry of Education with the following grades:

Science 10	75%	B
English 10	72%	B
Math 10	70%	B–

Whether the Arrowsmith Program is successful for a child can be determined in several ways. For parents, success is often measured by how well their child is able to transition back into the regular school system. Samantha is now in a public high school in Vancouver and doing very well. She is considering which college she wants to attend after high school.

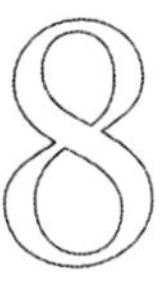

Dyslexia and the Arrowsmith Program

I would like to emphasize to families of dyslexic children that genetics is not a life sentence. The brain is a "plastic" organ, which constantly changes and rebuilds itself and for which ***genes and experience share equal importance.***

—STANISLAS DEHAENE, AUTHOR, *READING IN THE BRAIN*

Letter-Sound Confusion

Kyle was a happy preschooler and enjoyed his primary grades. He had a wonderful smile, a good sense of humour, a delightful disposition, and his large bright eyes were evidence of his great curiosity for life. He had a natural drive to do well in school and sports, was very social, and generally thrived. In her interview, Vicki, his mother, said, "Everybody liked Kyle. He was happy and outgoing. He was a hard worker, determined to accomplish what he set out to do. He loved school and he loved his family." His father, Tom, noted, "Kyle's self-esteem, at that time, was totally intact."

Though Kyle was happy at school, his parents both knew something was not quite right with how his language development was progressing. He was always keen to participate verbally, but his speech was unclear and he was not picking up the sound/symbol associations of the English language. In his early school years, he was struggling with all aspects of language arts (reading, writing, spelling, and copying).

Vicki and Tom's concern for their son's education was one associated with family history. Tom had seen this problem before. He had a brother who had struggled in school, and the painful memories of that experience were close to his heart. Tom did not want his son to repeat these frustrations at school. Vicki was well aware of the family history, and was determined to provide Kyle with all the necessary support to find success in school. Both Tom and Vicki knew that not addressing the issues Kyle had with language development could result in long-term life functioning problems for their son. "In my mind," Tom said emphatically, "I knew I was never going to let this happen to my kid."

Tom and Vicki recalled the similarities between Tom's brother and Kyle. "My brother had a lot of trouble with reading," said Tom, "and I was conscious at the time that he wasn't doing very well in school. I think the public school system pushed him along to grade five. A new teacher finally called my parents into a meeting and told them that my brother could not read at all!" When Tom realized that Kyle found learning math concepts easier than learning to read, he found the similarities between his brother and Kyle even more striking.

Awareness of a family history of learning difficulties does not always make acceptance of them any easier. Vicki realizes now that she knew Kyle was struggling in preschool, but was probably in some sort of denial. But as more months passed, the evidence kept building that Kyle was not picking up reading skills.

"In preschool, Kyle could not learn his alphabet, no matter what. He would seem to know some letters on one day and then on another day he would guess because he didn't remember any of these letters," Vicki recalled. "I remember going to Save-On-Foods on a little outing with the preschool. All the kids stood in a line and looked at the word *prescription*. It was a large neon sign, bright as can be. When asked to identify letters in the word they could all pick out several letters." Vicki paused for a moment, recalling the significance of that event. "I knew there was not a chance Kyle could do that, yet he was so smart and capable in other ways. It just blew me away that he could not get that *E* is *E*. We didn't even get to the sound an *E* makes. He didn't understand the importance of the connection."

Vicki also recalled that Kyle was not good at rhyming, another common difficulty for many children with dyslexia. Kyle received some speech therapy in preschool. Vicki said, "Throughout preschool and kindergarten he spoke out a lot, but he was not easy to understand if you were not accustomed to how he spoke."

Some Background on Dyslexia

While a reading disorder is the most commonly discussed and researched type of learning disability, it is important to recognize that there are various kinds of learning disabilities and attention disorders. Not all children with learning disabilities have reading problems. There are difficulties with mathematics and written expression. Some children and adults may have two or even all three of these learning disability types. However, a study conducted by Susan Mayes and Susan Calhoun in 2007 entitled, "Challenging the Assumptions about the Frequency and Coexistence of Learning Disability Types"[37] placed learning disabilities with written expression as the most common type. This is surprising, considering that our intervention focus in schools today is still primarily focused on reading and less on written expression. Schools tend to rely on the use of technology and accommodations to bypass the neurological disorders associated with written expression disabilities. Children with this learning disability type often require the use of a computer, keyboard, and/or note-taker for classroom lectures. If these accommodations or technologies are not available, the child can experience serious trouble trying to manage classroom learning requirements.

Even with reading disorders, there can be many subtypes. For example, researchers have discussed subtypes such as auditory dyslexia, visual dyslexia, and combined visual/auditory dyslexia. These subtypes are based on which specific neurological deficits the child may have and how they are expressed in their reading problems. Unfortunately, labels such

---

37. D.S. Mayes and S. Calhoun, "Challenging the Assumptions about the Frequency and Coexistence of Learning Disability Types," *School Psychology International* 28, no. 4 (2007), 437–448.

as *dyslexia* are thrown around so easily that even children with mild or moderate intellectual disabilities are sometimes called dyslexic.

The International Dyslexia Association provides a definition of dyslexia. When reviewing this definition, it is important to consider the type of intervention that could most directly affect each of the symptoms of dyslexia highlighted. The association states:

> Dyslexia is a language-based learning disability. Dyslexia refers to a cluster of symptoms [that] result in people having difficulties with specific language skills, particularly reading. Students with dyslexia usually experience difficulties with other language skills such as spelling, writing, and pronouncing words. Dyslexia affects individuals throughout their lives; however, its impact can change at different stages in a person's life. It is referred to as a learning disability because dyslexia can make it very difficult for a student to succeed academically in the typical instructional environment and, in its more severe forms, will qualify a student for special education, special accommodations, or extra support services.
>
> Some dyslexics manage to learn early reading and spelling tasks, especially with excellent instruction, but later experience their most debilitating problems when more complex language skills are required, such as grammar, understanding textbook material, and writing essays.
>
> People with dyslexia can also have problems with spoken language even after they have been exposed to good language models in their homes and good language instruction in school. They may find it difficult to express themselves clearly, or to fully comprehend what others mean when they speak. Such language problems are often difficult to recognize, but they can lead to major problems in school, in the workplace, and in relating to other people. The effects of dyslexia reach well beyond the classroom.[38]

It is clear that learning problems related to dyslexia can go far beyond reading and spelling difficulties. Intervention programs for dyslexia

---

38. International Dyslexia Association website, "Frequently Asked Questions" page. http://www.interdys.org/FAQ.htm.

often focus on reading and spelling. The other neurological weaknesses connected with dyslexia, such as problems with spoken language and the understanding of more complex language, are often not addressed. The child with dyslexia may learn to read and improve spelling ability through the use of a phonics program, but may still struggle with reading comprehension, find it difficult to memorize auditory information and instructions, and have limited expressive language ability.

Researchers now consider the former subtypes *developmental dyslexia* and *specific language impairment* (SLI) to be the same problem, differing only in severity and developmental stage.[39] A specific language impairment is a developmental disorder than can affect expressive and receptive language. Researchers studying this association have stated that:

> In the field of dyslexia, there has been an overwhelming emphasis on poor phonological processing as a cause of reading difficulties. However, a study of children with oral language problems indicates that difficulties with semantics, syntax, and discourse will also affect literacy acquisition; in some children (so-called poor comprehenders) these difficulties may occur without any phonological impairment. In more classic cases of SLI, there can be both phonological and nonphonological language impairments that affect learning to read.[40]

Oral language problems affect not only literacy, but classroom functioning as well. If a child with dyslexia struggles with receptive language, he or she may experience numerous problems following classroom instructions and understanding general information. If the child has expressive language difficulties, he or she may not speak up in class, self-advocate, or share knowledge with peers.

It should also be noted that dyslexia may be caused by additional neurological deficits not addressed through phonological training. Reading and spelling require not just sound discrimination processing, but also the ability of the child's brain to process, memorize, and retrieve the

39. D. Bishop and M. Snowling, "Developmental Dyslexia and Specific Language Impairment: Same or Different?" *Psychological Bulletin* 130, no. 6 (2004), 858–886.

40. Ibid., 858.

orthographic patterns (letter patterns) of words. Researchers have used the terms *visual dyslexia* or *orthographic dyslexia* to describe children who struggle with this area of neurological functioning. Nathlie Badian, in an article entitled, "Does a Visual-Orthographic Deficit Contribute to Reading Disability?" stated:

> In spite of the significant roles of phonological awareness and naming speed in reading development, these two variables [visual dyslexia and orthographic dyslexia] leave a considerable proportion of the variance in reading unexplained, which leads to the logical hypothesis that other, unspecified, variables are contributing additional variance to reading. Basic visual-orthographic skills such as the accurate recognition of letter orientation may be among those variables.
>
> This study indicates that there are some children whose reading development continues to be hampered by a problem in orthographic memory for the orientation of letters (and numerals) long after most children have easily mastered this task. The problems of such children require special attention, but may be overlooked, especially if, as is frequently the case, they also have naming speed and/or phonological awareness deficits.[41]

The cause and symptoms of dyslexia are varied, and depend on the specific neurological strengths and weaknesses of each child. Phonological awareness training is not the only intervention for students with dyslexia, and it does not address all causes and symptoms of dyslexia. However, it is an important intervention and, if used, should be implemented at the early stages of reading instruction. Phonics-based reading remediation programs are valuable and provide a critical component of an intervention program.

The problem for children with dyslexia today is that these intervention programs do not provide the necessary cognitive training required to improve language impairments and possible visual-orthographic weaknesses. In some cases of severe dyslexia, the number of neurological

41. N.A. Badian, "Does a Visual-Orthographic Deficit Contribute to Reading Disability?" *Annals of Dyslexia* 55, no.1 (June 2005), 28–52.

deficits may be so great that a phonics-based reading program may not be immediately helpful for that child. Cognitive training to strengthen these neurological capacities is required *prior* to the effective utilization of a phonics-based reading program.

The Arrowsmith Program is a unique cognitive training opportunity available to children with dyslexia and other learning disabilities. The program focuses on the underlying causes of dyslexia, including the specific language impairments often observed (namely, receptive and expressive language problems). The Arrowsmith Program also recognizes the different subtypes of dyslexia that can exist—auditory, visual, or combined auditory/visual neurological deficits. The primary goal of the program is to improve the underlying neurological dysfunctions that are causing dyslexia. For example, if a child with dyslexia struggles with receptive language (i.e., difficulty processing speech sounds and difficulty processing and memorizing general information and instructions) or expressive language, specific cognitive exercises are implemented to improve that particular neurological capacity.

Many areas of the brain are responsible for success or difficulty with reading and spelling. The Arrowsmith Program assessments first identify which of these neurological functions are weak. For example, when analyzing the activity of reading, three brain regions are considered including Symbol Recognition (orthographic), Broca's (speech sounds), and Motor-Symbol Sequencing (visual scanning and tracking of symbols). It has been observed in Arrowsmith Program research that a higher number of neurological weaknesses correlate with more severe reading disorders.[42] Moreover, as these neurological weaknesses improve and move to an average range of functioning, the child begins to develop an ability to learn to read and spell. Phonics-based programs can then be introduced and the child can further develop reading and spelling skills. The Arrowsmith Program recognizes the importance of teaching the sound/symbol structure of the English language once these neurological deficits are improved. Some children working on the program had

42. Dr. William J. Lancee, "Report on an Outcome Evaluation of the Arrowsmith Program for Treating Learning Disabled Students" (November 20, 2005). http://www.arrowsmithschool.org/images/Arrowsmith_study_11_20_05.pdf.

previously received years of phonics training with little success but were able to return to the phonics-based programs after their neurological capacities were increased with cognitive training.

In summary, the Arrowsmith Program does not focus on one particular reason why children with dyslexia struggle to read and process language. Rather, the program looks at all the neurological functions required for these abilities and generates a cognitive training program specific to each child's profile. Recognizing the relationship that exists between strengthening cognitive capacities and the acquisition of skills related to academics is an important step in ensuring the success of each child's educational plan.

Kyle's Ongoing Difficulties

Numerous cognitive functioning weaknesses resulted in Kyle's reading, written expression, and oral language problems. He also had a variety of cognitive functioning weaknesses that affected classroom functioning beyond just reading and writing. For example, his Arrowsmith Program assessment showed cognitive weaknesses with Memory for Information and Instructions, Motor-Symbol Sequencing, and Symbol Relations. He had received phonemic awareness training and phonics instruction, yet he still had a variety of learning challenges. As we have seen, this is often the case for children with learning disabilities.

Kyle's difficulty with early speech development was initially attributed to hearing problems that he was expected to outgrow. In preschool, kindergarten, and Grade 1, Kyle had tubes placed in his ears. Vicki and Tom wondered if this was why their son found it difficult to make sound/symbol associations. Was this why he did not seem as capable as his peers? Said Vicki, "Kyle had many appointments with an ear specialist. He was always with me in the room, and I found it awkward to emphasize to the doctor that he was struggling in school. I didn't want to make Kyle feel bad. The doctor, at some point, must have realized I was frustrated and suggested getting a second opinion about his hearing difficulties and their connection to reading acquisition. This second specialist made it very clear that he believed there was no way Kyle's hearing issues would account for the reading difficulties. This was the first time I had a professional opinion that supported my own instinct. It was upsetting, but a relief to have the clarity."

Until this point, Vicki had felt frustrated and confused about Kyle's difficulties. Many people in the education system suggested being patient, that he would eventually catch up. "He's a typical boy," they would say.

Vicki disagreed. "Kyle has two older siblings so I was very aware that he was not learning the things they had. As a parent, you are torn in two directions. It's an emotional journey to face the fact that your child is struggling. You want to believe that nothing is really wrong so there is some tendency to try to believe anyone who gives you a message of reassurance. It's also uncomfortable to be seen as an overly concerned, high-maintenance parent who wants special attention for their child. However, you know the importance of early intervention and that it's your job to advocate for your child. Gaining sufficient understanding about learning disabilities in order to be confident enough to effectively advocate for your child can be difficult."

By the time Kyle was in Grade 3, Vicki had spent countless hours trying to understand the difficulties her son was experiencing with reading. She would select books from the library about reading development and difficulties associated with acquiring language. One night while reading, she came across a checklist on dyslexia. "I had Tom take a look at it, and he said, 'That's Kyle.'" That was a turning point for Tom—accepting that this was a serious issue, similar to his brother's problems.

Tom recalled a strategy Kyle would use to pretend he was reading. "I remember when Kyle was in Grade 3, sitting down and reading books with him. He would have already heard the story from his mother, or at school. He wanted to show me that he could read. So I would sit down with him, half asleep after coming home from work. Kyle would start reading the book to me and I would turn the pages. It all looked fine until I skipped ahead two pages and the words he was pronouncing didn't connect to those on the new page." Tom continued, "Kyle had memorized the words, having read the story twice that day with his mom or the teacher."

Vicki recalled another trick in Grade 1. "Kyle had a system for the books he had to bring home from school to read. He frequently brought home a certain book that was missing the pages. At the time, I didn't realize he was doing this on purpose." Chuckling, she continued, "It was missing most of the pages and it would only have about three words on each page. Kyle would come home and have only two pages to read."

Kyle received some early intervention. His hearing issues qualified him for one-on-one instruction time with a hearing impairment specialist at school. As well, for Grades 2 and 3, his classroom was set up with an FM speaker system to amplify the teacher's voice, making it easier to hear and follow instructions and directions. Kyle also received special instruction during a school trial with the Earobics Program, a software program that helps children develop phonological awareness and phonics skills. Tom and Vicki recalled that Kyle did well with this program, and was beginning to develop decoding skills as a result. He was sounding out words and trying to spell them, though his word decoding was slow. Kyle was also not recognizing words he had just read on a previous line. Vicki noted, "It was like a completely new word to him. Reading was backbreaking work for him, and it was heartbreaking to watch him have to work so hard with so little success."

Vicki was helping at home as best she could. She would have Kyle read to her as often as possible. She said, "I am a bit of a taskmaster, but Kyle was very coachable and willing to do whatever I asked of him. He is the hardest worker."

By the end of Grade 3, his parents were not sure what to do for Kyle. He was receiving support from the hearing-impaired resource teacher twice a week during school. He still had a lisp in his speech. He had also just finished the Earobics Program, with some success. Tom and Vicki wondered if another educational placement would be helpful for their son. They were hoping to find a school that would focus on his reading and writing weaknesses, and they considered both public and private schools.

Kyle's Psycho-educational Assessment

It was 2002, and by this time I had met Kyle and his family. Five months earlier, in January of his Grade 3 year, my assessment team at the Eaton Learning Centre conducted a full psycho-educational assessment for Kyle. I discussed the results with his parents several weeks later. Kyle had average intelligence, which met part of the criteria for diagnosing a learning disability under the regulations put forth by the British Columbia Ministry of Education. To be diagnosed as having a learning disability, as defined by the Ministry of Education, one needs both average or above average intelligence *and* significantly low scores on measures of achievement (reading, writing, spelling, and/or math). Kyle scored within the average range on almost all tests of IQ measurement. He showed average verbal and nonverbal/visual intelligence compared with his peers. In fact, some of the subtests of IQ showed excellent neurological functionality. His achievement scores in reading, writing, and math were considered average compared with his peers.

Although Kyle showed a weakness in spelling (66 percent of children had better spelling skills), and he decoded words slowly, the early intervention at school and considerable home support had likely helped him develop basic reading and spelling skills. Thus, Kyle did not meet the Ministry of Education's criteria for diagnosing a learning disability because his achievement scores were not low enough. He needed to have a larger discrepancy between his intelligence measure and his measures of achievement to qualify for learning disability services. His weakness in spelling was just not weak enough.

We suggested that Kyle should be tested again in three years. At this time, he might meet the criteria for having a learning disability. Sadly, this is often the case as children get older and their achievement difficulties become more apparent. It was also noted that he had weak visual-motor coordination, slow visual scanning speed, and poor memory for visual symbols/designs. This could hinder written expression as he grew older, but with assistive technology to bypass these cognitive weaknesses, their negative impact would likely be reduced. We recommended the development of effective keyboarding skills so he could use a computer to write. Using a keyboard increases the ease for producing written expression compared with the tasks of writing and spelling in longhand. We also recommended Orton-Gillingham tutoring for Kyle to help with his specific areas of difficulty.

We recommended that Vicki and Tom meet with the public school Kyle was currently attending to discuss the assessment. Vicki said, "Looking back, I realize I was really intimidated by the school administration and education specialists. I didn't go in there and shake the bushes the way I should have to get them to address Kyle's learning issues." Vicki informed the school that she would be getting Orton-Gillingham training and would tutor her son one-on-one to further improve his reading and spelling skills. She would keep him out of school some mornings in order to get the tutoring accomplished. Vicki said, "I'd been reading everything I could get my hands on about Orton-Gillingham." At one point, referring to Orton-Gillingham tutoring, one of the special education teachers said to Vicki, "With all due respect, Vicki, I think you are barking up the wrong tree." Vicki went home that day and cried. Tom recalled this event: "I remember being so angry. I wanted to go in there and just tell them the way it was going to be."

Vicki disregarded the comments of the special education teacher and began working with her son using the Orton-Gillingham method. Kyle would make excuses to his friends that he had doctor and dentist appointments to explain why he was not there many mornings. Tom said, "Vicki tutored Kyle in Orton-Gillingham for a year. I was more on the sideline. I mean, I would sit down and read with Kyle after work, but Vicki did the tutoring." He continued, "I was noticing huge improvements in his reading by the end of grade four. I remember being really impressed."

Kyle was feeling good about himself, but Tom continued to be aware of how his brother had fared in elementary school and did not want Kyle to start experiencing the same feeling of failure. Because Kyle was not in school many mornings, Tom wanted to ensure the teacher would not fail his son. Tom recalls, "They didn't want us to pull him out. I remember saying to his teacher, 'You are not going to give my son Ds. You are not going to give my son low marks. Marks at this age don't really mean anything. The last thing Kyle needs is to have something that isn't successful this year. You have to give him good marks.'" Tom continued, "I don't remember how I said it. I do recall the principal supporting me, saying she would look at his report card and just make sure [the marks] were not going to be harmful to his development."

In Grade 4, Kyle also began receiving some Arrowsmith Program cognitive exercises. Vicki had heard that the Arrowsmith Program was in use at an adult continuing education school near their home. The William Lucas Centre in North Vancouver offered a full-time and part-time program; it was the first educational facility to bring the Arrowsmith Program to Western Canada. Vicki decided to use the part-time Arrowsmith Program, which accepted younger students, to improve Kyle's written expression difficulties—he struggled to get ideas on paper and found it almost impossible to copy from the board quickly. He was registered for the Arrowsmith Program's Motor-Symbol Sequencing class.

The Motor-Symbol Sequencing program required Kyle to repetitively practise visual-motor integration movements that emphasized both accuracy and speed in daily Arrowsmith homework. Vicki recalled, "In school, at the end of that year he wrote a story about a dog. He was able to get the words on the page. There were lots of errors, but I was just blown away that he actually could get his thoughts written down into some sentences and connect them together in a paragraph." When she asked her son how he was able to do it, he responded, "I don't know. It's just easier. It just comes out and gets onto the page easier."

At the end of Grade 4, impressed with the progress Kyle had made, Tom and Vicki decided to enrol their son at a private school for children with dyslexia. The school provided daily Orton-Gillingham tutoring. Kyle spent Grades 5 and 6 at this private school, making progress in reading, writing, and spelling.

Kyle Works on Cognitive Exercises

Tom and Vicki learned that the Eaton Arrowsmith School would be opening in September 2005. Because Kyle had already worked successfully with the Arrowsmith Program, Vicki was interested. In March 2005, she attended an EAS information session about neuroplasticity and learning disabilities, and, like many other families that attended, the concept of a full-time program devoted to cognitive exercises was a leap of faith for her and Tom. The idea of neuroplasticity was new; research into the plasticity of the brain was just beginning to reach the mainstream market through newspapers, magazines, television, and the Internet.

Vicki was the parent most interested in having Kyle attend Eaton Arrowsmith School. Tom said, "I would probably have been quite happy bringing Kyle back into the public school system." When asked about his understanding of the Arrowsmith Program at the time, Tom recalled, "I didn't really understand it. I didn't understand it that well." However, both Vicki and Tom trusted me by this time, and that made them take the leap of faith. I had met with them several times, analyzed Kyle's cognitive profile through a verbal interview, and then considered whether Kyle's profile was a match for the Arrowsmith Program. Even with his three years of Orton-Gillingham tutoring, he continued to show difficulties with copying, written expression, spelling, reading comprehension, memory for information and instructions, and speech production. These problems were due to six cognitive weaknesses that could be improved through Arrowsmith Program cognitive exercises.

Vicki was persistent about Kyle attending the Eaton Arrowsmith School. As Tom said, "It got to the point where Vicki really wanted him to go there, so it seemed the decision was made." Vicki recalled that she understood what the Arrowsmith Program was about, although she did not understand or completely trust in the science behind the exercises. However, she had seen some of the results and she did not want to take the chance of Kyle missing the opportunity to try this new approach. The idea that the brain can build stronger neurological pathways made sense to Vicki. She said, "In a demonstration about the Arrowsmith Program, the presenter talked about a dog running back and forth through the woods. The dog gradually creates a pathway. The more the dog runs along the pathway, the more worn in it becomes. The dog can then find the pathway more easily and use it more efficiently. I just thought, yeah, that makes sense." Vicki continued, "The other thing that really made sense to me—and I try to explain this to other people—is that we all have weaknesses. It's when you pile weakness on weakness on weakness that the system breaks down."

Kyle's Arrowsmith Assessment

The Arrowsmith assessment is not for labelling a specific learning disability or for gathering information for establishing student qualification for educational funding. The Arrowsmith assessment is about identifying cognitive dysfunctions or weaknesses, and then designing a cognitive exercise remediation program that will improve those weaknesses to the point where they are functioning at the average range.

Kyle's formal Arrowsmith assessment went well beyond what could be provided by a regular psycho-educational assessment given by a private psychologist, psychiatrist, or school board psychologist; these would not be comprehensive enough to identify the kinds of problems Kyle was experiencing. Although he was making progress, he was still struggling with reading, spelling, and writing. The Arrowsmith assessment identified *why* he was struggling, pinpointing his neurological weaknesses. This information can change the direction of remediation for any child.

Table 16 shows Kyle's specific cognitive dysfunctions identified by the Arrowsmith assessment in May 2005.

TABLE 16. KYLE'S INITIAL ARROWSMITH ASSESSMENT RESULTS

Cognitive Function	**Description**	**Kyle's Level of Difficulty**
Motor-Symbol Sequencing	Problems associated with printing neatly and copying quickly. Careless errors in math, slow reading speed, inconsistent spelling.	Moderate to Severe
Symbol Relations	Problems understanding concepts and cause-and-effect reasoning. Logical-reasoning problems.	Moderate to Severe
Memory for Information and Instructions	Trouble remembering oral instruction, difficulty following lectures or extended conversations.	Moderate
Broca's Speech Pronunciation	Mispronouncing words, avoiding using words, speaking in incomplete sentences.	Moderate to Mild
Artifactual Thinking	Problems understanding and interpreting social cues.	Moderate to Mild

Cognitive Function	Description	Kyle's Level of Difficulty
Symbol Recognition	Poor word recognition, slow reading, difficulty with spelling, trouble remembering symbol patterns such as mathematical equations.	Mild to Moderate

One of Kyle's key weaknesses was in the Motor-Symbol Sequencing area. This was the same area Kyle had worked on in Grade 4 when enrolled in the part-time Arrowsmith Program. It was evident that Kyle's brain still struggled to effectively utilize the motor cortex area associated with speech, reading, writing, and copying, which was not surprising given that he had not completed this cognitive exercise in his part-time program. He scored at the moderate to severe range, which was well below average. In fact, his copying-text speed had fallen to below average for his age group (at the 10th percentile ranking). Another problem area was Broca's Speech Pronunciation, in which he scored at the moderate to mild range. Kyle also struggled with Memory for Information and Instructions—in other words, listening skills. It was difficult for him to retain information he heard in class. Reading comprehension appeared weak due to problems with Symbol Relations, the ability to relate concepts or see cause-and-effect patterns efficiently. Because of this weakness, Kyle was also struggling with reading comprehension. Kyle's weak spelling was also influenced by a weakness with Symbol Recognition, the ability to hold letter patterns in visual memory. He scored at the mild to moderate range, which again was below average. Additional weaknesses were noted with visual perception of social cues as he scored at the moderate to mild range on Artifactual Thinking. If Kyle could remediate these weaknesses through daily drills of cognitive exercises, school success would be much more attainable, and the need for learning resource help or learning assistance could be eliminated.

A cognitive remediation program was designed for Kyle's first year at Eaton Arrowsmith School—Grade 7.

Kyle at Eaton Arrowsmith School

Kyle worked hard in his first year at Eaton Arrowsmith School. He progressed through his cognitive exercises and did well in the program. As we have noted, speech pronunciation was a problem for Kyle, and he was assigned exercises that would assist him in this area of neurological ability. Mark Watson, one of Kyle's two cognitive teachers, discussing Kyle's first year at Eaton Arrowsmith School, noted, "The change I most noticed in Kyle was his ability to express himself. Though he could still get overexcited, he became much more articulate and to the point. I perceived a noticeable difference in Kyle's attitude—the edge wasn't there anymore and he was much more confident and genuine."

Mark also noticed improvements in written expression due to progress with Motor-Symbol Sequencing. He said, "Part of Kyle's challenge was getting on paper what he wanted to say. He never wanted to show his work, by which I mean print it on paper. Instead, he did all the work in his head. If pressed, Kyle would show his work, but he saw it as a waste of time. He was very convincing—*almost* to the point of arrogance—but you couldn't help but like Kyle. There was no attitude or disrespect. He could talk his way out of most situations, usually with an air of humour. Nevertheless, as the year went on, Kyle started to write more in his daily journal, showing less frustration with written expression."

The Symbol Relations cognitive exercises also transformed Kyle's ability to read with comprehension. Kyle's reading comprehension jumped from Grade 5 to Grade 8 level in one year. Word recognition went from grade level 5.2 to 7.5, another considerable leap, and this was without giving him a phonics-based reading remediation tutor. These changes occurred through a strictly brain-based exercise program that focused on sound/syllable manipulations, symbol recognition, and visual-motor tracking.

Near the end of his first year, Vicki told us that Kyle wanted to transfer to his local high school that September. Though he was positive about EAS and his friends and teachers there, Kyle wanted to keep up with his neighbourhood friends. After all, he had been out of the regular loop for three school years. Vicki and Tom were experiencing a problem that some parents find when their child is confronted with another year of the

Arrowsmith Program: children wish they did not have to do this cognitive work. Not all children experience this—some enjoy the cognitive exercises and do not want to leave. However, the work can get repetitive and tiring, and it can be difficult to sustain focus. It takes masterful cognitive teachers to keep each child engaged, motivated, and goal oriented. Vicki reported that "Kyle remembers the important role his teachers played in the program. For him, the teachers' use of humour and lightheartedness was an important tool for motivation and for relieving the stress of the hard, repetitive exercises."

Kyle found it difficult to notice changes, especially as they happened gradually. In the Arrowsmith Program, one cannot expect a higher cognitive capacity to appear quickly. Rather, progress is usually slow and incremental; noticeable and observable changes are sometimes not seen for three to four months. Some children do not even notice changes until someone tells them, "Wow! You couldn't do that before."

I empathized with Kyle and his wishes to return to his neighbourhood school, but hoped he would finish his full-time program. I asked Barbara Arrowsmith Young in Toronto to look over his results, and she agreed that Kyle should remain at Arrowsmith. Vicki and Tom also reviewed them with me, and we discussed them with Kyle. Slowly he came around, recognizing that the cognitive changes he was making would benefit him once he returned to public school. We held another family meeting, during which Kyle, even though it was difficult for him to work through the emotional and logical issues in addition to feeling pressure from us, finally agreed that the best course of action would be for him to return to EAS. His teachers were delighted when they learned Kyle was returning.

Kyle's second year was one of continued building of cognitive functions and preparing for his transition to a public high school. He worked very hard, and his focus on the cognitive exercises was exemplary. He was determined that his final year at EAS would be a productive one. During this year, Kyle began noticing changes in his ability to write. "In English class we were doing essay writing," he said. "I just felt it was easy now. I could just start writing." Kyle noted that before the Arrowsmith Program he had many ideas, but could not get them on paper.

Mid-year, we discuss with parents their child's transition plans to regular public or private schools. By then, we usually know whether a child will need a further year or two years. These transition meetings are important; parents are often legitimately worried about how their child will handle the curriculum of their new school because their previous experience with regular programs was often disastrous. The idea of going back is frightening.

In addition, while doing the brain-based cognitive remediation programs at EAS, the children cover only math and English as curriculum subjects. Parents are concerned their children will be behind in other subjects such as science and social studies. Though this appears to be a justifiable concern, in reality Arrowsmith graduates transition into a regular curriculum with all core subjects with few problems; having missed subjects such as science and social studies for several years does not affect their overall marks. Like any other student trying to earn good grades, they need to do their homework and study for exams. Still, parents worry and their worries must be addressed.

Kyle's mother expressed four areas of concern prior to Kyle's transition. Could Kyle handle a second language—perhaps introductory Spanish? Should he enrol in a learning support program? Should she tell the school about his past learning problems? Finally, should she get a tutor for Kyle?

The answers to Vicki's concerns were straightforward. First, if Kyle wanted a language exemption, he could apply for it, although graduates of the Arrowsmith Program have been able to successfully take second languages after improving their cognitive weaknesses related to language processing. Second, if Vicki wanted to have Kyle enrol in the school board's learning assistance program, then he should be encouraged to do so—it might be a good time for him to do his homework. Learning assistance can benefit any student. Third, it would be important to inform his new school of his past educational experiences, and it would also be important to update Kyle's psycho-educational testing. Changes in his learning profile would provide valuable information to his new school. We also welcomed a new psycho-educational profile because Kyle's spelling was not yet at grade level, and his reading speed was still slower than his peers (with half a year to go, he had not yet completed the Motor-

Symbol Sequencing cognitive exercise). If Kyle wished, he could use the updated testing for a language exemption, which is otherwise an entrance requirement of many Canadian universities. Last, Arrowsmith graduates most often do not need extra support in the form of learning assistance or a tutor because their cognitive weaknesses no longer exist. Kyle no longer needed a tutor, though we advised that he should seek teachers' help whenever necessary.

Kyle was accepted by his high school for Grade 9. He was excited about this opportunity, and with this future in front of him, he worked even harder at his cognitive exercises during the last half of his final year at EAS. He was a role model to all his friends in class. As a result, the entire staff elected him as valedictorian for our graduation ceremony. His parents and friends were thrilled, and Kyle did an outstanding job as class valedictorian.

In June 2007, before Kyle left, his Arrowsmith assessment was updated, as shown in table 17, as well as measures of academic achievement.

TABLE 17. KYLE'S FINAL ARROWSMITH ASSESSMENT RESULTS

Cognitive Function	Description	Kyle's Level of Difficulty
Motor-Symbol Sequencing	Problems associated with printing neatly and copying quickly. Careless errors in math, slow reading speed, inconsistent spelling.	Mild to Moderate
Symbol Relations	Problems understanding concepts and cause-and-effect reasoning. Logical-reasoning problems.	Average
Memory for Information and Instructions	Trouble remembering oral instruction, difficulty following lectures or extended conversations.	Moderate to Mild
Broca's Speech Pronunciation	Mispronouncing words, avoiding using words, speaking in incomplete sentences.	Average

Cognitive Function	Description	Kyle's Level of Difficulty
Artifactual Thinking	Problems understanding and interpreting social cues.	Mild
Symbol Recognition	Poor word recognition, slow reading, difficulty with spelling, trouble remembering symbol patterns such as mathematical equations.	Above Average

The results highlighted just how much Kyle's hard work had paid off. His reading comprehension was at grade level now, and his spelling had moved up two years. Most importantly, his problem with Motor-Symbol Sequencing had moved out of the severe range, although he still needed to move this area to the average range to increase reading speed. He also rated average on Broca's Speech Pronunciation. An option would be to work on these cognitive areas in EAS's part-time program, but Kyle was certain that once he was finished with his full-time program, he wanted to focus on his high school studies.

Tom had noticed great improvements during his son's second year in the Arrowsmith Program. "Kyle was now reading books that were far more advanced than he'd ever read before," said Tom, but he clarified by noting, "The real measure [of the Arrowsmith Program] was going to be how he did when he was back in the public school system. I was still worried that Kyle would not have success. That he would become disappointed."

After Eaton Arrowsmith School

After Kyle finished Grade 9, his parents reported that his lowest mark was 84 percent and his average was over 90 percent. Further, Kyle had taken Grade 10 math. His father simply said, "Wow!" in an e-mail to EAS. Kyle had done an outstanding job of self-advocating and seeking extra help when needed. He would meet teachers after school to get clarification on homework tasks or examination points.

Kyle's Grade 10 results were no less impressive. He earned an A in all subjects, including a Grade 11 math class. His principal wrote in his report card: "An outstanding year." Kyle accomplished this without any subject tutoring, and he managed all aspects of his schoolwork without any parental involvement.

While at Eaton Arrowsmith School, Kyle had built his brain, changed himself, developed more neural connections in weak areas, and used this new neurological efficiency to succeed in his neighbourhood public high school. Kyle always had a strong work ethic, and now, combined with his stronger neurological pathways, academic success was the only possible option.

Tom's ongoing concern that Kyle might struggle in school as his brother had was now diminished—when Tom's brother was at school the educational system had not provided the support and understanding that was available to Kyle. Tom's parents had had no options or guidance to help their son. Sadly, Tom's brother died shortly after Kyle was born. He would not know the importance he was to have in ensuring that Kyle received all the help he would need to succeed in school. Though Kyle realizes this, he said, "My [grandmother] has never talked to me about this. I think it probably hurts her inside that one of her sons couldn't get the amazing help that I had." But Kyle's grandmother could be proud that her grandson had achieved so much success in areas where her son had not had the resources to do so.

Kyle is now motivating other students at Eaton Arrowsmith School to complete their cognitive programs. In May 2010 he was asked to e-mail one of our students at Eaton Arrowsmith School in Victoria, British Columbia, who was struggling to complete one more year in the program. Kyle's writing in this e-mail has not been altered:

> *Hey Jared,*
>
> *My name is Kyle and i am a former student of Eaton Arrowsmith. I have been told you are having some trouble understanding the benefits of finishing your program at Eaton Arrowsmith. I went to Eaton Arrowsmith in Vancouver for my dyslexia and i am very happy with the results.*
>
> *Five years ago (one year before my first year at Eaton Arrowsmith) i had a meeting with Howard Eaton who brought Arrowsmith to*

Vancouver. Me and my mom were very interested with how you could actually change the brain to make it run better, but i had one big worry. My worry was that if i changed the way my brain thinks, would i lose all my gifts from my dyslexia, as my flaws are fixed. Mr. Eaton told me that Arrowsmith would fix the flaws in my brain, and keep everything else the same or make them better, which is exactly what happened.

I had the same troubles as you after my first year at EAS *but seeing my program through to its end has been a life changing choice for me. In my experience i found that the first year at* EAS *is the hardest, its sort of like you're climbing up a hill and sometime during your second year you will win the uphill battle and start going down hill. That means its possible that if you had a flat out bad experience this year, next year could be better.*

Eaton Arrowsmith:

- *changed my reading level and speed by multiple grade levels*
- *made it easier for me to put my thoughts on the page and have it makes sense (example: this email)*
- *made me be 100% independent from my parents with ALL my homework (its a great feeling)*
- *got me an entire year ahead in math (currently in grade 11 but doing grade 12 math)*
- *helped me get better at spelling (instead of having to remember tricks of how to spell words now they just come to me naturally)*
- *helped me multitask and get huge projects done instead of just freaking under the pressure and getting intimidated by all the work i had to do*
- *helped me achieve academic success*

After considering all that i have said, i think it is most important to take in mind that if you do decide to attend next year, but slack off and do the exercises half-ass then you are wasting your parents money and your time. You got to give it your all.

If it helps at all i would like to tell you that after Eaton Arrowsmith i have got honours with distinction every year since. Last year i got straight A's for the entire school year, right now in my senior years of high school i have an average around 90 and got 100% in chemistry last term. I did all this with help from Eaton Arrowsmith, hard work, and the determination to show the world that it doesn't matter if you are Learning Disabled.

My experience at Eaton Arrowsmith has been really rewarding and if you had any questions or just want to talk feel free arrange a time to call me.

Good Luck,

—Kyle

The Irish Dancer

These bright children, discovered within the population of students who are identified as learning disabled, are often failing miserably in school. They are first noticed because of what they cannot do, rather than because of the talent they are demonstrating.

—DR. SUSAN BAUM, CO-DIRECTOR, INTERNATIONAL CENTER FOR TALENT DEVELOPMENT

No Learning Disability

The test results from psychologist Margaret Lancaster were ready to be reviewed by Rory's parents, Clare and Michael. Rory had been attending the Eaton Arrowsmith School for the past three years. He had worked hard to improve the weak cognitive capacities that had caused his learning problems. Progress reports from EAS had shown that his program was almost complete. It was Rory's last year at EAS, and an updated psycho-educational assessment conducted by a psychologist would give them a better idea of how he had improved cognitively and what kind of program he would be capable of transitioning to. Dr. Lancaster had conducted Rory's first psycho-educational assessment before they knew of the Arrowsmith Program.

Dr. Lancaster informed Clare and Michael that Rory had substantially improved specific areas of previous cognitive weaknesses. Dr. Lancaster had compared the first psycho-educational assessment conducted on Rory in November/December 2006 with this current assessment. She noted that Rory's motor coordination measure on the Beery Test of Visual Motor Integration had gone from the 14th percentile to the 96th percentile (superior). His processing speed on the Wechsler Intelligence Scale for Children (WISC-IV) had also improved, shifting from the 16th percentile (low average) to the 79th percentile (high average). Finally, on the WISC-IV measure of working memory, he had moved from the 55th percentile to the 94th percentile (superior) in cognitive functioning. In short, Rory had made some remarkable shifts in his cognitive capacities over the last three years.

Clare and Michael were delighted with these cognitive improvements, but Clare still needed answers. "I asked Dr. Lancaster specifically if Rory was learning disabled," she said. "Some other parents had said it was possibly a good thing to still have a learning disability designation to ensure extra support once you are back in the public school system. So I thought we should consider that as well. I wanted to ask that question—did he have a learning disability? Dr. Lancaster responded, 'Not according to the data I've collected.'"

Rory was also very happy with the results of Dr. Lancaster's assessment. "I think having been told by Dr. Lancaster that he had improved so much in specific cognitive functions was validation for him," said Clare. "He was very proud of that."

Tutors, Interventions, and Magic Ears

Rory wanted to do well in any activity in which he was participating. If he could not do well, he would become frustrated and stubborn. As his mother said, "He did have a low tolerance for frustration. He would refuse to do things if he thought he couldn't be successful." This led to struggles at home, but to his parents this was just part of raising their beautiful boy. They loved him no matter what.

Rory was social, though he struggled in various group learning situations at school. He enjoyed playing sports but did not find it easy to acquire the motor skills for each. Being of Irish heritage, his parents introduced him to Irish culture; working with his mother, he began to enjoy Irish dancing at the age of four. In short, their outgoing, tall, blond, freckle-faced, five-year-old boy was not someone who they thought had learning challenges. He did have some fears such as elevators and small rooms with closed doors, but other children seemed to have their quirks as well.

Rory's school's philosophy on the issue of low frustration level and stubbornness was not so tolerant, and teachers were having difficulties with him. However, Clare and Michael would not fully understand the level of their concerns until the end of the Grade 1 school year. As Clare put it, "Through kindergarten and Grade 1 there did not seem to be a problem. The report cards were fine, but I think they're very careful in how they phrase things. The report cards always seemed to be full of optimism."

Near the end of Grade 1, Rory's parents were called in for what they thought would be a standard meeting. Walking into Rory's classroom, they were greeted by the principal as well as the classroom teacher, and they suddenly realized the meeting would not be routine. Clare recalls, "I think the principal just sort of really let the hammer down then, and then we got it. They were struggling with him. Maybe he needed to have tough love or something. The principal said, 'Rory basically doesn't meet the expectations of Grade 1.'" Rory was having trouble behaviourally and academically. In terms of behaviour, he was not consistently listening to the teacher or following classroom routines. As well, his numeracy and literacy skills were not within expectations for the end of Grade 1. Clare and Michael listened and agreed that something needed to be done. At this point, they had no idea that Rory was in fact very bright (high intelligence) but had specific cognitive capacity weaknesses that in combination resulted in his behaviour—high levels of frustration and stubbornness. Thus, they were operating from the mindset that Rory was deliberately being troublesome.

The principal recommended that a speech-language pathologist in the school district test Rory. As well, a psycho-educational assessment was recommended to test for any learning disabilities. Clare and Michael had no idea what a psycho-educational assessment was, nor how a speech-language assessment might help their son. However, as Clare said, "We agreed with everything they wanted. We wanted to help our child. He was our baby."

The ball was rolling. Clare and Michael would be flooded with assessments and recommendations for Rory. Since both were goal-oriented people, they took it upon themselves to make sure anything that was recommended was completed, reviewed, and implemented.

The psycho-educational assessment came first, conducted by Dr. Margaret Lancaster. The results of the assessment and the insight into their son's learning profile would dramatically shift their understanding of why he was so frustrated at school and home. "After the assessment was completed and Dr. Lancaster met with us, the lights started to come on for us. That's when we realized we needed to take charge of the situation. Dr. Lancaster said that he was a gifted child with a learning disability, that some of his capacities were quite high."[43] Dr. Lancaster also stated that Rory had cognitive weaknesses with processing speed, working memory, and visual-motor integration. Both his Processing Speed and his Letter-Number Sequencing subtest scores on the Working Memory index fell at the 16th percentile. These cognitive weaknesses, combined with his high intelligence, resulted in his frustrations in school.

Rory was gifted in certain areas. His verbal comprehension IQ on the Wechsler Intelligence Scale for Children (WISC-VI) fell at the 92nd percentile (superior) and perceptual reasoning IQ at the 96th percentile. But this giftedness itself caused problems because very bright children are often sensitive to learning difficulties. If a bright child has specific cognitive weaknesses that make certain learning activities challenging, emotional flare-ups can happen. Clare and Michael gradually began to understand that this was the nature of Rory's problems, thanks to a psychologist who specialized in gifted children with learning disabilities.

Dr. Lancaster had made various recommendations on which Clare and Michael were to follow through. For Rory's reading, spelling, and writing, Clare said, "She recommended an Orton-Gillingham tutor,

---

43. A child deemed both gifted and as having a learning disability is considered *twice exceptional* in the learning disability community. This is sometimes referred to as "2E."

which worked really well, actually. He responded well to that. That's when we knew interventions worked. He just needed more private attention." Dr. Lancaster also recommended other achievement-skill instruction strategies for bypassing Rory's cognitive weaknesses such as keyboarding, teacher instruction, and possibly attending a school that could alter instructional design to best meet his cognitive capacity strengths and weaknesses.

Dr. Lancaster's final recommendation was for an occupational therapist's assessment of Rory, which Clare and Michael began with. The assessment was conducted through Vancouver Pediatric Occupational Therapists. Stunned by the results, Clare said, "The assessment . . . talked about how awkward he was because of low muscle tone, hypermobile joints, weak core strength, poor eye control, deficient shoulder stability, difficulty with motor sequencing and motor planning of novel tasks, eye-tracking issues, and all sorts of really upsetting things." It was particularly upsetting for the family as they were keen participants in sports. They were concerned that these findings might mean Rory could not succeed at sports and have an active lifestyle. But the OT assessment was thorough, and the family appreciated the recommendations; they knew the findings were important. Again, they were going to do what they could to get the recommendations in place. However, as Clare said, "It was kind of devastating. We were trying to figure out what this frustration was that he always had. You know, he was smart enough to realize what he wanted to do and what he couldn't do. That was a huge source of frustration for him. He could see what other kids could do."

The speech-language assessment came next. Cynthia Chan, a registered audiologist and speech pathologist, conducted a full auditory assessment on Rory. He was diagnosed with central auditory processing disorder. Children with auditory processing disorders have difficulties making sense of speech if listening conditions are not ideal. Cynthia Chan noted that "In environments where the external redundancy [background noise] has been reduced [such as in noisy environments or with distance or unclear speakers], Rory's compromised listening abilities are less pronounced." Rory was showing an auditory closure deficit. He would struggle listening in noisy environments and could experience auditory fatigue or overload. In a classroom of twenty or twenty-five students this could happen quickly and often.

Cynthia Chan also used the diagnosis *hyperacusis* to describe Rory's difficulties with noise sensitivity. A child with hyperacusis is oversensitive to sounds in his environment.[44] A loud classroom could result in auditory fatigue and overall rising frustration levels for Rory. Cynthia Chan made several recommendations. To try to reduce Rory's sensitivity to sound in his learning environment, she fitted him with a listening device that filtered white noise from his hearing, reducing any oversensitivity to the excess noise in the classroom and allowing him to improve his focus and active engagement. Clare and Michael agreed with Cynthia Chan that their son had a pronounced sensitivity to noise. "He really had a low threshold for noisy environments. He would get further distracted if the noise level increased," Clare said.

Rory was not keen on his new listening device, and he certainly did not want to wear it in the classroom. Clare and Michael decided to call it Magic Ears to make it more appealing to the seven-year-old boy. Rory wore the set for four months and was then retested by the audiologist. The tests showed much less sensitivity, which surprised Cynthia Chan. However, Clare and Michael suspected that Rory had quickly realized that if he reacted less strongly to the various noise levels, he would not have to wear the Magic Ears. His parents decided not to push the issue, with Clare saying, "We were pretty much flinging everything at him at that point."

Rory's Grade 2 teacher was perhaps not ideal. She was not keen on supporting the recommendations offered by the professionals. Clare and Michael felt she thought all these classroom recommendations and gadgets such as Magic Ears were nonsense. As Clare said, "I got the impression that my child was annoying her." She had been teaching for some time, and it became clear as the year went on that she seemed set in teaching only in ways she was familiar with. She felt she also knew how to handle boys like Rory. After one conversation with this teacher, Clare realized

44. For more information on hyperacusis and white/pink noise intervention, see www.hyperacusis.net.

that getting the professionals' recommendations implemented in the classroom was not going to be easy. She said, "I went to speak to the teacher about where Rory's desk was being placed. The recommendation was near the classroom teacher's desk. Well, Rory's desk was in the back corner. The teacher said, "That is his personal learning environment—if he's too close to me, he will ask me questions." On another occasion the school psychologist said to Clare, "I don't know your child, but I know of your child." Clare found this ". . . pretty upsetting as you know your child is being talked about because he annoys teachers in the classroom because he can't cope."

Clare and Michael were doing everything they could to follow all the recommendations set out by the professionals. Each had identified important issues that needed addressing, starting with Rory's high intelligence, moving through his auditory processing problems, and on to his fine and gross motor concerns. However, because of the great focus on behavioural difficulties and cognitive capacity deficits, often the child's gifted abilities are not addressed. At school, the notion of providing Rory with a challenging curriculum was not on anyone's mind, while at home, Clare and Michael were focused on finding ways to help bypass his cognitive weaknesses through the recommendations made in the reports. They even had Rory attend social skills intervention groups after school. The process was exhausting, with Clare admitting, "We were worn out." She continued, "You know, you get in the car at 3:30 p.m. and you drive him to the next thing. In fact, we didn't actually know that we could pick and choose from all these suggestions. We just thought we had to do them all. So we had the occupational therapist, the Orton-Gillingham tutor twice a week, the Magic Ears, and Social Skills intervention all going. Rory couldn't cope with it and we were becoming the enemy. Fortunately, he still had loads of friends, his soccer, his hockey, and his Irish dancing. There were things to keep his self-esteem from crashing."

Clare and Michael were determined to keep up the physical activities. Rory loved to play hockey, but he had difficulty handling abstract verbal instruction. A drill could not be described; it needed to be demonstrated. They could not say, "You're playing left wing"; rather, they needed to say, "We're going in this direction and you are playing forward on this side." Clare and Michael would need to become their son's advocate and enlighten the coaches. In Irish dance, a demanding physical art form, Rory was starting to see some accomplishment. Clare said, "It took him a long time to get it. It took him a long time to follow the patterns. [The dance] is first presented in a group environment, then the teacher works with the children individually. It's very methodical, with repeating patterns. Rory is naturally musical and very rhythmic but is also very tall, so he had trouble with balance and control. We would practise at home, and he would pitch himself down on the floor if he made a mistake. He just hates making mistakes."

Big Brain Academy

Clare was out of town on a business trip when she caught the *Vicki Gabereau Show* on television on December 17, 2001 (episode 371). Gabereau's guest that day was the founder of the Arrowsmith Program, Barbara Arrowsmith Young. Gabereau was fascinated with Arrowsmith Young's work and so was Clare. "I actually saw that show," she said. "It seems so long ago! I must have tucked the memory of that show in the back of my mind. It just stuck in my mind. You see, I never liked the idea of work-around solutions to things. For example, with Rory one person said to me, 'Well, if he can't tie his shoes, get him slip-ons.' You see, in my world, if you can't do something, you keep doing it over and over until you can do it. You don't find a work-around. Too many programs are work-around programs."

Both Clare and Michael were exhausted with their current approaches, and Rory was becoming increasingly frustrated at school. Another solution was needed. Clare recalls, "I thought, okay, there must be another way of doing this. I think we were really put off by the public school experience, and the fact that there was a limited amount of resources. If your child doesn't fit in somehow, there really isn't a good solution for them. Then it falls on your shoulders as a parent. You think you send your kid to school and they're going to get educated—well, that's not what happens when they don't fit in either end of those extremes. You have to do it yourself. We got exhausted trying to do it ourselves."

The idea of considering a private school for children with learning disabilities was developing in the minds of Rory's parents. They began exploring the alternatives in the Vancouver area. When they examined in what ways those private schools focused on improving the cognitive weaknesses that resulted in the learning problems, there appeared to be only two options. One school was designed to bypass the cognitive weaknesses by using instructional strategies, teaching achievement skills, providing accommodations, and using assistive technology. Another school was the recently started Eaton Arrowsmith School, designed to improve cognitive capacities that cause learning disabilities and move the child back into mainstream education as fast as possible. Clare and Michael decided to focus on improving cognitive capacities rather than bypassing them.

Next, their problem was persuading Rory to change schools for Grade 3. Using the positive words approach as they had done with Magic Ears, they came up with a solution. Clare describes what happened: "We told Rory that there was a school called the Big Brain Academy. We said it was a school for kids who are really smart but have trouble with some things at school. Rory didn't wear all his negative feelings about school on his sleeve, probably because he didn't have the verbal capacity to define how he felt about his struggles. But he knew he wasn't happy and he couldn't do certain things other kids were capable of. We told him that this new school was going to help him with things he struggled with so he'd be as good at those things as he was at some of the things he was already very amazing at."

Rory also liked the uniform. Students at Eaton Arrowsmith are required to wear a golf shirt with the school's logo on it. This was very appealing to Rory. Clare laughs as she recalls this event. "He got the uniform, which was pretty exciting because he's a uniform guy, I think from sports. Things like his hockey jersey, soccer jersey, soccer socks, and new gloves—the more equipment, the more he wants to do it."

Rory's Arrowsmith Assessment Results

Rory was given the Arrowsmith assessment in August 2007 prior to the start of the new school year. In September, Clare and Michael met with EAS school administrators to go over Rory's results, described in table 18.

Table 18. Rory's Arrowsmith assessment results

Cognitive Function	Description	Rory's Level of Difficulty
Motor-Symbol Sequencing	Problems associated with printing neatly and copying quickly. Careless errors in math, slow reading speed, inconsistent spelling.	Very Severe
Symbol Relations	Problems understanding concepts and cause-and-effect reasoning. Logical-reasoning problems.	Severe
Memory for Information and Instructions	Trouble remembering oral instruction, difficulty following lectures or extended conversations.	Moderate
Broca's Speech Pronunciation	Mispronouncing words, avoiding using words, speaking in incomplete sentences	Mild
Artifactual Thinking	Problems understanding and interpreting social cues.	Moderate to Severe
Symbol Recognition	Poor word recognition, slow reading, difficulty with spelling, trouble remembering symbol patterns such as mathematical equations.	Moderate to Severe
Object Recognition	Trouble finding objects, difficulty remembering faces and recalling visual details of pictures.	Severe
Supplementary Motor	Trouble with finger counting and retaining numbers in memory, difficulty making monetary change, problems learning math facts, poor sense of time management.	Severe to Moderate

The results supported the findings from the various professionals regarding cognitive capacity weaknesses. Some additional weaknesses appeared that had not been identified in Rory's original psycho-educational assessment. It was evident in the Arrowsmith assessment that he continued to show severe weaknesses with Motor-Symbol Sequencing—his ability to learn and produce a written sequence of symbols. He showed severe cognitive capacity weaknesses in Symbol Relations—his ability to understand the relationships between two or more ideas or concepts. He struggled to develop and maintain plans and strategies through the use of language—Symbolic Thinking. His weakness with remembering chunks of auditory information was identified on the Memory for Information and Instructions cognitive function assessment. He showed moderate to severe difficulties with Artifactual Thinking—registering and interpreting nonverbal information—and in planning and nonverbal problem solving. He also struggled to visually recognize and remember the details of objects. Finally, with respect to mathematics, he struggled to carry out internal sequential mental operations as observed on the Supplementary Motor cognitive function.

Rory's Arrowsmith assessment identified eight areas of deficit of the nineteen cognitive capacities the program assesses. His new goals consisted of:

- Working on cognitive exercises that would improve his ability to understand the relationships between multiple concepts
- Doing daily visual-motor integration activities to improve his ability to learn and produce a written sequence of symbols
- Strengthening his ability to hold oral language in memory
- Increasing his ability to improve his planning and strategic thinking
- Improving his ability to hold mental operations in his mind
- Strengthening his ability to process and interpret nonverbal information

Clearly, Rory had a great deal of work ahead of him.

Rory's Program Begins

Rory's first two weeks at Eaton Arrowsmith School were smooth and free of problems. "He put on his [golf shirt] and stood by the door ready to go every morning for the first two weeks," said Clare. "We thought, 'who is this kid, and what's happened to Rory?' There he was, waiting with his uniform on and his bag lunch the first two weeks of school." This was the boy who had previously found distractions every morning on the way out the door that consistently made him late for school.

After two weeks, Rory began to show resistance to doing the Arrowsmith Program exercises, a common pattern of behaviour for him. Once he reached a certain level of frustration, he would begin to resist. He feared failure, and did not want an activity to be so difficult that he would fail. This time Clare and Michael were prepared. As Clare recalled, "We signed up for this and we were here for the duration. We were not people who were looking at it every day, wondering, did we make the right decision? We'd made a commitment to the program. We were not going to look back, and that was that. But Rory was going to see how far he could push it. No matter what he did, though, [we would not allow him to give up]."

There were some positives—Rory made sporadic progress and made friends at Eaton Arrowsmith School. Nevertheless, for the most part, his first two years at Eaton Arrowsmith were tumultuous for Rory's teachers. He would quickly become frustrated if he was not mastering a level. He required patience and empathy as he worked through his anxiety over failure.

After two years at EAS, Clare and Michael decided to enlist the help of a registered clinical counsellor who provided in-class behavioural therapy for Rory. She provided his teachers with insight into supporting Rory in the classroom environment. Interestingly, Clare noted how Rory's training in the Arrowsmith Program helped the behavioural therapy to work in reducing his anxieties and frustrations. She said, "Rory could not have done this work with his counsellor two years ago. He could have gone through the process, but he wouldn't have come as far. The Arrowsmith Program exercises made him more capable of doing the work needed for his emotional regulation issues." The combination of the Symbol Relations, Symbolic Thinking, and Artifactual Thinking exercises made the work with the behavioural therapist even more beneficial. A bonus for Rory was a decrease in his need for perfection as well as his general anxiety issues—crowds, elevators, and other phobias were greatly reduced. "Rory's over so much of that now," Clare noted.

Clare and Michael also used various motivational strategies to keep Rory's goal setting high in his cognitive classroom. A good example is the story of the ribs. Rory's father is a vegetarian and his mother does not like cooking raw meat, so Rory lives in an essentially vegetarian home. "Our kids will order steak the minute they're in a restaurant," said Clare. Rory really enjoys ribs, so Clare and Michael used this as a way to get him over the obstacle of mastering a very difficult level of the Supplementary Motor exercise. Clare knew Rory was frustrated with both this mastery level and the fact he couldn't have ribs. Clare smiled as she continued, "Rory said to me, 'Mom why can't you make me ribs? Uncle Chuck eats ribs and you're his sister, so you should know how to cook ribs.' I said, 'Okay. I don't really want to, but if you'll master Supplementary Motor, I'll cook ribs for you—all-you-can-eat ribs.' So sure enough, he mastered Supplementary Motor. He was a guy on a mission." Rory tried to reach his mother by phone the moment he mastered Supplementary Motor. Clare recalled, "I was out seeing clients in another part of town, so he called Michael. He said, 'Phone Mom and tell her I mastered Supplementary Motor and I need ribs!' I got the message from Michael, who was laughing as he told me this. Of course, I didn't want to cook meat, so I had to figure out what to do. I decided to go to a specialty grocery store and pay about five times as much as I should for deli ribs. I brought them home, heated them, and presented them to him. He ate them—with huge pleasure!"

Rory's Irish dancing was also progressing, and he frequently competed. His repetitive practicing over the years had improved his gross motor coordination and sequencing skills. From a variety of levels of ability—beginner, advanced beginner, novice, and prizewinner—Rory was now dancing at the prizewinner level in the jig, reel, and hornpipe dances. "He's on the cusp of moving into the preliminary championship level, which he wants really badly," said Clare. "The championship level is for dancers who've accomplished the basic skills in their bag of tricks, and then they're on to more difficult rhythms in timing and footwork. He appears to get new patterns quite quickly now. He's now working to master the slow treble jig in his hard shoes!"

Equally as important, Rory was learning to accept that success does not necessarily mean winning at a competition, but giving his best effort to everything he undertakes. He was also learning that not everything is in his control—something often difficult for perfectionists to learn. Clare and Michael felt this applied equally to the other sports their son participated in such as soccer and rugby. Along with gains in cognitive functions, Rory's sportsmanship had improved. Clare and Michael also noticed that compared with three years earlier, their son was capable of following abstract verbal instruction and no longer required a parental advocate.

Final Assessments

Rory's final year at Eaton Arrowsmith School was a productive one. He graduated in June 2010. Table 19 highlights the significant gains he had made in his eight cognitive weaknesses:

TABLE 19. RORY'S FINAL ARROWSMITH ASSESSMENT RESULTS

Cognitive Function	Description	Rory's Level of Difficulty
Motor-Symbol Sequencing	Problems associated with printing neatly and copying quickly. Careless errors in math, slow reading speed, inconsistent spelling.	Severe to Moderate
Symbol Relations	Problems understanding concepts and cause-and-effect reasoning. Logical-reasoning problems.	Average
Memory for Information and Instructions	Trouble remembering oral instruction, difficulty following lectures or extended conversations.	Moderate to Mild
Broca's Speech Pronunciation	Mispronouncing words, avoiding using words, speaking in incomplete sentences.	Average

Cognitive Function	Description	Rory's Level of Difficulty
Artifactual Thinking	Problems understanding and interpreting social cues.	Mild to Moderate
Symbol Recognition	Poor word recognition, slow reading, difficulty with spelling, trouble remembering symbol patterns such as mathematical equations.	Average
Object Recognition	Trouble finding objects, difficulty remembering faces and recalling visual details of pictures.	Mild to Moderate
Supplementary Motor	Trouble with finger counting and retaining numbers in memory, difficulty making monetary change, problems learning math facts, poor sense of time management.	Mild to Moderate

During his stay at EAS, Rory showed noticeable improvements in cognitive, academic, and behavioural areas of functioning. He had moved to the average range in many cognitive functions initially identified as at the severe level in the Arrowsmith assessment. In particular, he was now average in Symbol Relations and Symbolic Thinking. He had also moved closer to the average range in all the other areas of cognitive capacity weakness.

Rory's challenges with math were addressed by first strengthening his mathematical reasoning through the Symbol Relations (Clocks) exercise. He was now capable of understanding complex relationships between multiple concepts quickly and efficiently. He improved his ability to do mental math through the Supplementary Motor exercise. He could now hold numbers in his mind without losing them or needing to write them down on paper. He reduced careless errors in math by improving his visual-motor integration ability through the Motor-Symbol Sequencing exercise. Math was now far easier for Rory. His improved cognitive capacities for math enabled him to do the math curriculum at advanced levels.

Because Rory's Symbol Recognition capacity was already in the average range prior to starting the Arrowsmith Program, he did not have severe challenges with reading and spelling. The Orton-Gillingham program had been needed to help him with the sound/symbol systems of the English language; however, he could not be considered dyslexic.

Rory had the intelligence to do well academically, but his processing speed and working memory had been weak, as identified by psychologist Margaret Lancaster in his first assessment. After he completed the Arrowsmith program, Dr. Lancaster performed an updated psycho-educational assessment, in which she noted that the most significant changes for Rory related to his ability to manage information and keep up with activities in a classroom environment. At graduation, Rory's processing speed and working memory had moved from areas of cognitive weaknesses to strengths, allowing him to keep pace with instruction. Table 20 shows Rory's cognitive improvement results from Dr. Lancaster from December 2006 to January 2010.

TABLE 20. RORY'S PSYCHO-EDUCATIONAL ASSESSMENT RESULTS BEFORE AND AFTER ARROWSMITH

Psycho-Educational Assessment Measure	Description	Before Arrowsmith Program (2006)	After Arrowsmith Program (2010)
Thinking Ability *-Long-term retrieval* *-Visual-spatial thinking* *-Auditory processing* *-Fluid reasoning*	A sampling of different thinking processes that might be used when information cannot be processed automatically.	34th %ile	85th %ile
Cognitive Efficiency	Ability of the cognitive system to process information automatically.	32nd %ile	81st %ile
Phonemic Awareness	Ability to analyze and synthesize speech sounds.	43rd %ile	95th %ile

Psycho-Educational Assessment Measure	Description	Before Arrowsmith Program (2006)	After Arrowsmith Program (2010)
Working Memory	Ability to hold information in immediate awareness while manipulating that information.	74th %ile	97th %ile
Oral Language	Ability to follow directions and recall story details.	23rd %ile	41st %ile

Note: The average performance range on psycho-educational assessments is considered to fall between the 25th and 75th %ile ranking.

Rory's ability to reason and use language to plan and strategize had also improved (these are cognitive functions not often accurately assessed in psycho-educational assessments). Finally, his ability to make sense of nonverbal information, such as in social situations, through the use of the Artifactual Thinking cognitive exercise had improved. In September 2010, Rory was ready to make a transition to a mainstream classroom. Even more important, he could now use his intellectual gifts and explore learning without cognitive weaknesses hindering his self-confidence.

French Immersion

Clare, Michael, and Rory decided that his next step would be a French immersion public school. Such a late immersion program would require a great deal of work for Rory. Clare noted, "Some of our friends looked at us and said, 'Are you crazy? You have a kid who had a learning disability status and you're going to do that to him?'" Clare and Michael felt Rory would succeed, and Rory did as well. "In December [of 2009], we went to the open house for the program," Clare explained. "Rory came too. They had a little girl from Grade 6 stand up and talk about the program so far. It was only three months into the year and she said they all have to work really hard, doing an hour of homework every day. I looked at Rory when the girl mentioned this and he sort of snorted—like, 'That's no big deal. You should see the homework I do at EAS.'" Rory began practicing his French in an effort to have an advantage in September when his new school year would begin. As his mother said, "He's always been very determined."

I asked Clare to sum up her thoughts on the Arrowsmith Program. She said, "The way I describe it to people is that it's based on our own philosophy of not making compensations for learning disabilities, but rather attacking them head on and trying to overcome and strengthen the things that are weak for these children, so that their learning profiles are more even. I think that's the crux of the whole thing. And it's a safe environment, it's a supportive environment, and the kids feel very successful when they master cognitive levels and they gain that confidence in their own abilities. They feel that success."

10

Is It Really an Attention Problem?

Once you get a feel for ADD, *you might start to think almost everybody has it.*

—DRS. EDWARD HALLOWELL & JOHN RATEY, AUTHORS, *DELIVERED FROM DISTRACTION*

Talents for Music and Humour

Cameron loves music. His parents, Bruce and Valerie, played all kinds of music in the car when he was young. Today, Cameron is a double bass musician for the Vancouver Youth Symphony Orchestra. He is also an accomplished sailor. Sailing a Laser, he won the Royal Vancouver Yacht Club Commodore Cup in his category. He has always been the kind of boy who likes a challenge.

Humour is a striking personality trait of Cameron's. "He sees the sunny side of everything," said his mother. His cognitive teachers at Eaton Arrowsmith School, Mark Watson and Sarah Cohen, also noted this. Said Mark, "Cameron has a great sense of humour. He's one of those students people immediately like because his personality is so kind and caring, and [he's] very giving and respectful of others. All the students in our class really liked him."

Sarah remarked, "Cameron loved to laugh, and luckily so did Mark and I. This humour really kept him going when things got hard. If there was a low moment, Mark would make a really funny comment, which would make the whole class feel lighter and enjoy being there all over again. I became a teacher in part because I find it fun, and hearing Cameron laugh was fun—he made *me* laugh. Having a student like Cameron was such a joy."

When Cameron started at Eaton Arrowsmith School he was entering Grade 8. His hair was often dishevelled in the morning, his clothing askew, and he moved around constantly. Cameron's parents were Vancouverites originally from South Africa. When their son was four years old, they moved with their children from Vancouver to England, then to Scotland for five years. When Cameron was nine, they returned to Vancouver, hence his accent was an interesting mixture of Scottish and South African. Sarah noted, "It was challenging to understand him because he also mumbled a bit when he spoke. Most of the time I understood most of what he said, but one day around Halloween he was trying to tell us a story about something that had happened on his bus ride to school, and we couldn't understand him. After repeating himself four times, we finally understood that he had seen a man in a watermelon costume. He laughed and said to us, 'That's why I have to come here.'"

Cameron has a twin sister, Stephanie, which made it easy for Valerie and Bruce to notice early that Cameron was struggling with various tasks at school while Stephanie was not. Valerie recalled purchasing a singing times-table recording that she would play in the car because Cameron could not learn his times tables. Valerie said, "We would all start singing the times tables in the car, but Cameron could not do it." He was also struggling with telling time on a three-handed clock and could not tie his shoelaces. At the time, Cameron was attending primary school in Scotland and was receiving learning support, but there was no diagnosed issue.

He was seven years old in 1999 when Valerie and Bruce decided to have their son tested for learning difficulties or disabilities at the Royal Edinburgh Hospital. To his parents' surprise, the professionals could find nothing of concern in Cameron's intellectual, cognitive, and achievement profile. In fact, his vocabulary level was above most other children his age, although fine motor skills issues were identified that were linked to his speech problems and maturity. Of course, his parents were also pleased there was nothing terribly wrong with their son.

When the family moved back to Vancouver, Cameron was entering Grade 4. Valerie and Bruce decided to enrol him at a private school in West Vancouver that was known for its strong academic program. Based on the learning assessment at Royal Edinburgh Hospital, there was no real need to be concerned about Cameron's ability to perform well academically. Perhaps, they thought, he just needed to mature a little more. This was not to be the case.

It did not take long for homework to become a problem for Cameron. "I used to sit with him mostly every night and do homework," Valerie said. "If I left him to work on his own, it just would not get done." The situation led to frustration for more than just Cameron. Valerie said, "Bruce would become frustrated and tell me, 'Cam is not working and he should be working,' and then we'd all be yelling and everybody would be upset. And Cam would start crying. It was just difficult for him, but we never realized it. I just thought he was easily distracted."

Completing homework was not Cameron's only problem. Learning foreign languages was also difficult. (In Canadian schools, French is the most popular second language taught in public and private schools.) Mathematics also continued to be a problem for him. "I had a lot of trouble understanding the concepts," he said later.

Valerie and Bruce went to the school administrators to state their concerns. The response was, "Oh, he's just a regular boy." In short, they seemed to be telling Cameron's parents that he was just goofing around, trying to avoid homework, and not concentrating because he was a boy, and that is what boys do. This did not sit well with Valerie and Bruce, and they decided to have their son tested again for possible learning difficulties. Valerie knew someone whose child had been tested at Eaton Learning Centre. In June 2004, Valerie called our office and spoke with Sandra Heusel, then the assessment manager at EAS, to arrange for testing.

Cameron was just completing Grade 6 and school had become even more challenging. At our first meeting, his love for music was evident as he said, "My dream job would be to go to a music university and then join an orchestra in double bass. It would be interesting for me to be involved in music for my career and get paid for it. I'd also like to do some teaching on the side." Cameron was knowledgeable about music and could talk about it for hours. My immediate impression was that he was a social, happy, and friendly boy.

Cameron's psycho-educational assessment noted that math and French appeared to be his most challenging subjects. It was also difficult for him to focus in class. He was easily distracted by the noise and movements of others and had trouble remaining still. Also, he became anxious when approaching exams, even if he was prepared and had enough time to complete the tasks. He was aware that he tended to miss details in his answers, which caused him to lose marks. Finally, it was difficult for him to follow instructions. At home, though he was keen to begin his homework, he had trouble focusing for long periods, so he took many breaks. Although he spent a great deal of time on his assignments, and he and his family were often frustrated during homework sessions, particularly math-related tasks. Table 21 outlines how severe some of his cognitive weaknesses were, based on the 2004 psycho-educational assessment.

TABLE 21. CAMERON'S INITIAL PSYCHO-EDUCATIONAL ASSESSMENT RESULTS

Psycho-Educational Assessment Measure	Description	Before Arrowsmith Program
Visual-Auditory Learning (Woodcock-Johnson Tests of Cognitive Ability—Third Edition—WJ-III)	A measure of long-term retrieval/ memory.	20th %ile
Coding Subtest (Wechsler Intelligence Scale for Children—Third Edition—WISC-III)	Ability to scan and copy visual symbols under timed conditions.	5th %ile
Verbal Ability (Woodcock-Johnson Tests of Cognitive Ability—Revised—WJ-R)	A measure of vocabulary knowledge and word reasoning.	67th %ile

Psycho-Educational Assessment Measure	**Description**	**Before Arrowsmith Program**
Working Memory (WJ-III)	Ability to hold information in immediate awareness while manipulating that information.	12th %ile
Motor Coordination (The Beery-Buktenica Developmental Test of Visual-Motor Integration)	A measure of motor coordination when copying symbols.	7th %ile
Nonverbal Intelligence (Test of Nonverbal Intelligence—Third Edition—TONI-3)	A measure of fluid intelligence. Ability to recognize visual patterns and relationships.	50th %ile

Note: The average performance range on psycho-educational assessments is considered to fall between the 25th and 75th %ile ranking.

For any parent of a child with attention problems, Cameron's problems are familiar. They have seen them repeatedly, often to the point of exasperation, even desperation. The symptoms are clear:

- Difficulty staying seated
- Difficulty listening to instructions
- Difficulty completing homework within reasonable time limits
- Classroom behaviour disruptions
- A need for frequent breaks
- Easily distracted both at school and at home

As an educational assessor, I was also familiar with the symptoms. I emphatically concluded that Cameron must have some kind of attention problem. He showed all the textbook symptoms, and the behaviour noted by his teachers and his parents supported my conclusion. However, I realized that if he also had learning disabilities, they would make it all the more difficult for him to cope in school.

Several of his classroom instructors had completed checklists indicating that Cameron was below grade level in writing, reading, spelling, and math by either one or two years. One of his teachers felt there was no problem and wrote, "Cameron is a warm and caring student. He is very eager to please his teachers. In my opinion he is a typical boy having fun at all times." However, the majority of his teachers disagreed with this and were concerned, requesting interviews with his parents. They wanted to develop solutions to the problems.

Cameron noted on a self-evaluation checklist completed prior to his psycho-educational assessment that he struggled to print and handwrite neatly. In reviewing the testing results, I wrote in his assessment: "It is very difficult for Cameron to neatly print or write. It is also challenging, at times, for him to copy notes from the board and to take notes in class. The writing process is also difficult for Cameron. It is hard for him to write enough about a topic, and to use correct grammar and punctuation. Spelling is also an area of difficulty. Math is an ongoing challenge. He finds it difficult to remember his times tables, to remember math facts, to understand word problems, and to remember the steps necessary to work out a word problem. Surprisingly, even though Cameron enjoys talking, he has difficulties with an oral presentation. At times he struggles to find the right words to explain what he means."

I continued: "Cameron has had difficulty focusing on his schoolwork during the past school year both in class and at home during homework sessions. Although he works hard at math, Cameron's math examinations were disappointing. He tends to miss details, such as the unit of measurement. As a result, his parents asked me to help them develop strategies that would help their son achieve greater success in Grade 7."

We concluded that Cameron had a combination of issues: an attention problem, a math-based learning disability, and a written output learning disability. His math scores were weak due to his slow recall of math facts. He had severe problems with visual-motor integration and speed, so his ability to use his hands or fingers to copy and get ideas out on paper efficiently was impaired. His fingers worked in slow motion to replicate symbols of the English language. I wrote in Cameron's assessment: "There are some indicators of attention inconsistencies (ADHD – Inattentive Type) based on a review of the Child Symptom Inventory forms filled out by Cameron's parents and teacher. His scores are not highly positive for an attention disorder, but he does show some of the characteristics such as becoming easily distracted, having difficulty paying attention in general, and exhibiting failure to pay close attention to details. Nevertheless, it is possible that his neurodevelopmental weaknesses with visual-motor integration, processing speed, cognitive efficiency for numerical information, working memory for digits, and visual-spatial organization result in the behaviours we observed. That is, when faced with tasks that stress his cognitive weaknesses, he shows increased inattention or distractibility, which is not unusual for any child or adult. He may also feel some anxiety during exams or tests. Providing Cameron with extended time and a distraction-reduced testing environment could ease his anxiety and improve his processing."

Arrowsmith Program and Attention Disorders

As an educational assessor, even before my immersion into the Arrowsmith Program, I was beginning to realize that behaviours related to attention disorders such as ADHD might indeed be related to other cognitive weaknesses. For instance, if a child has difficulty getting ideas down on paper or copying from the board, his brain can become fatigued and shut down, and he will appear to have an attention problem. Similarly, when listening to someone speak, if a child has trouble remembering, he will also become neurologically fatigued, shut down, and look "spaced out." A child with several cognitive weaknesses can be constantly tuned out in class.

Barbara Arrowsmith Young's work made me further aware of the fact that cognitive weaknesses can result in mild, moderate, or severe attention disorders. Most importantly, her work helped me realize that many children with attention disorders can improve their attention problem by improving their weak cognitive capacities. Children can improve weak memory for oral language and then be able to listen for longer periods. They can improve visual-motor functioning for printing and copying symbols, thereby improving their ability to get ideas on paper or copy notes from the board. They can improve their reasoning, making it easier to follow a lecture, understand the concepts stated, and not feel disconnected from the topic. These were all new and startling revelations to me as an educator. In fact, I had seen medication help children become more focused in class, but often they still struggled with taking notes from the board, listening to instructions, and understanding concepts. The medication allowed them to focus on their schoolwork and be less impulsive, but their cognitive weaknesses remained, and because of this school continued to be frustrating.

The Arrowsmith Program is designed to remediate attention weaknesses caused by weak cognitive capacities. For over thirty years, Barbara Arrowsmith Young had already recognized that many children are misdiagnosed with ADHD because their combination of cognitive capacity weaknesses causes them to display behaviours associated with this diagnosis. Over the years, Eaton Arrowsmith School has observed that approximately 60 percent of children who enrol in the school with medication for ADHD can come off their prescriptions upon completion of the program. These children have improved the specific cognitive weaknesses that in combination or on their own caused attention problems.

For example, a child might come in with oral language problems, or difficulties with listening to information and instructions. If that same child has a visual-motor output problem resulting in slow printing and copying using paper and pencil, there will be serious learning problems. The combination of these two cognitive weaknesses results in behaviours associated with ADHD such as poor listening, not completing tasks, being distracted, and so on.

Traditionally, the parents meet with the teacher and principal, where they are told their child may have ADHD and should see their family doctor. The doctor will then look at the teacher checklists, see that the behaviours fit the diagnosis, and prescribe a stimulant medication such as Ritalin. The medicated child is more focused but still cannot keep up with her peers in class. I learned from Arrowsmith Young to approach things differently.

At the start-up of Eaton Arrowsmith School, in admissions meetings I was having difficulty determining if certain children with ADHD were appropriate candidates for the program. As well, I needed to know whether candidates with ADHD should continue their medication. With remarkable insight, Arrowsmith Young categorized "attentional" problems in the following ways:

- ADHD behaviour that is possibly neurochemical or subcortical and most amenable to drug therapy, and is not treatable with Arrowsmith Program work.
- ADHD behaviour that arises out of too many cognitive deficits that require the child to focus more energy on completing tasks, resulting in mental fatigue and confusion, and the outcome is trouble sustaining attention once this occurs.
- ADHD behaviour that arises out of an emotional etiology, making it hard for the child to stay present; thus, attention wanders.

Arrowsmith Young noted that the second of these causes is directly addressable by Arrowsmith Program cognitive exercises. Many students in Arrowsmith Programs have a mixed bag of the above factors with different weights given to each factor, resulting in highly individualized profiles. For students who have separate subcortical or neurochemical attention problems as well as specific cognitive deficits, medication is often necessary in order to get the requisite level of attention directed toward the cognitive exercises. Medication is carefully monitored for dosage and specific type before the desired effect is achieved. Arrowsmith Young confirmed my thinking about ADHD for children with a variety of cognitive weaknesses, but her confirmation brought to light many more issues that I had not fully realized.

At Eaton Arrowsmith School, approximately 30 percent of admission applicants have been diagnosed with ADHD *and* learning disabilities. It is both fascinating and challenging trying to discover why they have ADHD and whether ADHD is the appropriate diagnosis. All applicants to the school must undergo an Arrowsmith assessment, and in many cases, after the assessment is completed, we discover that there are at least five or six cognitive weaknesses or dysfunctions that affect the brain's attentional ability.

Prior to the Arrowsmith Program, my approach to attention problems was to either medicate the child, try neurobiofeedback, use natural supplements (e.g., omega 3), and/or accommodate the attention weaknesses. In fact, some of my recommendations for Cameron at the time included the use of a note-taker, extended time on tests, use of a computer for written tests, taking tests in distraction-reduced environments, use of a calculator for math tests, and possibly a foreign language exemption. Essentially, I worked to find a way to support his weak cognitive capacities with outside help—by bypassing them. I did not think about neuroplasticity, about improving these specific cognitive capacities. When I first tested Cameron, I had no idea this was an option. When I saw Cameron one year later in the spring of 2005, my thinking had changed to include neuroplasticity, and I was about to open Eaton Arrowsmith School.

Cameron's Arrowsmith Assessment

Bruce and Valerie had heard about the Eaton Arrowsmith School from Sandra Heusel, a former assessment manager at Eaton Learning Centre who had became a cognitive teacher when EAS opened. By this time, Cameron was in Grade 7 and still struggling, even with accommodations, learning strategies, and technology. For Bruce and Valerie, the idea of improving weak cognitive functions sounded logical, but removing Cameron from his private school was not an easy choice. Said Valerie, "It was really scary. It was something foreign. I had to take him out of the regular system for Grades 8 and 9."

Cameron's marks had been steadily declining. Valerie said, "Cameron's academic struggle was starting to show not only in his marks but in his relationships and self-confidence. He dropped down to a C in English. In math, he was struggling, [even though] he was getting extra math help. There were still lots of debates at home as to why this was happening." But Cameron seemed to accept the idea of going to Eaton Arrowsmith School with trust and without protest. "Cameron could see that he was starting to struggle. I spoke to him about this alternative program and said that it would help him in the long run. He was willing to try. He never put up a fight." Cameron added, however, that after the Arrowsmith Program he "was worried about jumping into Grade 10 without Grade 8 and 9 science and social studies."

At Eaton Arrowsmith School, science and social studies are not on the curriculum. EAS graduates rejoining the regular school system are usually introduced to science and social studies for the first time. Initially, some parents and children are concerned about this because society's mindset is that school must include a full curriculum. Nevertheless, when it is explained to parents that their children have been trying to learn these subjects with little success due to their weak cognitive capacities, and the new goal is to improve those cognitive capacities, they understand it may not be worthwhile to teach all subject matter until their cognitive capacities are ready. If all the core subject material (the entire curriculum) were taught, no time would be left for a comprehensive cognitive program. So many children with learning and attention weaknesses fumble through their school day not understanding the concepts being taught. And evidence is strong that Arrowsmith Program graduates transition back into science and social studies with little difficulty, although occasionally there may be some transition time necessary to get used to a full curriculum.

Cameron's June 2005 Arrowsmith assessment examined why he struggled with attention and focusing, and why he was struggling in other areas academically. The assessment results revealed his weak cognitive capacities, as shown in table 22.

TABLE 22. CAMERON'S INITIAL ARROWSMITH ASSESSMENT RESULTS

Cognitive Function	Description	Cameron's Level of Difficulty
Motor-Symbol Sequencing	Problems associated with printing neatly and copying quickly. Careless errors in math, slow reading speed, inconsistent spelling.	Severe to Moderate
Symbol Relations	Problems understanding concepts and cause-and-effect reasoning. Logical-reasoning problems.	Severe to Moderate
Memory for Information and Instructions	Trouble remembering oral instruction, difficulty following lectures or extended conversations.	Moderate
Broca's Speech Pronunciation	Mispronouncing words, avoiding using words, speaking in incomplete sentences.	Severe to Moderate

Cognitive Function	**Description**	**Cameron's Level of Difficulty**
Auditory Speech Discrimination	Inability to discriminate between similar-sounding speech sounds.	Severe to Moderate
Kinesthetic Speech	Lack of awareness of the position of lips and tongue.	Severe to Moderate
Artifactual Thinking	Problems understanding and interpreting social cues.	Mild to Moderate

The psycho-educational assessment Cameron had taken one year prior to the Arrowsmith assessment had highlighted some but not all of these problems—psycho-educational assessments are not as comprehensive as the Arrowsmith Program's. With the new Arrowsmith results, we could now explain to Bruce and Valerie why their son did not want to speak up in class or take part in conversations that were unfamiliar to him. A look at his cognitive weaknesses with speech pronunciation showed it was very difficult for him to feel comfortable about how a word is pronounced. He also struggled with Symbol Relations, causing him problems with seeing relationships between multiple concepts and utilizing cause-and-effect problem solving. This would affect mathematics, social studies, science, and English classes. Cameron's visual-motor difficulties were significant, affecting his reading speed, speech, copying, and accuracy of written output. Furthermore, two to four cognitive weaknesses could be affecting his writing, mathematics, listening, and reasoning skills because these functions do not operate in isolation. A problem with mathematics can become more severe when multiple cognitive weaknesses are involved. Cameron struggled with math because of:

- weakness in understanding relationships between two or more concepts at a time
- weak Motor-Symbol Sequencing (he would make careless errors in math when printing or copying math notes)
- weak memory for instructions and information

We were eager to present Cameron's cognitive profile to his parents and explain how the Arrowsmith Program could deal with his learning disabilities and attention difficulties at the underlying cognitive weakness level. While two years would be needed to fully address the most important deficits, the main thing was that Cameron *could* improve. We would be pleased to tell his parents that Cameron's attention problems were likely not the primary problem, but instead caused by underlying cognitive weaknesses.

Understanding the Arrowsmith Program takes time and commitment. In fact, an understanding of aspects of neurology, psychology, and neuroplasticity is required to fully appreciate the Arrowsmith Program's premises. Unfortunately, many educators today are not provided with this training at their teacher colleges or universities, nor is the average parent aware of these areas. Rather, both educators and parents are focused heavily on achievement in the math, language arts, and science curricula. Teachers studying special education may get a course on aspects of cognitive functioning, but it is usually not comprehensive. Thus, a gap exists in our ability to communicate the concepts of Arrowsmith to educators and parents. Large gaps also exist between the fields of education and neuroscience at the university level. Slowly, this relationship will develop, but considerable hurdles remain.

Fortunately, many parents (and teachers) are willing to look for alternatives if their child's current program is not helping. They often want to learn about and understand how the Arrowsmith Program can change their child's life.

Cameron at Eaton Arrowsmith School

Cameron made excellent progress throughout his first year at Eaton Arrowsmith School. However, as his teacher Sarah Cohen noted, he did not have an easy start. "Cameron worked at a consistent level but was not what I would call a goal setter or achiever, right away. I believe he was afraid to try, but over the course of our first year, I saw him slowly trying to push himself more as he got closer and closer to major milestones in his cognitive exercises." Cameron's daily homework included writing in a journal, and this caused him problems. Sarah wrote, "Cameron completed his homework regularly, but the quality and quantity of his work was far below what I knew he was capable of as the year went on. Each student is asked to write a one-page journal entry each night, and getting him to do his was not easy—he would skip four lines at a time to make it a full page, would barely stick to one topic, would never put the date on his work, and would often not complete this part of the homework."

Cameron began working on the Symbol Relations exercise to build the cognitive capacity to understand relationships between two or more concepts. This weakness had seriously hindered each of his academic subjects in the past as well as his current achievement skills in reading, writing, and mathematics (the psycho-educational assessment conducted a year earlier had not identified this as a problem). Cameron was also working diligently on his speech, using the Broca's Speech Pronunciation exercise, and his auditory memory, using the Memory for Information and Instructions exercise. Finally, he spent dozens of hours improving fine motor for printing and copying with the Motor-Symbol Sequencing exercises. This would improve his reading speed and written output fluency as well as reduce careless errors in written mathematics.

Valerie noticed changes within the first month of the program. "Cameron started to express himself," she said. "In the past, we would be sitting at the dinner table as a family or if the grandparents were around, and he wouldn't speak. He never joined in the conversations. After about one month in the Arrowsmith Program, he started to express himself more. His confidence just improved dramatically. He started to believe in himself." Cameron also noticed changes. He said, "In the first two months I noticed that my handwriting was improving. I was also beginning to understand what the teachers were saying a lot more."

Cameron had made very good cognitive progress in his first year in the Arrowsmith Program, and during his second year (Grade 9), his cognitive teachers, academic teachers, and parents stayed in continual contact. Cameron again made good progress during his second year. It was possible he would be able to make the transition to private or public school for Grade 10.

Sarah Cohen recalls, "In his last year, Cameron became more focused and goal oriented in his cognitive exercises. He was greatly motivated by competing with his friend Kyle—anytime Kyle would master a level, Cameron would push himself and master it too. Anytime Cameron mastered something, Kyle would push himself and master it just to catch up and try to pull ahead. Kyle was naturally more goal oriented than Cameron, and Cameron learned a lot by example from him. Cameron also started to really shine academically in his last year at EAS. He was in a Grade 9 mathematics class where the teacher, Meagan Trayers, motivated the students by challenging them. She gave them Grade 9 exams with questions from Grade 10 provincial exams, she shared her love of math with them, and her sense of humour encouraged them to be themselves with her."

Critical for Cameron was that the cognitive capacities he needed for developing math concepts were now within the above-average range. By November of his second year he had completed the Symbol Relations program. His last Arrowsmith assessment in May 2007 highlighted his cognitive functioning improvements, as shown in table 23:

TABLE 23. CAMERON'S FINAL ARROWSMITH ASSESSMENT RESULTS

Cognitive Function	**Description**	**Cameron's Level of Difficulty**
Motor-Symbol Sequencing	Problems associated with printing neatly and copying quickly. Careless errors in math, slow reading speed, inconsistent spelling.	Mild to Moderate
Symbol Relations	Problems understanding concepts and cause-and-effect reasoning. Logical-reasoning problems.	Above Average
Memory for Information and Instructions	Trouble remembering oral instruction, difficulty following lectures or extended conversations.	Moderate
Broca's Speech Pronunciation	Mispronouncing words, avoiding using words, speaking in incomplete sentences.	Average

Cognitive Function	Description	Cameron's Level of Difficulty
Auditory Speech Discrimination	Inability to discriminate between similar-sounding speech sounds.	Average
Kinesthetic Speech	Lack of awareness of the position of lips and tongue.	Moderate to Mild
Artifactual Thinking	Problems understanding and interpreting social cues.	Average

In addition to the results in table 23, an updated psycho-educational assessment conducted during the last months of Cameron's second year at EAS highlighted greatly improved reasoning. Table 24 is a comparison of some of Cameron's cognitive capacities on the psycho-educational assessment before and after the Arrowsmith Program.

TABLE 24. CAMERON'S PSYCHO-EDUCATIONAL ASSESSMENT RESULTS

Psycho-Educational Assessment Measure	Before Arrowsmith Program	After Arrowsmith Program
Coding Subtest—WISC-III to WISC-IV	5th %ile	75th %ile
Working Memory—WISC-III to WISC-IV	12th %ile	50th %ile
Verbal Ability—WJ-III	67th %ile	94th %ile
Visual-Auditory Learning—WJ-III	20th %ile	47th %ile
Motor Coordination—BEERY	7th %ile	53rd %ile
Nonverbal Intelligence—TONI-3	50th %ile	88th %ile

Note: The average performance range on psycho-educational assessments is considered to fall between the 25th and 75th %ile ranking.

On the updated psycho-educational assessment, it was evident that some of Cameron's cognitive abilities had moved from average to above average and even into the superior range of ability. For example, on the Verbal Ability cluster of the Woodcock-Johnson Tests of Cognitive Abilities he went from the 67th percentile to the 94th percentile (superior ranking). He moved from the 50th percentile to the 88th percentile on the Test of Nonverbal Intelligence—Third Edition. Other cognitive abilities moved from low percentile rankings into the average range, and his motor coordination ability was improving through the Motor-Symbol Sequencing exercises. The updated assessment now showed average motor coordination abilities, a great improvement from three years earlier when his ranking had been at the 7th percentile. The updated psycho-educational assessment was showing the cognitive changes in Cameron over the last two years of Arrowsmith Program intervention.

Every result from both the updated Arrowsmith assessment and the updated psycho-educational assessment highlighted positive changes in Cameron's neurological profile. He had improved the efficiency of his visual-motor output ability for copying and written output, which would decrease careless errors in mathematics and spelling and increase reading speed. His spoken language had also improved: the difficulty he had been having with speech pronunciation (limiting his ability to express his knowledge of English vocabulary) was remediated. Because of his work on Broca's exercises, his overall language ability had moved from average to the superior range of functioning, a remarkable achievement. Finally, his results on measures of reasoning showed improved conceptual thinking skills.

Transition to Private School

Five months before Cameron would graduate from Eaton Arrowsmith, we met with Bruce and Valerie to discuss his transition to Grade 10. Valerie had been in touch with two private schools. Both schools had asked for a recent report card; one asked that Cameron write the entrance exam the following month, and the other had openings available only as children left, with a waiting list for preferred students.

Valerie was worried about this transition. When asked about her primary concern, she replied, "Well, he hadn't done science and social studies, only math and English. I thought, how do you go from not being in a full-curriculum school for two years to suddenly being in one? That was terrifying for Bruce and me."

Valerie and Bruce were not unusual; most parents worry about moving their child to a new school. In this case, the concern was that their child had struggled before in mainstream education, and they would be devastated to have this happen again. When the Arrowsmith Program is over for a child, parents want to ensure that their child will be successful. In EAS's second year, ten graduates went on to high school. All of them are doing well, receiving Bs and As. In EAS's third year of operation, thirty graduates went on to high school. However, even with the evidence of success of our graduates and those of the Toronto school for thirty years, every parent is fearful that their child will struggle again. Valerie and Bruce were experiencing the same feelings that had overwhelmed them for most of their son's education.

Cameron was also worried about his future. He said, "I was really nervous. I was especially nervous about science, because I had not done it since Grade 7. I was worried that I would be too far behind to catch up and I would struggle my way through again. I was also worried about languages, which were a major issue for me in the past. At that point, I hadn't taken French in two years."

Even Sarah Cohen and Mark Watson were somewhat worried about Cameron's transition. Sarah said, "He was one of my first students to graduate from the Eaton Arrowsmith School, and while I had seen him progress in cognitive exercises and in his math and English classes, I didn't know how this would translate to another school setting, let alone an advanced academic classroom [where Cameron had decided to attend]. I relaxed a bit in June of his last year with us. By the end of the year he was taking our coaching about studying for exams, organization, test writing, and hard work. He came to school each day focused and more determined than ever to show us, himself, and his parents that he could be successful. He even started to take more pride in his appearance and insisted that his mom get him the full kilt and Scottish formal dress for his graduation ceremony. But even with all this positive growth, I don't think I fully exhaled until I heard from his mother how well he was doing at his new school. He refused any accommodations in his new school, proving that he was no longer a learning-disabled student."

These were Cameron's marks at the end of Grade 10:

English	80%	A–
Maths	75%	B
Science	76%	B
Social Studies	81%	A–
IT	84%	A
Planning	81%	A–
PE	74%	B
Outdoor	71%	B–
Drama	80%	A–

When Valerie reflected on Cameron's progress after the Arrowsmith Program, we asked her if her worries had come true. She said, "Actually, there was no problem. He just was right in there with the other kids." There were inevitable bumps during the first few months as Cameron got used to a full curriculum. Yet even without accommodations, gradually his marks went up. He needed no extra time on tests, no use of a laptop, and no note-taker.

As far as Cameron's concern about science, he told us proudly that he'd received an 87 percent on his final Grade 10 science exam. He noticed big changes in his cognitive capacities after his two-year Arrowsmith Program. "My understanding of concepts improved. That was the major change. I could also structure my writing and write a lot more. I could focus a lot more now."

I asked Valerie if she felt the program had improved Cameron's cognitive weaknesses. "I recommend it to everybody," she said emphatically. "I think it's incredible. I think I put him on a par now with his twin sister, academically."

Cameron finished Grade 12 and graduated from high school in 2010. He showed no signs of any attention problems and received As and Bs with no accommodations. To make sure he had the second-language requirement for a major university in Canada, he enrolled in Spanish and did well. He was accepted by several major Canadian universities and decided to pursue a degree in economics, though music was still a passion for him. He chose to attend a university in British Columbia.

11

Can IQ Change?

Genius is nothing but continued attention.

—CLAUDE ADRIEN HELVETIUS, FRENCH PHILOSOPHER (1715–1771)

Intelligence

Is intelligence fixed for life? Can IQ change? If I have low average IQ based on an intelligence test, is that my fate? Does this determine what I am capable of understanding, of learning?

From 1996 to 2008, our team of psychologists and educational assessors at Eaton Learning Centre tested children and young adults for learning disabilities. In order to be diagnosed with a learning disability (or learning disorder), a child requires at least average intelligence. Our team of psychologists would routinely administer intelligence tests—usually the Wechsler Intelligence Scale for Children depending on the specific age of our client.

In addition to intelligence testing, measures are taken of cognitive capacity and achievement skills. Nevertheless, the intelligence test is the key area of attention. The IQ scores would dictate our perception of what was possible for our client. If the IQ score was low, at borderline range, there was little we could do for that client. If the child had low-average

IQ—below the 25th percentile, meaning more than 75 percent of the population had higher intelligence—it was deemed not a learning disability, but worse, an *intellectual disability*, and in such cases there was also little we could do.

We needed an average or better score in order to label a *learning disability*, a diagnosis that would help the parents receive educational services—including accommodations and bypasses—at their school district. The intelligence test often determines exactly how much in-class support the child can receive.

If the IQ score was low, our psychologists would let us know that not much could be done. An academic focus would not work because reasoning was too low. Instead, we focused on the life skills the child would now need to try to survive in the world—to find a (usually low-paying) job, know how to go to the bank, use money properly, find a place to live, manage a home. There was never any discussion about that IQ score improving. Psychologists and educators assumed that intelligence was fixed, and the child must henceforth be "accommodated."

Some educational researchers, teachers, and psychologists have contended for years that intelligence testing should be banished from school districts, that an IQ label, whether high or low, does more harm than good. Despite these arguments, however, it continues in schools today.

Cody

Cody was experiencing significant struggles learning to read and write. He was seven years, seven months old when we first met, with curly hair, a slight build, and an infectious smile. He had been raised on Cortes Island, a tranquil island off the east coast of Vancouver Island, British Columbia, known for its pristine natural surroundings and its compassionate community. His mother, Lisa, was a certified elementary teacher, and his father, Scott, a highly skilled carpenter, builder, and sawmill operator. Cody was attending Grade 1 at a private school.

Lisa noted, "Cody loved his school, teachers, and friends." Lisa described her son as "a doer—busy, liked doing things outside, loved to explore nature and learn about the world with peers and teachers. He was happy, very social, but shy too. He liked to watch before leaping right in. He was cooperative, attentive, and an excellent listener. He was easy-going, fair minded, funny, and super compassionate."

Cody was tested at Eaton Learning Centre in 2005. (At the time of this psycho-educational assessment, Eaton Arrowsmith School was three months away from opening for its first year of operation.) The notes from the intake interview were revealing. "Cody struggles with letter/word recognition and activities that involve a great deal of visual memory. Everyone who works with Cody is interested in learning how much and what kind of academic support would best help him achieve his potential as a learner." Cody was considered to be a very friendly boy, and indeed, he had many friends. It was also noted that "If information is presented visually, Cody tends to disengage and withdraw; he becomes distracted. But he has a large spoken vocabulary and easily makes connections between concepts." Furthermore, "Cody struggles to recall visual symbols because of a weaker visual memory." In short, he showed a number of visual-perceptual weaknesses (memory, processing speed, and visual reasoning) that were interfering with his acquisition of basic skills and how he coped with school-related tasks.

Cody was given the Wechsler Intelligence Scale for Children (WISC-IV) as well as other measures of cognitive ability and achievement skills. There was a large discrepancy between his Verbal Comprehension IQ (vocabulary knowledge, word association knowledge, and awareness of social rules and norms through oral questioning) and Perceptual Reasoning IQ (solving puzzles, solving matrix patterns, and understanding social rules and norms through visual story cards). Cody had a Verbal Comprehension IQ of 112 (above average, 79th percentile). But his ability to solve puzzles, reason through matrix patterns, and perceive and understand social patterns through story cards was only 66 (borderline, 1st percentile). Explained another way, this large discrepancy in intellectual functioning showed that 99 percent of children Cody's age had stronger perceptual reasoning. On the other hand, Cody's Verbal Comprehension fell in the top 20 percent of his age group. His vocabulary, word reasoning, and social awareness of rules and norms through language was excellent. His Vocabulary subtest score on the WISC-IV fell at the 91st percentile (superior functioning), putting his vocabulary in the top 9 percent of children his age. Lisa and Scott were correct in their description of Cody. He had a strong language base but showed weak memory for visual symbols.

Cody scored at the 5th percentile on the Design Reproduction subtest of the Detroit Tests of Learning Aptitude (DTLA-3). On this test he was shown a design for several seconds, it was removed, and he had to copy it from memory. He also showed a weakness with visual-motor coordination for printing and copying, scoring at the 12th percentile on the Beery-Buktenica Developmental Test of Visual-Motor Integration. There was no doubt that Cody's visual reasoning, visual processing, and memory system were weak cognitive capacities within his learning profile. Researchers continue to be fascinated by how the human brain can be capable of considerable talent and at the same time show significant cognitive weaknesses.

Cody undoubtedly had severe dyslexia. He also showed serious written output issues and a math disorder. This was all due to the complexity and severity of his visual-perceptual cognitive weaknesses. I had seen this profile for many years; the result is usually slow or minimal progress in acquiring achievement skills. If the child, like Cody, has good verbal intelligence, good self-advocacy skills, determination, and has used accommodations and technology effectively, he can often make it to college or university. It would be difficult to achieve this level of success, however, with the severity of the cognitive weaknesses Cody displayed.

Fortunately for Cody's parents, the impact of Barbara Arrowsmith Young's work had reached Canada's West Coast. Scott and Lisa now had a choice. They could let Cody simply cope with his cognitive weaknesses, or they could move to Vancouver and have him attend the Eaton Arrowsmith School that September.

At the initial Arrowsmith assessment with Sandra Heusel, she outlined the options for Cody. Lisa recalled that meeting: "This was a really hard decision to make. I remember Sandra drawing a picture for us about the difference between getting tutoring and compensatory measures versus going to Eaton Arrowsmith School. She drew a picture associated with EAS that showed the pathway from the eyes and ears to the brain. She didn't push the EAS program, but was forthright when encouraged to give her opinion."

Lisa continued, "We went away and thought about it. We talked to Cody too—not that we would have let him make the decision—and we all agreed that the best approach would be to go directly to the brain route. The testing results had a lot to do with our decision to go for it. Because of my own background in education and experiences of the public system's approach to learning differences, I knew we would need to do something that explicitly addressed Cody's difficulties in a crucial way." Lisa also noted, "I kept wanting to know what was going on in his brain. What was making it different or more difficult for him to learn print tasks?"

Scott and Lisa talked more about this decision upon their return to Cortes Island. Lisa recalls, "Scott and I felt at that point in our lives our most important job was to parent. So we put decisions around parenting first before lifestyle or jobs, and in our case that meant making the move off Cortes Island to Vancouver."

Changing Perceptual Reasoning IQ and Visual Memory

Cody spent three years at Eaton Arrowsmith School, building his cognitive capacity for processing visual-perceptual information. He worked on symbol recognition, visual-perceptual reasoning, visual scanning speed, copying speed, and object recognition. Each school day he spent a total of two hundred minutes working on these cognitive areas, with ninety minutes of homework each evening. That works out to approximately 666 hours per school year.

It was not easy for Cody to sustain active engagement in his cognitive exercises each day. As with other children, it took encouragement to keep him at the school for his third year and continue improving cognitive weaknesses. One of Cody and his parents' frustrations was that his reading and spelling were not developing as soon as they hoped for. However, this would not happen until these cognitive weaknesses moved closer to average. Of course, less severe forms of reading disorders can often benefit from tutoring alone, but in many cases of severe reading failure even the best tutors cannot improve that skill. The more cognitive weaknesses are apparent—for example, in the case of reading acquisition—the more problematic it is to teach a child to read. Cody had severe cognitive weaknesses related to his ability to acquire not only reading, but also spelling, writing, and math skills. It would take time before these would develop to a level commensurate with his grade.

Toward the end of Cody's third year, Scott and Lisa informed me that this would be their son's last; they were moving to the city of Comox on Vancouver Island. We decided to have the psycho-educational assessment updated to see Cody's progress over the last three years. We assumed that, unlike many students who achieve grade level after three years at EAS, Cody's achievement skills would be two or three years below grade level. He had developed rudimentary reading, spelling, math, and writing skills, but we felt there was still a long way to go. Scott and Lisa would need to provide Cody with skill-based tutoring after the Arrowsmith Program. Yet we were still curious about his cognitive changes and how much progress the updated assessment would show.

We were not disappointed. Scott, Lisa, and I and my staff were amazed at Cody's cognitive improvements, which are summarized on table 25:

TABLE 25. CODY'S PSYCHO-EDUCATIONAL ASSESSMENT RESULTS BEFORE AND AFTER EAS

Psycho-Educational Assessment Measure	**Description**	**Before Arrowsmith Program (2006)**	**After Arrowsmith Program (2009)**
Wechsler Intelligence Scale for Children—Third and Fourth Editions		**WISC-III**	**WISC-IV**
Perceptual Reasoning Index	A measure of nonverbal and fluid reasoning.	1st %ile	47th %ile
Matrix Reasoning Subtest	A measure of fluid intelligence and a measure of nonverbal intelligence.	9th %ile	63rd %ile

Psycho-Educational Assessment Measure	**Description**	**Before Arrowsmith Program (2006)**	**After Arrowsmith Program (2009)**
Picture Concepts Subtest	A measure of abstract, categorical reasoning ability.	5th %ile	63rd %ile
Block Design Subtest	Ability to analyze and synthesize abstract visual stimuli.	1st %ile	16th %ile
Woodcock-Johnson Tests of Cognitive Ability—Third Edition		**WJ-III**	**WJ-III**
Phonemic Awareness Subtest	Ability to analyze and synthesize speech sounds.	38th %ile	88th %ile
Beery-Buktenica Developmental Test of Visual-Motor Integration (BEERY)		**BEERY**	**BEERY**
Visual-Motor Coordination Subtest	A measure of accuracy and speed of copying symbols.	12th %ile	74th %ile
Detroit Tests of Learning Aptitude—Third Edition (DTLA)		**DTLA**	**DTLA**
Design Reproduction Subtest	Short-term memory for reproducing visual designs.	5th %ile	75th %ile

Note: The average performance range on psycho-educational assessments is considered to fall between the 25th and 75th %ile ranking.

In three years, Cody's Perceptual Reasoning intelligence score had gone from the 1st percentile (an IQ of 66—borderline) to the 47th percentile (an IQ of 97—average). This was a dramatic improvement, a change in intelligence that I had not seen before. Cody had changed the capacity of his brain to process and reason with the visual-perceptual information coming from his environment. On each of his Matrix Reasoning and Picture Concepts subtests he had moved from low to average, and on his Block Design subtest he had moved from low to low average.[45]

Cody's visual-motor integration had also moved from low to average. With this improvement to his visual-motor coordination, he was now able to control pencil movement more effectively and write down information at a faster pace, though his spelling was still far from grade level. Finally, on the Writing Samples subtest, he had improved to his normal grade level, though spelling was not measured on this test.

Cody was one of the first cases I had observed at EAS where Perceptual Reasoning intelligence shifted dramatically after systematic and intensive cognitive remediation. His brain had improved its capacity to analyze and process visual-perceptual information and make sense of what he was observing, making a clear case for neuroplasticity. Barbara Arrowsmith Young had seen this before, but for me it was new and very exciting. The possibilities of cognitive remediation seemed infinite.

Despite the fact that Cody could have benefited from an additional two years at Eaton Arrowsmith, this boy had acquired the cognitive capacities to analyze and retain visual information. These capacities would be critical to him for the rest of his life. While we would have liked Cody to stay and complete his full-time program, we knew that Lisa and Scott would do whatever they could to make sure their son received the best tutoring and learning assistance possible.

Transition to Public School

We asked Lisa how the transition back to public school had gone for Cody. "It was smooth," she said, "but we did a lot of legwork to pave the way. We continue to keep in close contact with Cody's teachers, with

45. The Matrix Reasoning subtest measures ability to discover patterns within visual designs. The Picture Concepts subtest measures ability to recognize visual social concepts in pictures. The Block Design subtest measures visual-spatial awareness and ability to solve puzzles.

lots of meetings with the school now and before he started, trying to be really clear about his learning differences, where he was coming from academically, and the supports he needed. We met with professionals at all levels in the district who overlap with Cody, and we've tried hard to build positive relationships and ask for what we need. We have been blessed by incredibly wonderful and compassionate educators here in the Comox Valley."

Lisa went on to talk about how Cody felt. "I think Cody was pleasantly surprised by his transition to public school. He loved the variety, the learning, and to find himself among a wide spectrum of kids with all kinds of differences."

Lisa and Scott worked hard to plan effective tutoring services for Cody. With improved cognitive capacity for acquiring reading, spelling, writing, and math skills, he was ready to focus on skill-based training programs in these areas. Regarding phonetics programs, Lisa said, "We did phonics, multisensory spelling, repeated timed readings, independent reading and response, whole-word approach [building sight-word recognition], and a variety of short writing activities. This was a home-grown program that I created with help from Eaton Arrowsmith suggestions for Cody's learning and other suggestions from the learning assistance teachers in Comox and Vancouver. I also did some of my own research on this topic and utilized my teaching experience. We have a wonderful situation with an experienced teacher assistant who works at Cody's school and tutors him twice a day, for three days a week. I've given her some training, but she also brings a wealth of experience to what she is doing with Cody and we adjust the program as necessary through lots of communication."

In September 2010, as Cody entered Grade 7, Lisa noted that he was making increasingly faster progress in his reading. Nevertheless, because he still had more work to do on his achievement skills, he sometimes received help in the form of a reader and scribe. He also received extra support to develop his math skills. His Grade 6 report card showed Bs in science, social studies, health and career, and physical education. He received a C+ in language arts, core French, dance, and music. He received an A- in visual arts.

Cody's principal's comment on his Grade 6 report card: "A fine accomplishment, Cody. You have much to be proud of. Your inner strength and determination are noteworthy."

What Does Neuroplasticity Mean for Education?

There is no question in the minds of the Eaton Arrowsmith staff that intelligence can change. We have observed it. Research outside of the Arrowsmith Program is also highlighting this fact.[46] David Shenk's book, *The Genius in All of Us: Why Everything You've Been Told about Genetics, Talent, and IQ Is Wrong* (New York: Doubleday, 2010), is an insightful book into this specific issue.

Through our data-gathering efforts at Eaton Arrowsmith School, we are constant witnesses to intelligence changes among our graduates as they receive updated psycho-educational assessments from other learning centres. Intelligence tests show dramatic improvements in cognitive capacities such as perceptual reasoning, nonverbal intelligence, processing speed, and working memory. Beyond intelligence measures, we are observing improvements in visual-motor integration, motor coordination, visual memory for symbols, and expressive and receptive language abilities. Finally, depending on the type of learning disability, we have also observed significant shifts in mathematical reasoning, reading comprehension, reading speed, writing fluency, written expression, and math calculation skills. There is much research ahead of us. These are exciting times in neuro-educational developments.

What does it mean for education if intelligence is not fixed? In particular, what does it mean for the field of learning disabilities? First, the entire psychological and educational assessment business needs to be revisited in terms of diagnosing or labelling children with learning disorders or

46. Susanne M. Jaeggi, Martin Buschkuehl, John Jonides, and Walter J. Perrig from the Department of Psychology, University of Michigan, and the Department of Psychology, University of Bern, Switzerland, published a 2008 study entitled, "Improving Fluid Intelligence with Training on Working Memory" (http://www.ncbi.nlm.nih.gov/pmc/articles/PMC2383929/). The researchers concluded that fluid intelligence improvement occurs with training and is dependent on the amount of training. *Fluid intelligence* is the intelligence used to reason and solve new problems that do not require acquired knowledge.

disabilities. For example, if a child is tested and found to have severe perceptual organization intellectual deficits, one cannot simply assume that this is a lifetime sentence. Cody is a perfect example of this. A child can actually improve visual-perceptual cognitive functioning through intensive and systematic cognitive remediation. This will in turn dramatically improve overall intelligence for this child.

Before this kind of thinking becomes mainstream, several things must happen. First, professionals who conduct psycho-educational assessments for the purpose of diagnosing learning disabilities must assume nothing about what an intelligence score or measure is saying about future possibilities. Of course, a growing number of psychologists, psychiatrists, and educators already understand this. Second, teachers must be informed that intelligence is not fixed. It is too easy for a special education, learning assistance, or regular classroom teacher to review a child's assessment documentation, see an IQ score, and make assumptions about ability or possibilities. Teachers in training need to be informed of the limited predictability of intelligence measures and that intelligence can greatly improve through cognitive remediation. Teacher training is also important because children who are told that intelligence is fixed are vulnerable to negative feedback and may back away from educational challenges.[47] On the other hand, children who understand that intelligence is malleable recover more effectively from learning failures.

Teachers can lead the way in informing children and parents that intelligence is not fixed. For parents, teachers, and others in the education field to understand that intelligence can change based on experiences offers great hope for anyone struggling academically. Certainly, as we saw in the case of Cody, a severe deficit in a major category of intelligence as measured on the WISC-IV may require hundreds of hours of cognitive remediation, but the fact remains that intelligence can change. The greatest problem is integrating cognitive remediation programs into

---

47. Jennifer A. Mangels, Brady Butterfield, Justin Lamb, Catherine Good, and Carol S. Dweck, "Why Do Beliefs about Intelligence Influence Learning Success? A Social Cognitive Neuroscience Model," *Social Cognitive and Affective Neuroscience* 1, no. 2 (Oxford University Press, 2006), 75–86. http://scan.oxfordjournals.org/content/1/2/75.full.

school districts so more children can have access to them. One of Barbara Arrowsmith Young's dreams is that primary classrooms will have access to cognitive remediation programs so cognitive capacity weaknesses can be identified and remediated as early as possible.

12

She Inspires Me

Have you ever said things backwards, copied down the wrong math question in math class, or just forgotten how to spell simple words? Well, I did, until I started attending Eaton Arrowsmith School.

—EMILY, GRADE 10

Emily

French immersion was not working out for Emily. The happy, inquisitive, red-haired, freckled six-year-old was not learning to read and spell in French. She was much better at listening and speaking in French. Jeff and Michelle, her parents, were becoming increasingly concerned. Their older daughter had also struggled early, but eventually school had worked out for her. Would it be the same for Emily?

Over coffee in their kitchen on a sunny Vancouver day, Jeff and Michelle recalled those confusing days. Michelle said, "Our eldest daughter, Lauren, struggled in French immersion, particularly with reading. She wasn't learning the French alphabet the way other kids did in preschool and kindergarten. I remember thinking, 'Oh, I'll be so happy when Emily starts—she will be okay. It'll just come like it does with all the other kids.'"

It did not turn out that way for Emily. Michelle continued, "Emily was slower at picking up the French alphabet. It was kindergarten when it was pretty clear that she was struggling. I took her to a friend of mine who's a speech pathologist and [provides] Orton-Gillingham training. Well, she started doing the basic Orton-Gillingham training with Emily, without any formal assessment."

Jeff and Michelle knew Emily was struggling with French reading and spelling, and felt it was important to get English reading and spelling going as soon as possible. The learning assistance teacher at Emily's French immersion school was providing sound/symbol training for the French language, but Emily was not grasping it. Her parents did not want her to fall even further behind in her early acquisition of both French and English.

Jeff reflected on Emily's unbalanced acquisition of French. "Interestingly," he said, "in terms of the way the mind works, her acquisition of oral French was completely normal. She actually did fine with oral French. It's just in the reading and writing that problems showed up."[48]

Fortunately, Emily was not showing any signs of emotional distress at this time. By Grade 3, however, Jeff and Michelle needed to make a decision: keep Emily in French immersion or leave and enrol her in an all-English public school. They talked to both Emily's classroom teacher and the learning assistance teacher. The latter felt Emily could stay in French immersion; she noted that Emily's older sister, Lauren, had struggled early and eventually caught up. However, in the classroom teacher's opinion, explained Michelle, "It was quite clear that Emily wouldn't make it in French immersion."

Emily was enrolled at Lord Bradley Elementary School for Grade 4, in an English-speaking classroom. It was 2001, and by this time Michelle

---

48. In British Columbia, the French immersion programs experience children who drop out due to difficulties with reading and spelling acquisition. Dr. Monique Bournot-Trites, an assistant professor at the University of British Columbia's Department of Modern Language Education and Centre for Intercultural Language Studies, has studied this problem. Bournot-Trites noted that there needs to be more phonemic awareness training for children in primary French immersion grades and additional sound/symbol instruction. Bournot-Trites is working to further improve French immersion teacher training, so fewer children struggle with early acquisition of French reading and spelling. The problems faced by French immersion programs with early reading and spelling acquisition are similar to those of English-speaking public schools.

and Jeff had learned of the Arrowsmith Program. Michelle said, "I'd heard Barbara Arrowsmith Young speak. Somebody had given me a poster about a public school presentation she was giving." Jeff agreed, noting, "I'd read an entire article about her program and accomplishments."

At Lord Bradley, Emily was still behind her peers in basic reading, spelling, and writing skills, so the Orton-Gillingham tutoring continued. She was receiving three days a week of Orton-Gillingham tutoring and additional support in the school's learning assistance classroom. Michelle said, "We were hoping that might be enough." Jeff added, "This is what kind of worked for Lauren, though Lauren stayed in French immersion and went on to a French high school program."

To help Emily in the classroom, the teacher assigned a buddy to take notes. Emily was not only struggling with reading, spelling, and writing, but because of poor visual-motor integration output, she was slow at copying notes from the board. Her brain could not translate the messages she was receiving from her visual processing system to her motor system to coordinate the copying movement needed to form the symbols she was seeing on the board. This cognitive capacity weakness slowed her note taking and caused her to read slowly and make errors when copying math questions. Another problem was limited written output and poor spelling during writing activities—at school and at home. This would become more evident to Jeff and Michelle when Emily was given the Arrowsmith assessment to identify specific cognitive capacity weaknesses.

Michelle remembers Emily's classroom note-taking buddy. "In math, Emily's friend Amanda would copy the problems from the board. Emily was also supposed to be copying the questions, but she couldn't do that at all."

Emily had also begun to have feelings of isolation and of being different from her peers in the classroom. Jeff said, "For Emily, it was not so much an emotional frustration, as I remember it. It was more the feeling that she didn't like being the odd one out. She didn't like having to continue to ask for assistance. That's what I remember in particular."

Michelle continued her husband's thought: "I remember it—I think it was in Grade 4. It was night after night, putting her to bed. She'd seem fine in the day, and then she'd be crying and crying and crying at bedtime. She would say, 'I wish I'd never been born. I want to die.'" Michelle stopped for a moment and then continued, "It was hard for her to put words on it—why she felt that way. But she felt it. She had lots of support; her teachers were great, the kids were great. Nobody made her feel like she was stupid, but she could see everybody else reading. It was very hard. I remember it because we went through the same thing night after night."

Jeff and Michelle felt they had to do something to help Emily regain her confidence. They looked at Barlow Academy, a private school for children with language-based learning disabilities, as a solution for the start of Grade 6. For Emily, it was a saving grace at a time of self-confidence loss. Michelle said, "I credit Barlow Academy; it was the best thing. [Teachers told] Emily, 'You're special. You're smart. What you have is a learning *difference*.' It was like night and day for her. She actually came to think of her learning differences as something good about herself. She felt very validated."

By the end of Grade 7, Jeff and Michelle felt that Emily, now twelve and feeling more self-confident, might be able to handle a mainstream public school system. Could Emily transition to the Grade 8 high school program with success?

Jeff and Michelle knew Emily still showed some difficulties with independent reading and written expression, but she was certainly more confident and had learned some good organization and planning skills. Her marks at Barlow Academy were good in math, science, social studies, and English. However, progress in Orton-Gillingham was slow. Michelle said, "I thought she would always need scribes and readers—that she wouldn't be able to do it herself. We were still timing her to read every day and in the summer [as a way to get her to read independently for specific periods of time]. We'd always read to her and she loved books and stories. She'd listen to stories on tape endlessly. But to get her to read herself—it was just work."

Jeff and Michelle prepared their daughter's application for Grade 8 at public high school. Emily was interested in the Grade 8 Declan Arts Program. The application was sent in and she was accepted. Then Michelle heard that Eaton Arrowsmith School would be opening at a facility located on the University of British Columbia campus. Michelle noted,

"I ran into another parent. She'd been to one of the introductory evenings discussing the start [of EAS] and had told me about it. I already knew about the Arrowsmith Program, but wasn't aware then that a Vancouver school was opening. There was another talk two days later, and I went to that."

Jeff and Michelle were interested in having Emily take part in the Arrowsmith Program at some level. Jeff liked the idea of improving neurological functioning. He said, "I knew about child development, what brain functioning and brain plasticity were. I knew that it was a legitimate program. So that wasn't the issue."

The results of Emily's initial 2005 Arrowsmith Assessment, outlined in table 26, showed that Emily needed to be in the full-time program at the Eaton Arrowsmith School.

TABLE 26. EMILY'S INITIAL ARROWSMITH ASSESSMENT RESULTS

Cognitive Function	Description	Emily's Level of Difficulty
Motor-Symbol Sequencing	Problems associated with printing neatly and copying quickly. Careless errors in math, slow reading speed, inconsistent spelling.	Moderate to Mild
Symbol Relations	Problems understanding concepts and cause-and-effect reasoning. Logical-reasoning problems.	Moderate
Memory for Information and Instructions	Trouble remembering oral instruction, difficulty following lectures or extended conversations.	Moderate to Severe
Broca's Speech Pronunciation	Mispronouncing words, avoiding using words, speaking in incomplete sentences.	Moderate to Mild
Symbol Recognition	Poor word recognition, slow reading, difficulty spelling.	Average to Mild

Cognitive Function	Description	Emily's Level of Difficulty
Object Recognition	Trouble finding objects, difficulty recalling the visual details of pictures, problem remembering visual cues.	Moderate to Severe
Artifactual Thinking	Problems understanding and interpreting social cues.	Mild to Moderate

By this time, Emily was one week into her studies at Declan High School. Jeff said, "We let her get started at Declan because we hadn't heard back from [EAS] yet. We were a little concerned about her written output as well, though there was also a sense that she could potentially manage high school, because she had acquired a lot of skills in terms of writing and comprehension at Barlow Academy. So we were very much on the edge and having our fingers crossed—that kind of thing."

Michelle recalls that during Emily's first week at Declan problems arose with her written expression abilities. "I remember one thing about that week. In English, she had to write something about her summer and she brought it home. Jeff looked at it a few days later and he couldn't even tell what she was trying to say. That was her written output at the start of Grade 8."

Emily was told she would benefit from being in the Arrowsmith program, but she was also given the option of either staying at Declan or going to Eaton Arrowsmith School. She had friends attending EAS, which would make a transition easier. Interestingly, the issue that seemed to bother Emily most was having to give up the diagnosis of dyslexia she had carried for so long. Michelle explained, "If she went to Eaton Arrowsmith School [where programs are designed to remediate weak cognitive capacities that result in learning disabilities like dyslexia], she might not be dyslexic anymore, and she wouldn't be special. She really had that as part of her identity."[49] After some family discussion, she decided to attend the Eaton Arrowsmith School and improve her weak cognitive capacities.

49. A great deal of effort has gone into removing the negative connotations from the label or

Emily at Eaton Arrowsmith

Emily began her first day at Eaton Arrowsmith School near the end of September 2005. She appeared confident as she started on her cognitive exercises. Emily's Arrowsmith assessment results had highlighted moderate to severe problems with Memory for Information and Instructions, meaning she could easily miss oral information presented by a teacher in a regular education classroom setting. She showed moderate to mild difficulties with Motor-Symbol Sequencing, or ability to learn and produce a written sequence of symbols. This difficulty was hindering her written output, spelling, copying efficiency, and reading speed. As well, she showed problems with Symbol Relations—the ability to see cause and effect—at the moderate level. Emily also showed cognitive weakness with Object Recognition, which resulted in her having difficulty visually recognizing and remember the details of objects and thus struggling to find things and remember visual cues such as landmarks. This also affected her Artifactual Thinking, or social perception, in which she showed mild to moderate problems.

Sarah Cohen and Mark Watson welcomed Emily enthusiastically. They introduced themselves to her parents and learned more about the student with whom they would spend the next two years. "Emily came into our classroom after the school year had started and was quiet and serious," Sarah said. "She learned how to do the exercises, didn't complain, and worked hard. At the end of her first year, she exceeded many benchmark expectations of the Arrowsmith program, such as mastering the Symbol Relations exercise much more quickly than expected. She developed a solid group of friends who were positive and supportive of one another."

---

diagnosis of *dyslexia* for children and adults with this and other learning disabilities. It is important for children with these disabilities not to see themselves as just dyslexic or learning disabled, but to see their strengths or talents. In fact, Emily had been taught dyslexia was a positive trait, and the idea that the Arrowsmith Program wanted to improve the cognitive capacities that caused her dyslexia contradicted this. This issue is complex; the Arrowsmith Program has been criticized by those who are closely attached to the concept of dyslexia as positive. It needs to be emphasized that the Arrowsmith Program will not eliminate gifts that a student may have alongside the learning disability. Rather, the program improves dyslexia's various cognitive weaknesses.

Active engagement, or focus, drives the level of plasticity of the brain. Neuroplasticity does not occur if the brain is not focused on a task, usually a novel task. The EAS students who progress the most quickly are those who actively engage in their tasks every minute of the day, and this was the case for Emily. She made singular progress in her first year at our school.

Sarah Cohen described Emily's second year at Eaton Arrowsmith School: "She was able to see changes in her academic performance in both math and English, and she took up independent studies of both Grade 9 science and social studies through distance education [to prepare herself for entry into Grade 10 public school]. She flourished in math and became quite competitive with her peers, pushing them all to do their best—top score on a math test was the prize they all wanted, largely due to Emily's strength in leading them on."

Sarah continued, "Emily's spelling did not change much, though, something she would mention fairly regularly. All her cognitive areas of weakness to do with spelling improved, but she still had to learn the correct spellings for words. She definitely saw this as a weakness and was embarrassed about it. She used it to denigrate herself. It was like a reminder of what her limitations had been, a reminder of all the things she previously could not do.

"As her final year went on, we could count on Emily to do class presentations about her distance-education assignments, lead groups in games, coach students who were feeling discouraged, teach exercises to students who were trying out the school for a day, be vocal in class discussions, and try to work out disputes between friends by being empathetic but holding her ground. She always brought the best of herself to her schoolwork both in her cognitive exercises and in her academics. I believe it was this strength and determination that resulted in her dramatic cognitive changes and academic success. In my teaching career I have yet to encounter another student with the strength, certainty of purpose, and determination that comes close to matching Emily's. When I saw her final Arrowsmith testing I was indeed impressed, but I wasn't surprised. From Emily, I would have expected nothing less."

However, Emily was still a weak speller and would once again require content skill training in spelling rules and patterns, such as that provided by Orton-Gillingham. She had already received four years of Orton-Gillingham tutoring to improve spelling ability prior to the Arrowsmith Program, but because of the combination of her cognitive weaknesses for acquiring spelling, she had not progressed much. Now, after completion of the Arrowsmith Program, she had developed the cognitive capacity to acquire spelling ability, and it was time to reintroduce her to phonics, sound/symbol association, and spelling rules. Remarkably, her word-decoding skills had gone from Grade 5 to Grade 12 level in the first year of her program, but spelling mattered to her more as it was visible, something others could judge her on. Her weak spelling had a negative impact on her self-esteem, even though she was showing great cognitive progress otherwise. Unfortunately, in some schools today the emphasis is not on the reasoning mind, but achievements such as spelling abilities. Educators need to begin shifting this reality for their students.

Emily's final Arrowsmith assessment was conducted in May 2007, the results of which are shown on table 27.

TABLE 27. EMILY'S FINAL ARROWSMITH ASSESSMENT RESULTS

Cognitive Function	Description	Emily's Level of Difficulty
Motor-Symbol Sequencing	Problems associated with printing neatly and copying quickly. Careless errors in math, slow reading speed, inconsistent spelling.	Mild
Symbol Relations	Problems understanding concepts and cause-and-effect reasoning. Logical-reasoning problems.	Above Average
Memory for Information and Instructions	Trouble remembering oral instruction, difficulty following lectures or extended conversations.	Mild

Cognitive Function	Description	Emily's Level of Difficulty
Broca's Speech Pronunciation	Mispronouncing words, avoiding using words, speaking in incomplete sentences.	Mild
Symbol Recognition	Poor word recognition, slow reading, difficulty spelling.	Above Average
Object Recognition	Trouble finding objects, difficulty recalling the visual details of pictures, problem remembering visual cues.	Average
Artifactual Thinking	Problems understanding and interpreting social cues.	Average to Mild

Emily was now above average in Symbol Relations; her score on the Munzert Reasoning Test was at the 99th percentile (up from 45th percentile ranking) and her reading comprehension at the Grade 9 level. Before starting the Arrowsmith Program, she had been at the Grade 5 level in reading speed; because of her work on Motor-Symbol Sequencing, her reading speed was now measured at the Grade 10 level. Her parents noticed that, for the first time, Emily was enjoying reading—she was reading more books than she ever had before.

Michelle and Jeff were asked if they had noticed any major changes in their daughter after her first year in the Arrowsmith Program. Michelle said, "What was stunning for me was what happened during our summer holiday. Remember, before we used to have to time her to read, so she would at least try. We would say, 'You have to read ten minutes a day,' which didn't seem like much. That summer we did a road trip to the Grand Canyon. She would hike on ahead of us, and she'd be sitting there reading her book and waiting for us to catch up. Everybody was walking by her, thinking, 'Why is this girl reading a book?'"

Jeff added, "She must have read twenty-five books on that vacation. The previous year she'd read two or three books. She was now quite happy to switch from audiotape and CD books to the written word."

Emily was also now capable of recognizing and tracking letter patterns at a faster speed. Her work on Motor-Symbol Sequencing was also improving her copying text speed, in which she had moved from the 30th percentile to the 65th percentile after only her first year and to the 80th percentile after her second year. Her score on Memory for Information and Instructions (oral language memory) had moved from moderate-severe to mild. It was now much easier for her to follow oral directions and absorb information in class. She also had dramatically improved her Object Recognition ability, moving to the average range. Her Artifactual Thinking rating moved to average-mild. She had less likelihood of losing things and being disorganized with her belongings, and had improved her visual awareness for social interaction and patterns. Now she could transition to regular public school education and be able to listen to her teachers, remember what they said, and take notes from the board. She could more quickly read books or assignment documentation, get ideas on paper, and understand conceptual information. Her spelling, still a problem, would improve over time with her strengthened cognitive capacities for holding spelling patterns. In the meantime, she could make use of spell-check technology on the computer. We told Jeff and Michelle that because of her strength with active engagement, her program would end in two years, not four as we had originally predicted. They were delighted for Emily.

Emily One Year after Leaving Eaton Arrowsmith

Even more exciting was the letter I received from Jeff one year later, in April 2008. Emily had made a successful transition to regular public school. A copy of her report card was included in the letter, showing that she was getting Bs and As in her various courses. Jeff and Michelle had also updated Emily's psycho-educational assessment through the Vancouver School Board. Because of her spelling problem—her only achievement weakness—Emily was still allowed the diagnosis of a learning disability, making her eligible for tutoring.

The results from her intelligence testing were even more intriguing. Her psycho-educational assessment three years earlier had highlighted average to above-average intelligence, and now the school board psychologist had diagnosed Emily as gifted. That meant that her IQ score was now in the superior range, or above the 90th percentile ranking, in the top 10 percent for her age group. She was given the label Gifted–Learning Disabled because of high IQ and weak spelling ability. Not surprisingly, this designation confused many parents and teachers.

An analysis of Emily's different psycho-educational assessment results showed increased intelligence, ability to process visual information faster, and improvements in her reasoning capacity. A skeptic might attribute this to any number of factors, but the fact was that Emily had worked on these cognitive capacities for two years with the Arrowsmith Program. She had made cognitive improvements that directly affected her overall intelligence. She could begin working with an Orton-Gillingham tutor again as she now had the cognitive capacity to develop spelling skills. The proof of Emily's success was in her grades, her self-esteem, and her happiness at school.

One's IQ is not nearly as important as one's "I can do." Emily had a strong work ethic, high active engagement, and she was bright. This made her transition back to regular high school much easier. Prior to the Arrowsmith Program, even Emily herself was aware that she did not have the cognitive capacities to deal with her learning environments. She would not have used the term *cognitive capacities*, but she had simply felt she was not smart enough. Yet she had the potential; she just needed to fine-tune her brain and benefit from its plasticity. She focused on the cognitive exercises, and the results were impressive. She made profound cognitive shifts in her neurological ability.

Jeff and Michelle realize that a great deal of intervention took place between Emily's leaving the French immersion program at Lord Bradley and graduating from the full-time Arrowsmith Program. She received much support from Orton-Gillingham tutors, the Barlow Academy, and Eaton Arrowsmith School. Each teacher and program made a difference at various levels. As Jeff stated, "It's easy to measure what happened between the end of Lord Bradley and the end of Arrowsmith. I mean, it's just a stark difference in terms of Emily's ability to function in a public school classroom." Jeff continued, "And of course, within that time span, at Eaton Arrowsmith School there was that dramatic improvement in reading. Her desire to read, her ability to read, and of course, her written output. I just don't think it would have happened without the Arrowsmith Program." Michelle added, "I'm really glad we did the Arrowsmith Program. I've seen a number of kids, and we have friends who have kids who have a learning disability and haven't had a program like this, who just basically check out of school."

In June 2009, Jeff e-mailed EAS, stating:

> *Emily has just completed Grade 11 at Cadwell Creek Secondary School. She has been consistently on the honour roll. She uses a skills block to do assignments and rarely accesses help from the teachers or tutors in the room, yet she hasn't had any tutoring outside of school.*

Three months before her graduation, in March 2010, Jeff again e-mailed us:

> *Emily is completing her Grade 12 at Cadwell Creek Secondary. After the two years of impressive effort at* EAS, *Emily slowed down some for Grades 10 and 11 but still she made the Honour Roll. She's really keen to get into a school back east and has an average of around 92 percent. She has early acceptance at three universities and is hoping to go to McGill for Business Studies.*

I e-mailed Emily to congratulate her. She replied:

> *I have been accepted to Queens, Western, and McGill. Next year I will be going to McGill for business. This year I am taking math (93%), history (92%), philosophy (93%), geography (95%), comparative civilizations (97%), and law (83%). I also already completed English last summer with a 92. So far, Grade 12's not too bad, and I am very excited for next year.*

Emily had come a long way from leaving her French immersion program at Lord Bradley, crying at bedtime, and feeling that her life was not worth living.

During Emily's last year at Eaton Arrowsmith, she entered the YWCA Real Story Competition essay contest. The impact of the Arrowsmith Program on Emily's life had been so great that she decided her essay topic would be Barbara Arrowsmith Young. Emily was nominated as one of the finalists because of the following essay:

She Inspires Me

Have you ever said things backwards, copied down the wrong math question in math class, or just forgotten how to spell simple words? Well, I did, until I started attending Eaton Arrowsmith School, a school for children and young adults with dyslexia [and] other learning disabilities. Eaton Arrowsmith does this by using the Arrowsmith Program designed by Barbara Arrowsmith Young. She made this astonishing program to help other people like herself to strengthen cognitive weaknesses. She did all of this work with a severe learning disability herself. Barbara Arrowsmith Young inspires me because she created this amazing program despite her own weaknesses, and it has helped me and my peers immensely.

Ms. Arrowsmith Young created this unlikely program to help others like her overcome their learning disabilities. Her program was first met with disapproval from psychologists researching the brain because they believed that you could not strengthen areas of weakness. It was common belief that all people with learning disabilities could do was to find a way or ways to work around them. Ms. Arrowsmith Young discovered nineteen different deficits in the human brain and found different kinds of exercises to help strengthen each one, but the really incredible thing is that she has spent the last thirty years studying and improving her program, and still is. Now she is the principal of the school she set up, and is still devoted to helping kids and young adults overcome their learning disabilities. Her program is gaining respect and interest, and there are new schools popping up all over North America. One of these [is] the Eaton Arrowsmith School in Vancouver, which I attend, where she also helps with testing the students for learning difficulties. Ms. Arrowsmith Young did all of this unusual work with her own learning troubles.

Ms. Arrowsmith Young herself had an interesting array of mental strengths and weaknesses. For instance, she had an extraordinary visual and auditory memory, although she had a really hard time pronouncing words. As this is one of my problems, I can relate to the way it feels to not be able to say the thing you want, not because you don't know what to say, but because you cannot pronounce it. Ms. Arrowsmith Young could not tell left from right and could not read a map. This means that she had poor cause and affect [*sic*] skills, and she could not read an analogue clock. Most people don't think that planning ahead is that important unless you want to be a football or chess player, but in Ms. Arrowsmith Young's case she could not even clean her own desk, because of her inability to plan. She had a really hard time with kinesthetics, which means she could not recognize objects or tell where her body parts were in relation to her surroundings. She could not hold a glass of juice in her left hand without spilling. She had to replay simple conversations or movie scenes twenty times over in her head because by the time she got to the end of each sentence, she would have forgotten the meaning of the beginning. She had many different learning disabilities but she never gave up despite them.

I find Ms. Arrowsmith Young inspiring, not just because of her hard work and willpower, but also because of what she has done to help me. She has shown me that a lot of determination can go a long way, and that things are never impossible. I thought that I would never like to read, that it might get easier but it would always be a struggle for me. Now, since I have started attending Eaton Arrowsmith School where I work on Ms. Arrowsmith Young's program every day, I've started to read and even enjoy it. For the last few years, in the summer, I might have read one to two books and that was with my parents pushing me to continue. Last summer, after my first year at Eaton Arrowsmith, I read twenty books and my parents had to tell me to put my book down, to sleep and eat. I've always really enjoyed stories, and I'm so thankful that I can now enjoy them without struggle. Also, my printing and hand-eye coordination has improved immensely, and if someone tosses me a pen, I can catch it now. Ms. Arrowsmith Young's program has helped me unbelievably, and I will hopefully be able to attend normal high school next year and be able to keep up with everyone else.

I feel Barbara Arrowsmith Young is really brave and innovative for going against what psychologists had been saying for years and coming up with this new program. She also acted as her own guinea pig and started running her program in a one-room school that she set up in Ontario. Now she has her program running all over North America and it is becoming more and more well known throughout the world. Arrowsmith Young has also created such a warm and caring environment with her program [that] if you just walk into my school you are welcome and all the staff wants you to succeed. Barbara Arrowsmith Young has changed my life forever and I thank her so much for that.

Emily acknowledged that the Arrowsmith Program had changed her life academically. Perhaps equally important, she had found the program enjoyable. "I had fun," she said. "It was challenging, but I had fun."

Part III

The Outlook

13

Arrowsmith and the Future of Education and Neuroscience

When we seek for connection, we restore the world to wholeness. Our seemingly separate lives become more meaningful as we discover how truly necessary we are to each other.

—MARGARET WHEATLEY, ED.D., ORGANIZATIONAL CONSULTANT AND AUTHOR

Exceptions to Success

It must be emphasized here that the case studies in the preceding chapters have not been used because they are exceptional; rather, because they are the norm. In fact, in the process of selecting additional EAS graduates to interview for a second book, I am having difficulty deciding which ones *not* to use because their stories are all so uplifting. The overall success rate at Eaton Arrowsmith School is remarkably high, which continues to delight me and the other EAS staff members. Last year we polled seventy of the graduate families whose children had finished the full-time program, and 100 percent stated that the Arrowsmith Program had been very beneficial for their child. All but one said they would refer other families to our school.

From the data Eaton Arrowsmith School has gathered, the grade-point average of our graduates falls within the 75 to 80 percent range after they have completed one to two years of regular school studies. In 2007, the Toronto Catholic District School Board (TCDSB) in cooperation with the Arrowmsith Program completed a study that produced similar results: the grade-point average on the students' high school report cards was 79 percent.[50] Of the elementary school children who received the Arrowsmith Program in the TCDSB, 69 percent of them no longer needed special education support services. Prior to the Arrowsmith Program, 95 percent of them required resource assistance. Of the 5 percent who had not received resource support prior to entry in the Arrowsmith Program, all were waiting for either identification of their learning disorder or for resource support.

In fact, 90 percent of the students who graduate from the Arrowsmith Program at Eaton Arrowsmith School are succeeding academically. Seventy-five percent of the students achieve the levels described in this book's case studies and 15 percent of the students achieve a B− or C average in school.

There are students who have struggled after completing the Arrowsmith Program at Eaton Arrowsmith School. The numbers are low—approximately 10 percent of our graduates. Staff members have followed these students closely, giving advice, encouragement, and counselling to most of the families involved. A few need a year of the regular school environment before showing signs of integration. Other students are coping with emotional problems (e.g., family disruptions such as parental divorce or separation, which may cause anxiety or depression). Still others have families who have resisted medication for untreated ADHD symptoms not related to cognitive weaknesses. Finally, there are a few students who simply don't care enough about their education in public school. They have the cognitive functioning abilities but are not attending classes regularly or doing the homework. They don't feel connected with the educational

---

50. Arrowsmith School, "Report on the Arrowsmith Program in the Toronto Catholic District School Board" (January 25, 2007). http://www.arrowsmithschool.org/research.htm.

system. Success in school requires passion, motivation, and determination to concentrate in class, do homework, and study for exams.

Hope for Advancement in Neuroscience and Education

In September 2009, I was invited to speak at the 17th National Learning Disabilities Conference in Whitehorse, Yukon, on the topic of neuroplasticity and learning disabilities. This was the first talk about the Arrowsmith Program and its impact on the field of learning disabilities at a national conference in Canada. Psychologists, principals, teachers, and parents were present, as were representatives from learning disabilities associations throughout Canada. Included was the Learning Disabilities Association of Saskatchewan, which is offering the Arrowsmith Program in their facility in Saskatoon, Saskatchewan.

I began my presentation with a discussion of how, for decades, the field of learning disabilities throughout North America has focused almost exclusively on intervention for reading and spelling difficulties. Consequently, most research funding and practical applications have also gone into this area of academic achievement. While it is true that many children have reading-based learning disabilities, this focus means that the other types of learning disabilities such as written expression and mathematics are given less attention. As a result, thousands of children across North America are not given appropriate intervention for the variety of cognitive disorders that exist.

For example, written expression learning disabilities are the most common.[51] Yet there is little remediation for children with written expression disorders other than the use of assistive technology such as a laptop or scribe to bypass the learning problems. Math-based learning disabilities are another common problem for children, yet little cognitive intervention or support is available except extra tutoring and allowing students to use a calculator. Approximately 65 to 80 percent of children with learning disabilities struggle with social perception, and reasoning and

---

51. S.D. Mayes and S.L. Calhoun, "Challenging the Assumptions about the Frequency and Coexistence of Learning Disability Types," *School Psychology International* 28 (2008), 437–448.

critical-thinking learning disorders are also common, yet little cognitive intervention is available.

The Arrowsmith Program is the first cognitive remediation system that addresses *multiple types* of learning disabilities. This was a surprise to many attending the conference; they had viewed the Arrowsmith Program solely as a reading intervention, similar to the programs they had been using for years. This was the first time many of them had fully recognized the broad scope and potential of the Arrowsmith Program. The fact that the program addresses reading, math, written expression, reasoning, memory, spatial thinking, social perception, attention, executive function, auditory processing, planning, and organization was the main new idea attendees took away from the conference.

The Arrowsmith Program, founded on neuroscientific research, involves intensive and graduated mental exercises designed to strengthen the underlying weak cognitive capacities that are the source of the learning disabilities. Over thirty years of experience has demonstrated that these affected cognitive areas can be improved through these exercises, resulting in increased mental capacities and strengthened learning abilities. Research at Arrowsmith School has also shown that when the deficient area is improved, the individual's ability to perform complex tasks such as reading or writing also improves.

The Arrowsmith Program has conducted research showing its positive results, and we are excited about the possibility of further research. If future generations of educational researchers and policy-makers will embrace the contributions from the field of neuroscience and capitalize on scientists' abilities to measure the brain during learning activities, they will be able to measure the effectiveness of programs and interventions for students with learning disabilities in new ways. By recognizing the relationship that neuroscientists and educators can have, new measures can be developed to investigate claims made about the effectiveness of all intervention methods currently being promoted. In short, all of us involved in the education of children with learning disabilities need to continue improving our programs through rigorous scientific research.

The International Mind, Brain, and Education Society, established in 2004, was created to foster awareness of the importance of the relationship between education and neuroscience. One of the organization's mandates is to bridge the gap between education and neuroscience. Current research published in the *Mind, Brain, and Education Journal* in March 2009, in an article entitled "How Many Brains Does It Take to Build a New Light? Knowledge Management Challenges of a Transdisciplinary Project," investigated the challenges of bringing both educators and neuroscientists together for the common purpose of improving educational practice. It stated:

> Some educational researchers seemed to perceive neuroscience research as a potential threat to principles about learning established by social science research, which they had built their careers on. Furthermore, only a few education policy-makers accepted invitations to our meetings, possibly because some of them were intimidated by arcane neuroscience and some of them saw a political danger related to the concerns of educational researchers. Namely, that education had thus far always used the social sciences (psychology, sociology, philosophy, etc.) as reference disciplines and they feared that these disciplines would suddenly be neglected and replaced by neuroscience.[52]

Despite these challenges, many educators and policy-makers understand that, through advances in neuroscience, great progress in educational methods can be made. Advances in neuroscience increase our understanding of how to create and apply educational methods in order to better serve all students.

The final remarks in my presentation referred to the definitions of learning disabilities from both the Learning Disabilities Association of Canada[53] and the Learning Disabilities Association of America,[54] which both state that a learning disability is lifelong. Through the Arrowsmith

---

52. B. Chiesa, V. Christoph, and C. Hinton, "How Many Brains Does It Take to Build a New Light: Knowledge Management Challenges of a Transdisciplinary Project," *Mind, Brain, and Education* 3 (2009), 17–26.
53. http://www.ldac-acta.ca/learn-more/ld-defined/official-definition-of-learning-disabilities.html.
54. http://www.ldanatl.org/new_to_ld/defining.asp.

Program, we are observing that this is by no means always the case. In psycho-educational assessments conducted one or two years after completing the Arrowsmith Program, some children are no longer classified as having a learning disability. This is because their cognitive functions, intellectual abilities, and achievement abilities have improved to the point that there is no longer a large discrepancy between the three areas. Because of the brain's plasticity, the notion that a learning disability is lifelong needs to be held up for thorough questioning.

I was grateful for the chance to speak at the 17th National Conference on Learning Disabilities. It is exciting to see learning disabilities associations throughout Canada interested in implementing the Arrowsmith Program. The successes of the LDA Saskatchewan Arrowsmith Program, Eaton Arrowsmith School Vancouver, Eaton Arrowsmith School Victoria, the Eaton Brain Improvement Centre,[55] and other programs underway throughout North America are helping other associations realize what is possible for children with diverse learning disabilities. It is my hope that educational researchers and policy-makers will feel inspired by recent neuroscience research and visit schools that offer the Arrowsmith Program to witness the program in action for themselves. I believe so much can be learned by the combined efforts of educators and neuroscientists, and I hope a continued dialogue will further efforts to advance the field of learning disabilities.

Numerous intervention programs are available to children with learning disabilities. In Vancouver, for example, students with learning disabilities are offered a variety of services from tutors and typing programs to organizational coaches and occupational therapists. Parents whose children are struggling in school often request an assessment from a school psychologist or seek a private assessment from a registered psychologist. The psychologist then analyzes the student's profile and makes program or referral recommendations. Because of the breadth of learning disability subtypes a child may be diagnosed with, the number of recommendations

55. Eaton Brain Improvement Centre (EBIC), located in Vancouver, British Columbia, works with young adults and adults with learning disabilities and attention disorders. The Arrowsmith Program is used at EBIC to improve the cognitive functioning of the clients.

can be overwhelming. It can be difficult for parents and teachers to both plan and then implement the many recommendations from these psycho-educational assessments.

Two frequent questions I get from parents and professionals alike are: 1) How does the Arrowsmith Program fit into the array of services already available? and 2) How can the Arrowsmith Program help students in conjunction with other programs currently being offered? The broad answer is that the Arrowsmith Program strives to work toward a common goal of improving the educational and life outcomes of individuals with learning disabilities and attention disorders.

The Arrowsmith Program focuses on improving the underlying cognitive weaknesses that cause learning disorders. Put another way, it works on improving the neurological dysfunctions that hinder the acquisition of achievement skills in a classroom environment, including social perception and life functioning.

For example, take the skill of reading. The Arrowsmith Program targets the regions of the brain that are involved with the acquisition of this skill. Areas in the brain that recognize letter symbols, process speech sounds, scan visual symbols, and increase reasoning ability are targeted for neurological improvement. The Arrowsmith Program itself does not explicitly teach sound/symbol letter patterns in the English language. Rather, once the neurological areas for reading acquisition are improved, the student can be introduced to sound/symbol letter patterns through various reading programs available and will then be *neurologically* capable of acquiring reading skills such as decoding and comprehension. This is just one example of how the Arrowsmith Program focuses on improving the neurological weaknesses that contribute to learning disorders. Other areas of weakness are also targeted, with the same focus on improving the neurological ability to acquire language, motor abilities, social skills, reasoning skills, attention control, planning and organizational ability, and math and written expression skills.

Arrowsmith Program Benefits to Other Professionals

By strengthening children's underlying neurological capacities, the Arrowsmith Program lays the groundwork for other services that build academic skills. In harmonizing the Arrowsmith Program with achievement-based intervention programs, professionals in the field of learning disabilities can work together to improve the educational outcomes of their students. Following is a look at various professionals working in the field and a discussion of how the Arrowsmith Program creates a foundation that allows students to benefit from their expertise.

1) Classroom Teachers

A teacher's ability to succeed in a regular classroom environment is no easy accomplishment. Teachers deal with large numbers of students, each having a unique neurological profile. Often the teacher needs to instruct to the "average" student. That is, the teacher has to sense what the average rate of skill acquisition is in the student body. If certain children learn more quickly, the teacher may provide some form of enrichment. If a child learns at a slower pace, significant complications can exist in both instructional practice and ability to find solutions for that child.

Classroom teachers are often faced with large numbers of students to teach. A certain number of students in these classrooms will have learning disabilities and/or attention disorders. These students often have low self-esteem and struggle with organization, listening skills, and understanding ideas. Teachers can face real challenges as they must effectively balance teaching all students in their classrooms, no matter what their capacity to learn.

In 1997, the Toronto Catholic District School Board implemented the Arrowsmith Program at St. Patrick Catholic Secondary School. Since then, seven elementary schools in the TCDSB have also implemented the program. In order to research the effectiveness of the Arrowsmith Program, a quantitative and qualitative study was conducted and presented to the Superintendent of Special Services. Part of this research included teacher observations of changes in the students' academic performance. Fifty-five teachers were asked to participate and "observed and rated noticeable changes in cognitive abilities necessary for learning such as the ability to focus, understanding instructions, listening skills, organizational skills, remembering factual information, understanding ideas, and in skill acquisition such as reading comprehension, legibility of written work, telling time, and in areas of confidence, self-esteem and frustration level."[56]

The fifty-five TCDSB teachers filled out questionnaires, and the results were very positive. For example, 62 percent of these teachers stated that there was a noticeable change in these students' ability to understand and follow instructions. Thirty-one percent of these teachers stated that there was an extremely noticeable change. Not one of the fifty-five teachers indicated that there was no change. The remaining 7 percent of these teachers were never concerned with the students' ability to understand and follow instructions.

The TCDSB teachers were also asked if the Arrowsmith Program students in their classroom showed improved ability to understand ideas. Fifty-six percent of the teachers stated that there was a noticeable change, 35 percent stated that there was an extremely noticeable change, and only 2 percent indicated that there was no change. The remaining 7 percent did not see the students as having this problem before implementation of the Arrowsmith Program.

Classroom teachers do their best to work with students with learning disabilities and/or attention disorders. They provide extra time on tests, allow the use of laptops for written assignments, provide classroom lecture notes, and ensure that the pace of instruction does not overwhelm the students. Unfortunately, these accommodations are often not enough for children with learning disabilities and/or attention disorders. As a result, these students often need resource room support and special education classrooms to support regular classroom instruction. The Arrowsmith Program can make curriculum delivery much less problematic for the regular classroom teacher. As the TCDSB study highlighted, students returning from the Arrowsmith Program into the regular classroom environment require less or no special education resource support, learn more independently, and show stronger self-confidence.

---

56. Arrowsmith School, "Report on the Arrowsmith Program in the Toronto Catholic District School Board" (January 25, 2007). http://www.arrowsmithschool.org/research.htm.

2) ADHD Specialists

The number of children diagnosed with Attention Deficit Hyperactive Disorder is considerable. When Eaton Learning Centre was conducting psycho-educational assessments from 1996 to 2008, roughly 30 percent of the children diagnosed with learning disabilities also had symptoms of ADHD. We would often refer them to a medical doctor specializing in ADHD, and the diagnosis was indeed often ADHD, with intervention consisting of stimulant medication. For many children with the diagnosis of ADHD, the results are positive. The medication helps them at school and at home.

We also had cases where the medical doctor was unsure of the diagnosis of ADHD. Furthermore, in some cases we were unsure of whether the ADHD was the primary problem or a secondary result of the severity of the accompanying learning disability. For example, if a child has neurological weaknesses with reasoning, oral language, and visual-motor copying from the board, that child could exhibit ADHD-like behaviours.

Providing neurological remediation helps to determine if the ADHD symptoms are primary or secondary. Through the Arrowsmith Program, a student can work on improving the underlying neurological weaknesses that may be causing ADHD. Once these neurological weaknesses improve to near the average range of functioning, the signs of ADHD will either be eliminated altogether or remain constant. Many students who begin the Arrowsmith Program while taking stimulant medication for ADHD are able to stop taking the medication after one to two years since the ADHD was caused by their combined neurological weaknesses. Once these neurological functions are strengthened, the child no longer exhibits signs of attention related-problems.

However, some of the children who come in with ADHD do need to continue with stimulant medications even after Arrowsmith Program intervention. This is determined when the medication is gradually reduced or removed altogether, yet improved cognitive abilities through the implementation of the Arrowsmith Program *do not* result in increased active engagement or focusing ability in a classroom setting. In these cases, the ADHD is a primary problem and not a result of a combination of cognitive functioning weaknesses; it stands alone and requires ongoing medical intervention.

Medical doctors, teachers, psychologists, and parents can work with the Arrowsmith Program to determine if the ADHD diagnosis is a primary or secondary concern. Many children who currently take stimulant medication for ADHD may not require medication if the causes of their ADHD symptoms are underlying cognitive functioning weaknesses related to a learning disability. Parent and professional partnership with Arrowsmith can aid in determining the underlying causes of attention disorders in children.

3) Speech-Language Pathologists

Remediation of speech-language dysfunctions requires intensive and repetitive intervention. The Arrowsmith Program can be used both in preparation for and in tandem with a student's work with a speech-language pathologist. Through the use of specific and systematic interventions designed to target the weaker areas of the brain, the Arrowsmith Program can strengthen the cognitive abilities required for improvement in speech-language capacities. The program can be used to improve a child's ability to discriminate between speech sounds, to improve weak memory for information and instructions, and to facilitate the expression of ideas.

Progress made by these students is constantly monitored by Arrowsmith's cognitive teachers to ensure that they are not using bypass strategies, which would enable the student to complete the exercise without targeting the area of weakness. After a child has completed the Arrowsmith Program, speech-language pathologists can continue with further intervention to teach language skills.

4) Tutors of Orton-Gillingham or Other Phonics-Based Reading/ Spelling Programs

During graduate school at Boston University, I was trained as an Orton-Gillingham tutor. I took a summer course with Diana Hanbury King at the Kildonan School, tutoring at Kildonan's summer camp, Camp Dunnabeck, and then at the Fraser Academy in Vancouver. I also served on the International Dyslexia Association, British Columbia Branch, organizing conferences that often had an underlying focus on the Orton-Gillingham method.

While I continue to observe some cases of great success using this method of reading and spelling intervention, other students do not respond as well, and their progress is slow. I also recognized this when working with registered psychologists who conducted psycho-educational assessments. Many parents who hire an Orton-Gillingham tutor for several years notice slow progress. Even private schools in the Vancouver area that use the Orton-Gillingham method are puzzled that some children with dyslexia do not progress as well as others.

The Arrowsmith Program appreciates reading remediation programs; they are often necessary to help children acquire the code of the English language. However, at Eaton Arrowsmith School it is evident that some children with dyslexia first need to improve the underlying neurological functions used to acquire reading and spelling skills. This is based on the observation that many children, even after three or four years of intensive intervention at phonics-based private schools, are still struggling to read, write, and spell. A student attending the Arrowsmith Program will spend hours improving the cognitive areas related to the ability to learn sound/symbol correspondence, automatic visual recognition and memory of symbols, and ability to scan visual symbols. Then, when the sound/symbol system of the English language is introduced using the Orton-Gillingham or Wilson Reading programs, the acquisition rate is much faster.

Those using Orton-Gillingham and other phonics-based methods would do well to consider the Arrowsmith Program if the child is making slow or little progress. After the neurological intervention, the child can then be referred back to an Orton-Gillingham tutor or school. Children with reading disorders often have multiple learning disabilities including such areas as written expression, reasoning, visual-motor integration, and memory for information and instruction. In these cases as well, the Arrowsmith Program can assist in the areas where the Orton-Gillingham practitioner has had little success.

5) Occupational Therapists

Occupational therapists, who assess fine and gross motor abilities, know how important it is to improve the motor abilities of children with various learning disabilities. The Arrowsmith Program can support occupational therapists by providing motor dysfunction remediation in children with learning disabilities before, during, and after the child's work with the therapist. Errors in written expression such as miscopying, irregular spelling, careless written errors in mathematics, overall poor written performance, and handwriting ability can all be improved through those of the program's cognitive exercises that target the motor systems of the brain. Specific cognitive exercises in the Arrowsmith Program suite can also improve gross motor and kinesthetic abilities such as body awareness in space and the recognition of objects by touch. Once the Arrowsmith Program is complete, a child may be referred to an occupational therapist who can provide additional support. Conversely, a child's work with a therapist may be enhanced by a referral to the Arrowsmith Program.

6) Social Skills Training Practitioners

Children with learning disabilities often struggle with social acceptance. Research highlights the fact that a majority of children with learning disabilities struggle to make friends, tend to be bullied, and are often isolated from peers at school. As a result, self-esteem can be low and an increase in psychological problems such as anxiety and depression is possible. The need to improve these children's perception of their social interactions should not be understated.

To my knowledge, there are no cognitive programs that target brain areas involved in social perception to improve a child's ability to make sense of her world. Rather, the focus is on self-help groups or counselling. Therapists often tell the child to be proud of her strengths and to understand that we all have weaknesses. The hope is that this will provide enough encouragement for the child to accept her differences and not take social rejection so heavily. In some cases, group therapy or individual counselling can help a child with a combination of a learning disability and poor social skills.

When the Eaton Learning Centre conducted psycho-educational assessments, many parents asked what they could do to improve their child's social skills. We often made recommendations for group therapy or individual counselling. We stressed that teaching their child good self-advocacy skills would also be beneficial. At that time, however, we did not have cognitive remediation resources available that focused on improving the underlying neurological weaknesses that caused the social-skill deficits in the first place.

The Arrowsmith Program can help counsellors, psychologists, and psychiatrists in these situations. It is the only remediation system that offers the ability to improve the underlying neurological functions related to social perception. Children work on cognitive exercises that help them to interpret facial cues, body language and gestures, and social pragmatics and norms in various social environments, and to respond appropriately. With increased capacity for social skills, they can then better interact with counsellors, psychologists, and psychiatrists. A child's ability to function successfully in social situations is extremely important; those unable to cope socially are at a considerable disadvantage for general success in school, career, and relationships.

7) School Psychologists and Registered Psychologists

Psychologists spend many hours meeting with teachers, parents, and students, sharing their insights into why a child might be struggling at school. They are often knowledgeable about intelligence, cognitive ability, and achievement skills. They are aware of the emotional disorders that can get in the way of successful school outcomes.

When a child is struggling in school, the psychologist is asked to conduct a psycho-educational assessment. The psychologist will typically first talk to the team of teachers working with that child and then consult with the parents. The psycho-educational assessment consists of measures of intelligence, cognitive ability, and achievement skills. If the assessment shows discrepancies between ability (intelligence/cognitive levels) and achievement (reading, writing, spelling, and math), a learning disability may be identified. The psychologist will then make recommendations to the school and parents.

The Arrowsmith Program can provide psychologists with solutions to various learning disabilities previously not addressed in their practice. For example, the program offers help to children assessed with nonverbal learning disorders. These children often struggle with mathematics, written expression, and social perception. They show significant academic frustrations when they reach the higher grades, where conceptual reasoning is more critical. No longer can they trust their memories to do well on tests or exams.

The Arrowsmith Program is the first cognitive remediation program that improves the brain's capacity to acquire math skills, get thoughts on paper fluently, and understand social interactions. It provides children with nonverbal learning disorders the capacity to reason efficiently, thereby improving math problem-solving skills and reading comprehension. Children with severe verbal language impairments also often struggle to receive speech-language remediation because speech pathologists in school districts are often kept busy just trying to keep up with assessing children. The Arrowsmith Program can address the underlying cognitive problems that result in these language disorders. Children work on cognitive exercises related to speech pronunciation weaknesses, oral language processing and memory, and expressive language deficits.

As well, the Arrowsmith Program provides an intensive cognitive remediation program for children with visual-motor integration or motor-symbol sequencing deficits, which can lead to a written expression learning disability. Occupational therapists are well aware of the large number of children struggling in school due to these neurological deficits. In fact, research shows that a written expression learning disability is the most common type of learning disorder in North America. Children with this disability require intensive, repetitive cognitive exercises that improve visual-motor coordination required for printing and copying. These children may also struggle with speech and careless errors in mathematics, and they can be slow readers. Over thirty years, the Arrowsmith Program has discovered that, through cognitive exercises, each of these learning functions can be improved.

Finally, it is interesting to note that the definition of a learning disability often fails to clearly acknowledge reasoning problems as a cause of that learning disability. The Learning Disability Association of Canada definition states, "These disorders affect learning in individuals who otherwise demonstrate at least average abilities essential for thinking and/or reasoning."[57] In fact, we have learned in conducting psycho-educational assessments that many children diagnosed with a learning disability showed substantial reasoning problems. Psychologists may see these reasoning deficits on measures of intelligence such as on the Matrix Reasoning subtest of the Wechsler Intelligence Scale for Children or the Woodcock-Johnson Tests of Cognitive Ability measure of Fluid Reasoning and Concept Formation.

If children with reasoning deficits can receive the necessary cognitive remediation, their capacity to reason will improve. Cause-and-effect problem solving will become more fluent and accurate. In turn, achievement areas such as reading comprehension and math problem solving will improve without direct instruction and without tutoring or the use of workbooks.

Now, with the Arrowsmith Program, children struggling with these particular learning disability subtypes can receive the intensive remediation they so badly need. The program can assist educational and medical professionals who work with children with learning disabilities and attention disorders. Professionals who have worked with Arrowsmith students have found that, as students' capacities increase, learning occurs more rapidly and is a more rewarding experience. Their improvement in neurological functioning can then improve the intervention delivered by other special education professionals.

The Initiators of Change

It is not easy to shift thinking about learning disabilities or attention disorders. As I have noted, it took me some time to realize and acknowledge that the brain can change itself. I was stuck in the paradigm that the brain was fixed. I was focused on conducting psycho-educational assessments and recommending accommodations and assistive technology. I spent years developing self-advocacy training DVDs and workbooks. The idea

---

57. Learning Disabilities Association of Canada website, "Official Definition of Learning Disabilities" (January 30, 2002). http://www.ldac-acta.ca/learn-more/ld-defined/official-definition-of-learning-disabilities.html.

that children could improve their neurological weaknesses was not in my realm of thinking until I began to learn about a program designed specifically to improve those weaknesses—the Arrowsmith program.

It is only a matter of time before the field of learning disabilities changes. One day soon, the definition of learning disabilities will not state that they are lifelong, but that the severity of each specific case can improve dramatically. Recommended support for children with learning disabilities and attention disorders will include cognitive exercises to improve neurological functioning. However, it will take parents and teachers to create this awareness and sense of possibilities. Because they are focused on their own specialties, educational faculty at many universities and colleges throughout North America will take longer to develop an understanding of this reality. They are connected with associations and schools that have not yet developed a knowledge and awareness of neuroplasticity and cognitive remediation. These researchers continue to focus on skill-based achievement programs, assistive technology support, use of accommodations, and learning strategies intervention, while not acknowledging the field of neuroscience.

The idea of parents and teachers being at the forefront of educational change is not new. After all, they are at the frontlines of advocacy for children with learning disabilities and attention disorders. They understand that what professionals are doing does not always work. They see some of their children still struggling in school even after having been taught phonics and having shown improved reading levels. They see others having difficulties with attention and still others who do not have the cognitive abilities to keep pace with regular classroom instruction. They see that nonverbal learning disorders that affect social skills and reasoning are not being addressed adequately in schools today. Parents and teachers are encouraged to look into cognitive remediation programs such as the Arrowsmith Program. You are the initiators of change.

Appendix A

Arrowsmith Program's Nineteen Cognitive Dysfunctions and Common Features

Cognitive Area	Brief Description	Common Features
Motor-Symbol Sequencing	Ability to learn and produce a written sequence of symbols	Messy handwriting, miscopying, misreading, irregular spelling, speech rambling, careless written errors in mathematics, poor written performance
Symbol Relations	Ability to understand the relationships among two or more ideas or concepts	Difficulty with reading comprehension, trouble with mathematical reasoning, trouble with logical reasoning, difficulty reading an analogue clock, problem understanding cause and effect, reversals of *b–d, p–q* (in younger students and more severe cases)
Memory for Information and Instructions	Ability to remember chunks of auditory information.	Trouble remembering oral instructions, difficulty following lectures or extended conversations, problem acquiring information through listening

Cognitive Area	Brief Description	Common Features
Predicative Speech	Ability to see how words and numbers interconnect sequentially into fluent sentences and procedures	Problem putting information into one's own words, speaking in incomplete sentences, difficulty using internal speech to work out consequences, trouble following long sentences, breakdown of steps in mathematical procedures
Broca's Speech Pronunciation	Ability to learn to pronounce syllables and then integrate them into the stable and consistent pronunciation of a word	Mispronouncing words, avoiding using words because of uncertainty of pronunciation, limited ability to learn and use phonics, difficulty learning foreign languages, difficulty thinking and talking at the same time, flat and monotone speech with lack of rhythm and intonation
Auditory Speech Discrimination	Ability to hear the difference between similar speech sounds, e.g., *hear–fear* and *clothe–clove*	Mishearing words and thus misinterpreting information, difficulty understanding a foreign accent, extra effort required to listen to speech
Symbolic Thinking	Ability to develop and maintain plans and strategies through the use of language	Problem being self-directed and self-organized in learning, limited mental initiative, difficulty keeping attention relevantly oriented to the demands of a task necessary for completion, difficulty thinking, planning, problem solving, trouble seeing the main point
Symbol Recognition	Ability to visually recognize and remember a word or symbol	Poor word recognition, slow reading, difficulty with spelling, trouble remembering symbol patterns such as mathematical or chemical equations

Cognitive Area	Brief Description	Common Features
Lexical Memory	Ability to remember several unrelated words	Problem with associative memory, trouble following auditory information, trouble learning names of things such as animals, places, people, colors, days of the week
Kinesthetic Perception (Left and Right Side)	Ability to know where one's body is in space and to recognize objects by touch	Awkward body movements, bumping into objects due to not knowing where body is in space relative to objects, uneven handwriting with variable pressure
Kinesthetic Speech	Awareness of the position of the lips and tongue	Lack of clear articulation of speech, some speech slurring
Artifactual Thinking	Ability to register and interpret nonverbal information and plan and problem solve nonverbally	Problem interpreting nonverbal information such as body language, facial expression, and voice tone, weak social skills, difficulty perceiving and interpreting one's own emotions, difficulty with nonverbal thinking, planning, problem solving
Narrow Visual Span	Ability to see a large number of symbols or objects in one visual fixation	Slow, jerky reading with errors, eye fatigue when reading, problem navigating in the dark
Object Recognition	Ability to visually recognize and remember the details of objects	Trouble finding objects, problem remembering visual cues such as landmarks, difficulty remembering faces and recalling visual details of pictures
Spatial Reasoning	Ability to imagine a series of moves through space inside one's head before executing them	Frequently getting lost, losing objects, messy disorganized workspace, trouble constructing geometric figures

Cognitive Area	Brief Description	Common Features
Mechanical Reasoning	Ability to understand how machines operate and effectively handle and use tools	Difficulty understanding the mechanical properties of objects, problems constructing or repairing machinery such as taking apart and putting together a bicycle or repairing a car
Abstract Reasoning	Ability to carry out a task in the proper sequence of steps	Trouble understanding the proper sequence of steps in a task such as sewing, cooking, or computer programming
Primary Motor (Left and Right Side)	Ability to control muscle movements on one side of the body or the other	Poor muscle tone, which results in some degree of awkwardness and slowness of body movement
Supplementary Motor	Ability to carry out internal sequential mental operations such as mental mathematics	Finger counting, trouble retaining numbers in one's head, difficulty making change, problem learning math facts, poor sense of time management, difficulty with time signature in music

Appendix B

Differences between the Arrowsmith Assessment and the Psycho-Educational Assessment

The purposes of the psycho-educational assessment are different from those of Arrowsmith assessment. The psycho-educational assessment is conducted in order to diagnose a specific learning disability and to assist in determining achievement skill remediation, in-class accommodations, and use of assistive technology. The Arrowsmith assessment is for the sole purpose of designing the cognitive capacity training intervention through the Arrowsmith Program. Psycho-educational assessments often take about three to four hours to complete. They often consist of an intelligence measure, other cognitive ability measures, and achievement measures in reading, writing, and mathematics. In three or four hours only a limited amount of testing can be completed. This is especially the case for public school psychologists, who have limited time and resources. Private psychologists can spend more time conducting assessments, often spending four or five hours testing a client and several more hours working with the parents. The Arrowsmith assessment is different from a psycho-educational assessment in that the focus is not on finding percentile scores on measures of reading, writing, and math. No measures are taken of a child's reading, spelling, or mathematics abilities; however, some schools using the Arrowsmith Program may conduct their own tests of achievement, as does the Eaton Arrowsmith School. In short, the focus of the Arrowsmith assessment is to look at the cognitive capacities necessary for achievement acquisition. For example, if a child is weak in three cognitive capacities related to reading acquisition, it is often the case that the child's reading is impaired. Thus, it is not necessary to conduct achievement measures in this area.

Appendix C

ARROWSMITH SPECTRUM LINE

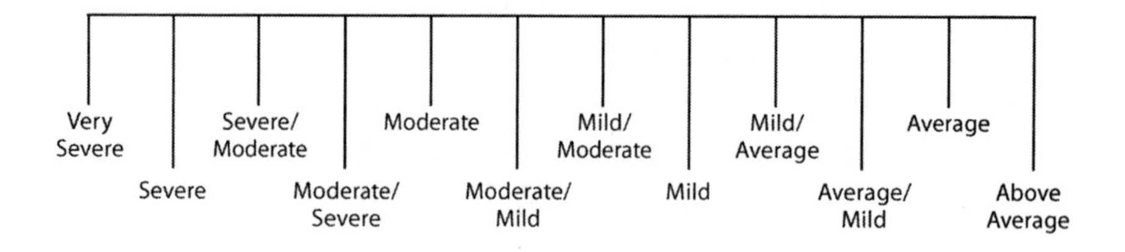

Index

"n" refers to notes; "t" to table

B

D

E

As the discoveries of neuroplasticity, and this self-directed neuroplasticity, trickle down to clinics and schools and plain old living rooms, the ability to willfully change the brain will become a central part of our lives—and of our understanding of what it means to be human.

—SHARON BEGLEY, AUTHOR, *TRAIN YOUR MIND, CHANGE YOUR BRAIN: HOW A NEW SCIENCE REVEALS OUR EXTRAORDINARY POTENTIAL TO TRANSFORM OURSELVES*

LaVergne, TN USA
15 February 2011
216511LV00005B/8/P

9 780986 749407